T0312648

TREASURE HUNTER

OTHER BOOKS BY W.C. JAMESON

Buried Treasures of America Series

Buried Treasures of the American Southwest
New Mexico Treasure Tales
Buried Treasures of Texas
Colorado Treasure Tales
Buried Treasures of the Ozarks
Buried Treasures of the South
Buried Treasures of the Appalachians
Buried Treasures of New England
Buried Treasures of California
Buried Treasures of the Atlantic Coast
Buried Treasures of the Rocky Mountain West
Buried Treasures of the Great Plains
Buried Treasures of the Pacific Northwest
Buried Treasures of the Mid-Atlantic States
Lost Mines and Buried Treasures of Arizona
Lost Mines and Buried Treasures of Old Wyoming
Lost Mines and Buried Treasures of Arkansas
Lost Mines and Buried Treasures of Missouri
Lost Mines and Buried Treasures of Oklahoma
Lost Mines and Buried Treasures of Tennessee
Texas Tales of Lost Mines and Buried Treasures
Lost Treasures in American History
Legend and Lore of the Guadalupe Mountains
Buried Treasures of the Ozarks and Appalachians
Lost Mines and Buried Treasures of the Guadalupe Mountains
Lost Mines and Buried Treasures of the Big Bend
Florida's Lost and Buried Treasures
Lost Mines and Buried Treasures of the Civil War
The Silver Madonna and other Tales of America's Greatest Lost Treasures
Finding Treasure: A Field Guide

Outlaw Treasures (audio)
Buried Treasures of the Civil War (audio)

BEYOND THE GRAVE SERIES

The Return of the Assassin, John Wilkes Booth
Billy the Kid: Beyond the Grave
Billy the Kid: The Lost Interviews
Butch Cassidy: Beyond the Grave
John Wilkes Booth: Beyond the Grave

Books on Writing

Hot Coffee and Cold Truth: Living and Writing the West
Notes from Texas: On Writing in the Lone Star State
Want to Be a Successful Writer? Do This Stuff
An Elevated View: Colorado Writers on Writing
The Seven Keys to Becoming a Successful Writer

Poetry

I Missed the Train to Little Rock
Open Range: Poetry of the Reimagined West (Edited with Laurie
   Wagner Buyer)
Bones of the Mountain

Food

Chili from the Southwest
The Ultimate Chili Cookbook
Fandango Cookbook

Fiction

Beating the Devil
Eulogy

Other

Unsolved Mysteries of the Old West
A Sense of Place: Essays on the Ozarks
Ozark Tales of Ghosts, Spirits, Hauntings, and Monsters

TREASURE HUNTER

A Memoir of Caches, Curses, and Confrontations

Second Edition

W.C. JAMESON

TAYLOR TRADE PUBLISHING
Lanham • Boulder • New York • London

Published by Taylor Trade Publishing
An imprint of The Rowman & Littlefield Publishing Group, Inc.
4501 Forbes Boulevard, Suite 200, Lanham, Maryland 20706
www.rowman.com

16 Carlisle Street, London W1D 3BT, United Kingdom

Distributed by NATIONAL BOOK NETWORK

Copyright © 2014 by W.C. Jameson

All rights reserved. No part of this book may be reproduced in any form or by
any electronic or mechanical means, including information storage and retrieval
systems, without written permission from the publisher, except by a reviewer
who may quote passages in a review.

British Library Cataloguing in Publication Information Available

Library of Congress Cataloging-in-Publication Data

Jameson, W. C., 1942–
  Treasure hunter : a memoir of caches, curses, and confrontations / W.C.
Jameson. — Second edition.
      pages cm
  ISBN 978-1-58979-992-9 (pbk. : alk. paper) — ISBN 978-1-58979-993-6
(electronic) 1. Jameson, W. C., 1942- 2. Adventure and adventurers—
Southwest, New—Biography. 3. Treasure troves—Southwest, New—Folklore.
4. Treasure troves—Mexico, North—Folklore. 5. Tales—Southwest, New.
6. Tales—Mexico, North. 7. Legends—Southwest, New. 8. Legends—Mexico,
North. 9. Southwest, New—Biography. I. Title.
  GR108.5.J36 2014
  398.20979—dc23

                                                        2014015120

∞™ The paper used in this publication meets the minimum requirements of
American National Standard for Information Sciences—Permanence of Paper
for Printed Library Materials, ANSI/NISO Z39.48-1992.

For Laurie

CONTENTS

INTRODUCTION

Never More Alive Than When on the Hunt

> Treasure! It's out there. It's whispering to me.
>
> —Anonymous

For over five decades I have been a professional treasure hunter. During dozens of quests to locate lost mines and buried treasures, I have faced death and injury, broken national and international laws, neglected my family, and occasionally found fortune. There are not many of us left, those dreamers and wanderers who find excitement and satisfaction in remote and sometimes unmapped regions of the globe. We are dedicated to the search for something that may or may not exist. We are a breed of men addicted to danger, adventure, and the quest.

The lure of treasure has captivated mankind since earliest civilization, and men who wanted more out of life than the ordinary, those whose hearts and souls pulsed and throbbed with a sense of daring, went in pursuit. Indeed, I'm convinced it was not so much the promise of wealth as it was the quest, the opportunity to journey to unknown lands, to confront obstacles and dangers, and not only to overcome and survive but to thrive in pitting one's skills and mettle against sometimes overwhelming odds.

The seekers of treasure have been with us for ages. Who can forget the mythical odyssey of Jason and the Argonauts in pursuit of the Golden Fleece? Who has not thrilled to the adventures that lay between the covers of Robert Louis Stevenson's *Treasure Island*, H. Rider Haggard's *King Solomon's Mines*, or B. Traven's *The Treasure of the Sierra Madres*? Who could read J. Frank Dobie's *Coronado's Children* or *Apache Gold and Yaqui Silver* and not be compelled to gather up maps and expedition gear and go searching for a buried cache or lost mine? We can't seem to get enough of these stories. For men of adventure, this kind of quest is as much a part of the culture as food, music, and religion.

During my teenage years, I lived with the memory of finding a cache of gold ingots in the Guadalupe Mountains of West Texas. I remembered the heft and texture of the bullion in my hands as it was passed to me from a small cave by the men who found it. The experience possessed me as I relived it every day. As a result, I seldom paid attention in my school classes. While public school faculty droned on about some dull subject, I drew stick-men adventures on scrap pieces of paper. I stared out the window at the bright sunshine-illumined West Texas landscape, imagining expeditions I could be participating in rather than being confined indoors. In my reveries, I smelled the creosote bush and cactus flowers, felt the desert breeze of the Guadalupes, and relished the heat of the sun on my skin just like I did on that day I stood outside the treasure cave.

I flunked algebra my freshman year in high school and barely passed my other courses. Bored by boring teachers who made everything boring, my ears perked up only occasionally in English class when some bit of literature or poetry caught my attention, when some compelling tale such as *Silas Marner* unfolded and captivated me. I was entranced by the rhythms found in "Miniver Cheevy" by Edwin Arlington Robinson, and by the stories of Jack London such as *White Fang* and "To Build a Fire."

Other than being a member of the football and track teams, I was a loner. The few friends I hung out with from time to time were loners too. What we had in common was our understanding of and craving for solitude, but their dreams, if they had any, seemed different from mine.

I barely graduated from high school. During the final hour of the last day of my senior year, I, along with a fellow student, was forced to seek permission from the principal to receive my diploma. I'm convinced he simply took pity on us because my friend sobbed like a baby during what amounted to an exit interview.

After being granted approval to graduate, I jumped into a car with friends who were determined to make some mischief that afternoon. During a high-speed police chase, the car slammed into a telephone pole. Knocked unconscious, I suffered broken ribs and bled from dozens of tiny cuts on my face as a result of my head going through the side window of a 1949 Plymouth. The policemen, concerned I was badly hurt, released us, and I walked through the graduation ceremony that evening in pain and looking like a victim of a knife attack.

After high school I worked at a variety of occupations—lifeguard, ranch hand, dockworker, disc jockey, boxer, rodeo rider, freelance writer, and artist—but these left me unsatisfied. While trying to make a living, I yearned to be exploring the wilderness in search of lost mines and buried treasures.

At nineteen and disgusted with dead-end jobs, I filled a small pack with some dry biscuits, jerked meat, and a denim jacket and, without telling anyone, crossed the Rio Grande into Mexico and walked nearly three hundred miles into the Sierra Madres. There, living among and working with Indians and *campesinos*, I got caught up in a civil war between the indigenes and the wealthy *hacendados* who coveted the native homelands. Siding with the outnumbered and outarmed Indians, I found myself involved in a fight between the mercenary armies of the landowners and ranchers. This adventure is detailed in my book *Beating the Devil* (2007). A year later, I returned to Texas, deeply scarred and saddened by the lengths to which men will go in order to acquire property and wealth. I was heartened, however, to experience the friendship and inspiration of people who would defend to the death what was dear to them.

Trying to make some sense of life, I read everything I could get my hands on: Plato, Darwin, Steinbeck, Forester, Twain, and others. I absorbed the words, the philosophies, the adventures, like a sponge, but had no one with which to discuss them. It occurred to me that college was where one found like-minded souls who read similar books. When I was twenty-one years old, I enrolled as a freshman at Texas Western College, now the University of Texas at El Paso. Who could have known that I would eventually graduate with honors, ultimately receive a Ph.D., and author more than ninety books?

During the summer following that first year of higher education, I undertook my first solo expedition: a search for the famous Lost Sublett Mine in the Guadalupe Mountains, some 110 miles east of El Paso. Before setting out on my journey, I read everything I could find on the subject and discussed my plans and preparations with other professional treasure hunters. I departed, alone, in search of the gold that had eluded many previous searchers for more than a century. I spent more than two weeks on foot in the range. The recovery of a small treasure from that venture funded my next hunt, then the next.

I have been involved in nearly two hundred expeditions, some lasting only a few days, some for more than six weeks. I have searched for treasure in the United States and Mexico and more than fifty years later I am still on the hunt. Many of my expeditions yielded little or no treasure but supplied an abundance of adventure. From a few of these excursions, my partners and I acquired enough wealth to pay off houses and purchase new vehicles. With some of the money, I paid college tuition for myself as well as for my children. Always, we set aside enough to fund the next venture.

I always attempted to pursue the quests in secrecy, but during the 1960s, I had the misfortune of being the subject of a newspaper report about a lost treasure that I was researching. The article was syndicated in dozens of papers around the country. The word was out, my identity known to thousands, and the calls started coming, followed by visits to my house by men who wanted to join me on my expeditions and/or fund them for a share of the recovered treasure.

I turned down every request. Anonymity is a great ally for a professional treasure hunter. Most often I have worked with the same three partners and we operated in total secrecy. We communicated our activities, often our destinations, to no one, not even family members. We carried no cameras, no video cams, and no tape recorders to any sites. Maps that we used to identify and locate specific treasures were destroyed because we wanted no evidence of what we found or where we found it.

Here's why: Far too many treasure hunters, particularly ones new to the business, cannot wait to make an announcement to the press about a discovery. Generally, this is a result of unbridled vanity, an uncontained ego that requires publicity and notoriety and comes to no good end. In almost every case that my partners and I are aware of, the existing laws forced the finders to relinquish their discovery. Most state and federal salvage recovery laws require that anything found that can be determined to have "historic" value be turned over to the respective government. Virtually everything recovered, whether gold and silver ingots and coins or artifacts that had been lost or cached during some bygone time, has historic value. Though the finders may have invested thousands of dollars as well as months, perhaps years, of time and energy into locating a treasure, they don't always get to keep it. Furthermore, if the find was on private, state, or federal lands, laws relating to trespass will likely have been broken. If a recovery is made, charges of theft often follow. Whenever we recovered a treasure in Mexico, we were forced to smuggle it across the border, often after paying hundreds of dollars in *mordida*, bribe money, to local officials and police.

It is important to understand that almost everything treasure recovery professionals like me do is illegal. Thus, the bizarre and unreasonable laws related to treasure recovery have turned honest, dedicated, and hard-working fortune hunters into outlaws. Announcing a discovery often leads to negative and unwanted developments, primarily the loss of any treasure that may have been found. As mentors explained to me years ago: The fewer people involved the better, and silence is the byword.

Most of the labor involved with any given treasure-hunting expedition takes place in libraries and archives studying research materials. "Research is the key," says author and recovery specialist Clive Cussler, "and you can never do enough." He goes on to state that research can either lower the odds or tell you that a quest may be hopeless. Sometimes 90 percent or more of my time was taken up with research on any given project. When I explain this to hopeful treasure hunters, they grow discouraged, preferring to believe that the life of a treasure hunter is all glamour, excitement, and wealth. However, the more work we did prior to an expedition, the more sophisticated the preparation, the greater the chances we had for success.

For years, my partners and I told anyone who wanted to join us on an expedition that they must be able to run seven miles carrying a full pack and a rifle, must be a marksman, must not be timid about shooting someone if necessary, and must not be afraid to die. Those criteria eliminated everyone.

This line of work can be dangerous. Treasure hunter Fain Donnelly once referred to treasure search and recovery as "blood sport." I have fallen from cliffs, had ropes break during climbs, been caught in mine shaft cave-ins, contended with flash floods, been shot at, watched men die, and had to deal with rattlesnakes, water moccasins, scorpions, and poisonous centipedes. I have fled for my life from park rangers, policemen, landowners, competitors, corporate mercenaries, and drug runners. My three partners and I each claim military experience, have earned marksmanship recognition, possess black belts in martial arts, and have engaged in warfare, and we are not intimidated by much. Still, we never courted danger and confrontation unnecessarily. At times, our primary goal was merely to get back home alive.

Over the years, friends, fellow treasure hunters, editors, and publishers have encouraged me to write about my adventures but I refused, turning down decent advances to tell these stories. Why? I didn't want anybody to know who I was, who my partners were, what we did, or where we explored. I could not write about these things for fear of incriminating ourselves and inviting legal action on a variety of levels.

Now over seventy years of age, while still active and healthy, I see my days as a treasure hunter slowing down. One of my partners has passed away. Another is unable to participate any longer for health and family reasons. The third is missing: following an attempted recovery of a sunken treasure off the coast of Jamaica, he disappeared and has not been heard from. Years ago these stalwart companions gave me their blessings and encouraged me to tell the stories, but I have taken some precautions. At their request, I have changed their names to protect them and their families from unwanted attention and scrutiny. In most of the following accounts I have changed the names of other principals and specific geographic sites. I have provided only cryptic directions and imprecise locations. All of this was done out of respect for privacy, but also because some treasures still lay where they were found, and I have plans to return for them. I have been purposely vague about other treasure locations, particularly in cases where they are on state or federal land or private property. I wouldn't want readers to get caught and punished while attempting to retrieve a treasure because they could wind up in prison for a long time.

People ask: Why do you do it? Why have you spent a great portion of your time breaking laws and risking your life pursuing elusive lost treasures?

The answer is easy: the challenge, the excitement of having the opportunity to live life to its fullest. The writer James Ramsey Ullman stated, "Challenge is the core and mainspring of all human activity." This is true for those of us who possess a sense of adventure, a zest for life and living that involves the mythic notion of the quest, the grand and daring experience of pursuit.

I am never more alive than when I am on the hunt.

1

GUADALUPE MOUNTAIN GOLD

There comes a time in every rightly constructed boy's life when he has a raging desire to go somewhere and dig for hidden treasure.

—Anonymous

It was an hour past sundown, and a three-quarter moon hung low in the sky, providing enough light for me to see my surroundings and make my way through the willows and into the fenced yard. Anyone surveying the grounds would be able to spot me in the moonlight, but I decided it was worth the risk.

A three-foot-high picket fence surrounded the yard. Lying just on the other side was my target—a twelve-by-four-foot patch of strawberries that had come to perfect ripeness that afternoon, the bright red fruits reflecting the moon's silver glow. It was 1953 and I was eleven years old. I had been thinking about those strawberries for a week, and now I was going after them. Gene Seitsinger had a reputation for growing the finest berries in West Texas.

I had thought about asking Seitsinger if I could pick some of the fruit, but knew I would be denied. He was known by all as mean, angry, and particularly hostile to youngsters. There were stories that circulated around the lower valley where we lived that the last time Seitsinger found a boy in his strawberry patch, he tied him to a tree and whipped him with a belt. There were other stories, supposedly true accounts, of boys who told their friends they were going to steal berries from Seitsinger's patch and were never seen again. As far as I knew, no one ever verified the accuracy of these stories, but it gave me pause. It also provided the temptation of a challenge.

The pickets were held to the bracing by small, thin nails. I pulled at the bottom of one and it gave easily, but the squeaking of the rusted and resistant nail broke the silence of the evening. I hoped the chirping of summer crickets and the peeping of frogs covered the sound. Moving aside the picket, I wriggled through. Crawling on my belly in the cool grass, I crossed the thirty-five feet to the patch, which lay only spitting distance from Seitsinger's back porch. Barefooted and summer-tanned, I wore a pair of threadbare Levis because it was all I owned and a green T-shirt because I thought it would help camouflage me against the plants. If Seitsinger or his wife, Ruby Lee, were to come outside and glance into their garden, they would spot me with no difficulty.

After squirming into the plot and wedging my skinny frame between rows of plants, I turned onto my back, reached out, and plucked a juicy fruit from a nearby cluster. I brought it to my face, regarded the beautiful red color reflected in the lunar light, and felt the firmness between my fingers. It was a large berry, one of the biggest I had ever seen. I inhaled the aroma. In those days, I thought nothing smelled as delicious, as sensual, as a fresh, ripe strawberry. I took a bite, savored the flavor for a full minute, took another, and then swallowed the remainder.

For fifteen minutes I plucked the fruits and ate, one slow berry at a time, careful to harvest them from several different plants in the hope that the pillage would go unnoticed the next day. I planned on returning every night until such time as the Seitsingers picked the crop. I extended my right arm beyond my head as far as I could reach and felt for berries among the leaves and stems. Finally, I found another large one, perhaps the biggest of the evening. As I was about to pull it from the plant, the back porch light came on and four men walked outside. I froze, arm still extended, moonlight shining on me less than ten feet from the porch.

I turned toward the sounds and saw Seitsinger accompanied by Hobie Schwarz, Tex Sanderson, and Simon McVay, neighbors, more or less, each living within a mile or two of the others. The men were holding drinks, bourbon I guessed from the color. They sat down around a wooden table. I tried to make myself smaller, to melt into the ground. I dared not move. For a few minutes, the men talked about the delicious meal they had just finished. Ruby Lee had fed them steaks, baked potatoes, grilled vegetables, and apple pie. Seitsinger then unrolled a large piece of brownish paper that appeared to be a map. The four men stared intently and then began speaking.

"The old man who used to own this told me the treasure is hidden in a small cave to the east of this arroyo," said Sanderson, jabbing at the map with a finger. "This spring over here keeps the arroyo running with an inch-deep flow of water most of the year. The cave is supposed to be southeast of the spring, somewhere about here."

"How did that old man know about this treasure?" asked McVay. "And where did he get the map?"

"He told me he stole the gold himself and hid it there more than fifty years ago. He drew the map, planning on returning at a later date and retrieving it, but he never got the chance. Between battling consumption and having to care for his crippled-up wife, he never could leave Bisbee, Arizona, long enough to go get it."

"How come he told you about it?" asked Seitsinger.

"I saved his son's life in the Korean War. He was badly wounded in the leg from a grenade explosion, couldn't walk, and was bleeding like a stuck hog. Our company was retreating from a hill we failed to take, so I picked him up and carried him a mile or more from the field of fire. His leg was mangled pretty bad. I cleaned out his wounds, bandaged him up, and got him to a field hospital. They sent him home a month later. They told him if I hadn't pulled him out and stopped the bleeding, he would have died in an hour."

I heard grunts of acknowledgment from the other men.

"Last year I stopped by to visit him and his family in Bisbee," said Sanderson. "His old man took me aside to thank me for all I done, and then told me about his outlaw past, about the treasure, and hiding it in the Guadalupe Mountains."

"What about the son?" asked Schwarz. "Isn't he entitled to some of this, if it's there?"

"The son doesn't know a thing about his father once living on the other side of the law and he doesn't know a thing about the treasure," said Sanderson. "The old man refers to the gold as ill-gotten gains and doesn't want the boy to have anything to do with it."

Pointing at the map, Schwarz asked, "What about this location? Can we just waltz in there and get this stuff or is it private property. What if we get caught?"

"It's part of the J.C. Hunter Ranch," offered McVay. "Hunter owns most of the front of the Guadalupe Mountains and a lot of the top. I know Hunter a little. Mostly, I know his foreman, a man named Noel Kincaid. I worked for him a couple of times stringing fence and branding cattle. We could stop by the ranch house where Kincaid lives and just tell him we're out hunting for arrowheads. He won't mind. People do it all the time out there, and he's real easy to get along with."

"Assuming we find the gold, it'll take a while to carry one hundred ingots from the cave to my car," said Sanderson. "It looks like the closest we can park is about a mile and a half away, and them bars are gonna be heavy, maybe thirty pounds apiece or more. We're looking at a lot of trips back and forth."

"Who cares?" said Seitsinger. "If this pans out, we'll all be pretty damn rich. Seems to me like it's worth the effort."

McVay rose, said he needed another drink, and went into the house. Seitsinger stretched, made some comment about the dinner, and then asked if anyone was in the mood for strawberries. He rose from his chair and walked out to the edge of the porch, hands on the railing, and looked down into the patch.

He stood thus for a full minute, then turned to Sanderson and said, "Tex, are you packing that boot pistol?"

In response, Sanderson reached down into his right cowboy boot and withdrew a custom .22 revolver and held it up.

"Toss it here."

Seitsinger caught the weapon in his right hand by the grip, swung around, and pointed it at me.

"Tex," he said. "It seems like we got a prowler." He clicked back the hammer.

At this moment, McVay walked back outside, a fresh bourbon in his hand. I could hear the ice clinking in the glass. He joined Seitsinger and stared at me lying on the ground. McVay, who had the vision of an owl in the dark, said, "That's the Jameson kid. He ain't no prowler. He's probably just filchin' strawberries."

"Stand up!" commanded Seitsinger.

I rose, heart hammering against my ribs.

"Get on up here," he said, gesturing at the porch. "And if you step on a single one of those berry plants, I'm gonna shoot you."

With extreme caution, I made my way across the rows and stepped up onto the wooden porch, my skinny arms raised above my head like I had seen men do in movies when held at gunpoint. Seitsinger grabbed my shoulder and pushed me toward the table. The pistol never swayed from my direction.

"Leave him be," said McVay, stepping between me and the gun. "I know this boy. He lives with his mom and brother and sister in the rock house on the other side of the big alfalfa field to the west. His dad ain't never around and they got no money. He was probably hungry."

"We got a problem, Simon," said Seitsinger. "This kid heard everything we said. We can't turn him loose to tell everybody what we're all about. Hell, we'll have enough trouble keeping things quiet as it is and we sure as hell don't need some kid blabbing about it."

"We don't have a problem," said McVay. "I've known this boy a long time and he's a good one. "

"What if he talks?"

"He won't talk if he's one of us. I say let's take him with us on the hunt, show him what we do, maybe give him a part of the action. At the very least, he might make a decent camp hand."

"I'm for it," said Sanderson.

Schwarz nodded agreement. Within seconds of being caught stealing strawberries and believing I was going to be shot and killed, I became a member of a clandestine team of treasure hunters. It was to change my life forever.

Two weeks later, I was sitting in the front seat of Sanderson's 1949 Chrysler sedan between him and Seitsinger. Schwarz and McVay rode in the back. On arriving at the Hunter Ranch, McVay got out and walked over to speak with Hunter Ranch foreman Noel Kincaid by some cattle pens. The trip to the Guadalupe Mountains in Culberson County, Texas, had taken about three hours from the time they picked me up at my house. It was my first time to travel eastward on Highway 62-180 and I thrilled at the journey through the Hueco Mountains and across the gravel and sand desert and salt flats to the foothills of the magnificent range.

After several minutes, McVay returned to the truck, squeezed in, and told us Kincaid said it was okay to camp over by Manzanita Spring. "That's about as close as we'll get the car to the search area anyway," said McVay.

We set up camp next to the spring, a pool of fresh water. Sanderson said we might be there for four or five days, depending on what we found, if anything, and how long it took to move the gold from the cave to the Chrysler. That evening, McVay prepared dinner, a delicious stew of beef, tomatoes, red chiles, onions, celery, garlic, and green beans, served with warmed corn tortillas and coffee. After dinner while the men sipped whiskey, I cleaned the dishes and put them away.

The next morning following a breakfast of scrambled eggs, sausage, flour tortillas, a delicious cheese they called *asadero*, and coffee, we hiked across the foothills and negotiated some deep arroyos, finally arriving at Juniper Spring. There, a trickle of water spilled from the brush-choked opening. Twenty yards down the shallow arroyo, the flow disappeared underground into the permeable rock and sand. Referring often to the map, Sanderson parceled out areas along the slope for each man to search. Flattered to be included, I alternately felt important and nervous. I didn't want to screw up. I still wasn't convinced that Seitsinger would not kill me.

We found dozens of caves; some were only large enough to allow entrance for a porcupine or badger. Others, though narrow and low ceilinged, could almost accommodate four or five men at a time. The deepest we encountered extended about twenty-five feet into the huge, bare expanse of limestone. We hacked away at the thick low brush covering some entrances and rolled away stones from others.

Rattlesnakes taking shade inside the cooler confines of the caves were a constant hazard. Using a stick, Sanderson flipped a rattler from the mouth of one cave and across several yards of hillside. It missed me by only a few inches, causing an adrenaline rush like I'd never experienced before, the first of many I would be exposed to. When the snake landed near my feet, I studied it, fascinated. Alive with some new and strange atavistic connection, I reached to pick it up when I heard a shout from Schwarz. He found the cave they were searching for.

Twenty-five yards away, bent over and hands on knees, Schwartz peered into a small opening. "I've got something," he called out. "Come take a look at this."

The rest of us clustered around the low, dark entrance. Schwarz dropped to his knees and started to crawl inside when a sharp buzzing caused him to scamper backward. Two feet inside the opening, a four-foot-long diamondback rattlesnake lay coiled, forked tongue darting in and out.

Using a length of juniper branch lying nearby, McVay dragged the serpent out into the sunlight and tossed it down the slope. He beat around the inside for a few seconds with the branch to make certain there were no more snakes. He backed out and told Schwarz, "You found it. You go first."

Schwarz crawled in, followed by Seitsinger, Sanderson, and McVay. Before he entered, Simon turned to me and said, "You stay out here."

At first I was hurt, disappointed, but then realized I was just a kid and they had their reasons. From inside the cave I could hear murmured conversation and the dull clank of heavy metal objects. Ten minutes later, McVay crawled out and took a seated position at the entrance. He pointed to a spot two feet away and told me to stand there. Leaning back into the cave he called, "I'm ready!"

A moment later, someone inside handed him an ingot that he, in turn, passed to me with instructions to start a pile like I was stacking firewood. The dust-covered bar was surprisingly heavy for being no bigger than it was. I stood transfixed by the dull yellow color and the texture. It was the first time I had ever held and hefted such a thing. Again, I felt a rush. I had only seen gold on jewelry worn by people outside my family. As I stared at the ingot, McVay smiled and told me it was probably worth over $15,000.

After ten bars had been passed from the cave and stacked, the men crawled out. Sanderson, Seitsinger, Schwartz, and McVay stood outside the entrance brushing fine dust and packrat nest debris from their clothes.

"Now comes the hard part," said Sanderson, "and that's carrying these heavy bastards down to the truck. We should have brought some packs."

Each man picked up two ingots and without a word started down the rocky slope toward the campsite. I tried to lift the last two but couldn't manage. I only weighed ninety pounds and together the two bars were well over half my weight. I yelled to Seitsinger that I couldn't carry them both. Without pausing, he said, "Carry one down, then come back and get the other." Mortified, I picked up one of the ingots and followed.

During the next two days, all of the bars were removed from the cave and carried down the foothill slope to the camp. Fifty of them were loaded into the trunk of the Chrysler and covered with a tarp. The back end of the car sagged and I thought the tires would burst. Seitsinger determined it would be best to bury the rest and return for them later. The ground near the spring, however, consisted of solid limestone and caliche and was impossible to dig. The nearest soil that was soft enough to excavate lay three hundred yards away in the middle of an abandoned orchard located several yards east of Kincaid's ranch house. We spent most of the night carrying the rest of the ingots to the middle of the orchard and quietly burying them in a shallow trench we scraped out.

We returned to El Paso about an hour before sundown and I was dropped off in front of my house with a caution: Never tell anyone about the gold. If I did, Seitsinger said he would deal with me personally. McVay explained that a closed mouth is the first requirement of a professional treasure hunter.

That night, I dreamt of gold, wealth, and adventure. I continue to have the dreams to this day.

POSTSCRIPT

I was never compensated for my role in retrieving the gold ingots from the cave and serving as a camp hand. I mentioned this to McVay a few years afterward and he laughed, saying that Seitsinger believed it was payment enough that he did not kill me for stealing his strawberries.

It had never bothered me that I didn't get a cut of what had been realized from the sale of the gold. I had grown up in a household with little money and had little to no experience with cash. I had become wealthy, however, as a result of the experience with the four treasure hunters. The event inspired and affected me in a number of ways that determined the course of my life.

I remained in touch with Simon McVay for the next three decades. When I was forty-five years old, I visited him at his house in Ysleta, Texas. As it turned out, it was only a few weeks before he passed away. We talked about the time I had accompanied him and his three friends to the Guadalupe Mountains more than thirty years earlier. He asked me if I was still upset about not being given a share of the treasure we hauled out of the cave. I told him I wasn't. He then asked me if I would like to be included now. I invited him to explain him what he meant, and he provided a fascinating piece of information.

Taking a sip of bourbon, Simon asked me if I remembered the fifty ingots we had carried to the old abandoned orchard and buried with the intent of retrieving at some later date. I said I did.

With a wink and a smile, he said, "They are still there."

2

INGOTS OF GOLD,
THREATS OF DEATH

Surprise is the lubrication of adventure.

—Rod Steiger

During the 1960s, I lived in Ysleta, Texas, the oldest settlement in the Lone Star State. I had a wife who taught public school and I worked at a variety of jobs to earn some money while I was taking classes at Texas Western College, now the University of Texas at El Paso. I had acquired a growing regional reputation as a young but competent treasure hunter among my peers as a result of some minor successes. I was known as a hard worker, dedicated to the research necessary for discovery and recovery, and an efficient and effective leader of expeditions. I was proud of the recognition as it came from longtime area fortune hunters I respected and admired. Reputations such as these circulate among a small circle of like men and are rarely heard of outside of the esoteric, somewhat secretive, and often dangerous world related to the search for lost mines and buried treasures.

I also earned a bit of a reputation among the general newspaper-reading public as the result of an overeager reporter who got wind of one of my adventures and wrote about it in an article that was syndicated in newspapers around the country. His exaggerations and misrepresentations made me appear far more successful than I was, mistakenly portraying me as equal parts Sir Edmund

Hillary, Jungle Jim, Trader Horn, and Percy Fawcett. It was a reputation I did not want and it caused me no end of trouble, not the least of which was people calling and inviting themselves to participate in one of my expeditions or offering insight into some treasure story or another. Ninety-nine percent of the callers had little idea of what was involved in a hunt for lost treasure.

That remaining 1 percent, however, sometimes provided information or opportunity that led to something interesting, adventurous, and occasionally lucrative. That is how I came to meet a woman named Ova Noss. The association with Noss had the potential of leading to the recovery of what many believed to be one of the largest lost treasure caches in the United States, if not the world. It also nearly got me killed.

Mrs. Noss phoned long distance from Truth or Consequences, New Mexico, and told me she believed she could use my help. She provided a brief backstory of the discovery of a multimillion-dollar treasure cache by her late husband, Milton "Doc" Noss, who had been, among other things, a mail-order-certified foot doctor though he had few patients.

For forty-five minutes she provided the details of the tale, the estimated size of the treasure, and her difficulties in recovering it. Her story sounded far-fetched, like something a Hollywood screenwriter might come up with, and I told her so. She berated me and informed me I would do well to listen to her. Then she invited me to come to her house. There, she told me, she would prove everything she said and more. Intrigued, and in between expeditions, I decided to travel to Truth or Consequences, some eighty miles to the northwest of my home, to meet with her.

When I arrived, Mrs. Noss, a brusque, excitable, and often angry woman, told me to call her Ova and lost no time in providing details of the story of a great treasure hoard hidden deep in a low, remote peak located about forty miles to the southeast of Truth or Consequences in the San Andres Mountains. Noss, Ova, and four companions had been deer hunting in the Hembrillo Basin in the

San Andres Mountains one day when Doc scaled Victorio Peak and found a vertical entrance into the mountain. He climbed down into the opening, using an aged tree trunk he found inside with notched footholds. Such a structure was long employed in early mines and was called a chicken ladder by the Indians. Noss entered a cavern large enough, he claimed, to house a locomotive and several boxcars and found it filled with treasure: gold ingots, golden church artifacts such as chalices and crosses, chests filled with jewels, Spanish armor, and more. He also found twenty-seven skeletons, several of them still tied to stakes driven into the ground. During successive months, Noss removed around two hundred of the gold ingots as well as numerous artifacts from the cave. In order to facilitate the recovery of the treasure, he attempted to widen the entrance using dynamite, but succeeded only in clogging the shaft with rock debris. As a result, he could then no longer enter the cave.

Years earlier, I had heard snippets and rumors pertinent to this story, but wasn't willing to believe most of it. I found it interesting and provocative, but I needed more than someone's version of a tale to get me involved. When I confessed my reservations and doubts to Mrs. Noss, she appeared insulted that I would even question her. She stepped into an adjacent room and brought out evidence: five crudely smelted gold ingots weighing about twenty-five pounds apiece, a chalice made from pure gold and similar to those in which communion wine is served, a Spanish sword with a jeweled handle, several gold coins bearing the date 1780, a gold ring mounted with what appeared to be an emerald, and a tiara festooned with jewels I took to be opals, garnets, and emeralds. Among these treasures was a human skull. All of these items, said Ova Noss, came from inside the cave. She said her late husband had buried many of the two hundred gold ingots he had taken from the cave in secret locations in and near Hembrillo Basin and sold several others on the black market. She estimated that hundreds, if not thousands, of gold ingots remained in the cave, along with the chests of jewels and more.

I became a believer. I asked Ova what she expected of me. She told me she had learned that the U.S. Army was attempting to dig into the mountain and remove the treasure she believed was rightfully hers. She showed me an extant mining claim with her name on it. Ova wanted me to enter the White Sands Missile Range by night, proceed to Victorio Peak, assess the progress made by the military, and report back to her. If time and opportunity were available, she requested I examine the entrance near the top of the mountain to see if it was still clogged and search the base of the peak for a possible second entrance that had been suggested by Doc Noss. Ova informed me I was to be part of a group of four men.

During the next hour as we visited, the three other participants in the scheme arrived and introductions were made all around. I knew one of them by reputation—an older man named Blake, about thirty-eight, and a professional treasure hunter who claimed some modest successes. The other two, local men named Garrish and Mendez, were only slightly older than I, claimed a few treasure expedition experiences, and came recommended by Blake. All were personable, and though I did not care to enter into an expedition with men I was not familiar with, I had a good feeling about these three. We agreed to make the attempt together and promised to meet at Ova's residence at 8:00 p.m. on the first Friday of October before leaving for Victorio Peak. We were to receive a percentage of anything we found during this trip or any subsequent ones, if such were to happen.

We left Ova's residence around midnight of the designated day and traveled in Blake's jeep along an unmaintained ranch road across several miles of washboard caliche. The road cut through rolling parched desert, and we finally arrived at a point along a four-strand barbed wire fence that separated the ranch from White Sands Missile Range on the other side. In the moonlight we could see the San Andres Mountains looming northeast of our position.

Blake parked the jeep next to a cluster of creosote bushes. We climbed through the fence and, after consulting a topographic

map, started toward the peak. Picking our way across the landscape was made easier by the illumination of a nearly full moon.
Hours later, as we made our way up a canyon that provided the
setting for the peak, the crepuscular light of a cool dawn enfolded
us and we proceeded confidently for several hundred yards. Then,
suddenly, we heard the distant whine of vehicles approaching
from the opposite side. From that point on, we took care to travel
with caution, moving from brush to brush, tree to tree, and trying
to stay out of sight of whoever was already at the low mountain.

As we arrived at the southwestern side of Victorio Peak, we
saw evidence of blasting and bulldozing: here, great chunks of the
side of the mountain had been removed, obviously an attempt
to gain access to something within. Nearby were parked several
earth-moving machines and other heavy equipment, as well as
several jeeps, all bearing U.S. Army identification. Formally or
informally, the military was trying to get at the Noss treasure.

After hearing the sound of the vehicles earlier, we heard
nothing more and grew concerned as to the whereabouts of
unknown others. We presumed they knew nothing of our presence, so we crept around the base of the peak in hope of spotting anyone before they spotted us. When we reached a point
that presented a relatively easy climb to the top, we decided to
go up and look for the entrance to the shaft Ova had described.
Without speaking, we made our way up the slope. Near the top,
it took another thirty minutes to find the opening. It was easy to
spot since there were jackhammers and other excavation equipment lying about. It was obvious that an attempt at reopening the
entrance had taken place here, but there were still tons of debris
filling the narrow shaft, making entry from that point impossible.

We crawled back down, determined to search for the secondary entrance alluded to by Ova. Once back at the foot of the peak,
we proceeded with caution, ever alert to the potential of others
nearby. Blake stopped and plucked something from the ground.
It was an arrowhead. Fifteen minutes of searching the ground
yielded four more.

Thirty minutes later as we rounded the northwestern flank of the peak, we heard voices. Finding a secluded place behind a cluster of rocks, we dropped down and watched as several uniformed enlisted men at a time entered a low, narrow shaft, each returning a few minutes later carrying two ingots. The ingots, which we presumed to be of gold, were placed onto a flatbed truck parked nearby. As far as we could tell, there were twelve enlisted men who were being directed by four in officer garb. Three of the officers wore the khaki uniforms of the U.S. Army while the fourth was in Air Force blue. During the time we watched from hiding, an impressive fortune passed out of the shaft and onto the truck. We counted two hundred and twenty gold ingots, each weighing, we estimated, between thirty and thirty-five pounds apiece.

Distracted by watching millions of dollars' worth of what we were certain was a portion of the Spanish gold described by Ova, we were unaware of the approach of others until it was too late. Startled by a loud command coming from several feet behind us, we jumped in response to a sharp voice ordering us to raise our hands and stand up. Two soldiers, each wearing combat fatigues and pointing automatic weapons, instructed us to step away from the rocks. In seconds they were joined by four others equally armed.

Blake, Garrish, Mendez, and I were pushed around, prodded with the tips of gun barrels, and thrown to the ground and ordered to lie on our bellies. We were handcuffed, searched, slapped, and kicked. One soldier took a cheap .22-caliber revolver from me and a .38 from Blake. Our wallets were pulled from our pockets and identifications examined. Then, we were jerked to our feet and shoved toward the four officers who stood waiting. Each had a nametag pinned above the left breast pocket.

It was clear the officers were upset, angry, and even a little nervous about being discovered emptying the treasure from Victorio Peak. While full of the usual military bluster one associates with the higher ranks, the men behaved as though they had been caught doing something wrong. One of the army officers stepped forward, and a soldier handed him our wallets. He examined the identifications within and asked us who was who. Caught red-handed, we gave our names while the soldiers held their weapons on us.

Speaking to Blake, the oldest, the officer asked what we were doing at the peak. In the instant between the asking of the question and any answer Blake might have provided, I had an inspiration. Before Blake could respond, I stepped forward and told the officer we were rattlesnake hunters, that we collected venom for a snakebite antidote laboratory in Albuquerque, and that this time of the year was best for finding rattlesnakes in this region. Blake picked up on my response and added that we wanted to get in one final harvest before the rattlers holed up for the cold season. He explained we didn't know anyone would be here.

The officer informed us we were trespassing on U.S. government property and by rights we could be shot where we stood. I told him where we had parked Blake's jeep and climbed the fence and mentioned we saw no signs alerting anyone to the fact that this was posted land. I figured the more ignorant we appeared, the less of a threat they would perceive us to be. We were lucky no one inquired about the absence of venom-collecting paraphernalia.

Another officer stepped forward and asked us how long we had been hiding behind the rock and what did we specifically see. With my mind still working in overdrive, along with a sense of survival kicking in, I answered that we had only been there a few seconds, only long enough to see the soldiers carrying "lead" bars out of a mine shaft. Continuing to play dumb, I told him we weren't aware that the military was using this old shaft to store lead. I asked if it was going to be used to make bullets.

The officers looked at one another, alternately amazed we were so stupid and visibly relieved that, to them, we were not cognizant of the treasure being removed. The four men asked us more questions, to which we responded with answers designed to validate our ignorance. Finally, one of them wrote down our names and addresses in a palm-size notebook, told us we would have to leave, and ordered us into two awaiting jeeps to be transported back to where we were parked. He warned us never to reveal what we had seen.

"If you do," he said, "you will be found and executed." With this, he held up the notebook containing our names and addresses and waved it in front of us. Since we had few options, we agreed.

We were turned over to the enlisted men with the automatic weapons, shoved roughly toward the jeeps, and ordered into the backseats. I rode with Mendez who whispered his concern that the soldiers were going to drive us out into the desert and shoot us. I had felt good about our chances of getting out of there unharmed until that moment. The soldier in the front passenger seat was turned, facing us, the barrel of his weapon pointed directly at Mendez's stomach. The other jeep was ahead of us, and we could see Blake providing directions to the fence crossing to the driver. Just as I was deciding on the best way to take our guard out and hoping Mendez could handle the driver, we arrived at the point where we had crossed the boundary.

By evening, we were back at Ova Noss's house giving her a full report of what we had seen at the peak and the events of the day. I provided her with the names and ranks of the officers who had confronted us. Enraged, Ova paced the living room cursing the military, the government, and anybody else she could think of. Never before or since have I ever heard anyone string together a series of curses and blasphemies as foul, or as impressive, as hers.

It was close to midnight when Blake, Garrish, Mendez, and I left Ova's residence, said our good-byes, and headed for our respective homes. I ran into Blake about five years later and visited with him about various expeditions. I never encountered Garrish or Mendez again.

Within days of our last visit, Ova Noss contacted her attorneys who, in turn, contacted government officials about the illegal excavation at Victorio Peak. Repeatedly, officials at White Sands Missile Range denied that there was any activity at the peak and declared that the Noss claim was being honored. We later learned there was a distinct possibility that the officers and enlisted men we saw removing the treasure were involved in an operation independent of government knowledge or blessing.

A short time later, the newspapers picked up the story of the treasure and the theft of the gold ingots by the soldiers. It was splashed around the country and mentioned the names of two of the officers. Because the wheels of government, especially the military, as well as the workings of what passes for justice, grind slowly, months went by with nothing accomplished save for delays. Years passed and it seemed as though Noss's claim to the fortune was going to be ignored forever. In the meantime, each of the four officers we identified had retired from military service. Private investigators hired by Noss learned that each of the officers had become wealthy far beyond what military service would have provided. The source of their wealth was never explained.

One of the officers was summoned to appear before several investigative boards but was never charged with violating Noss's claim. Once, when I was called to testify what I had witnessed at Victorio Peak at a hearing in Albuquerque, he and I came face to face outside the courtroom. We recognized each other immediately. He approached and spoke low enough so that only I could hear. Angrily, he told me he intended to have me killed for implicating him in the treasure recovery operation.

I never took the death threat seriously until four months later. Some court initiated a new series of hearings in an attempt to determine the legal owners of the mining rights at Victorio Peak and ascertain whether or not any violation of existing claims or laws had occurred. I was again summoned to provide a statement of what I witnessed at Victorio Peak.

I had two weeks to myself before the scheduled appearance, and I took the opportunity to travel to my father's ranch in Columbus, New Mexico. I packed a few things into my car, locked up the house, and left on the one-hundred-fifty-mile trip. As I pulled out of the long gravel driveway from my house to the highway, I noticed a late-model blue Cadillac parked across the macadam and about thirty yards to the east. Such a vehicle was uncommon in my relatively poor neighborhood. I could make out the form of a driver slouched down in the seat but was unable to note any details in the dark interior of the car. Thinking little of it, I proceeded toward Columbus.

After leaving Las Cruces and heading west toward Deming where I would turn south to get to the ranch, I glanced up into the rearview mirror and saw a blue Cadillac about forty yards behind me. I had no way of knowing whether it was the same car I saw on leaving my place, but a silent alarm went off in my brain. I didn't believe in coincidence.

I turned off the highway in Deming and stopped at a convenience store. I went in and, from my position next to a magazine rack, surveyed the outside. The Cadillac had pulled to a stop on the opposite side of the road about one hundred feet away. The driver was eyeing the building.

I exited the store with a small purchase, climbed into my car, and pulled away without haste, providing the driver of the Cadillac no opportunity to suspect I had spotted him. After making my way through Deming, I struck the paved highway that headed south to Columbus, about thirty-two miles away. I had covered only ten miles when I looked up and spotted the Cadillac once again, still maintaining a forty-yard distance behind me. Twenty miles later when I turned off onto the dirt road that led to the ranch house, the Cadillac continued on into town. I decided I needed to remain alert with regard to the mysterious car and driver.

The next morning around 10:30 a.m., I climbed into my father's pickup truck and drove to the mercantile in Columbus.

As I passed by the only operating motel in town, I saw the Cadillac parked in front of one of the units. At the hardware store, I purchased a fencing tool and a new pair of leather work gloves. On the way back I noticed the Cadillac was gone. Later that afternoon while I worked in the corral, I heard a car coming down the washboard road that went past the ranch house. Looking up, I spied the Cadillac. The driver saw me looking his way, sped up, and continued to travel toward the west until out of sight.

The following day during another trip to the hardware store, I was driving my car by the old abandoned cotton gin on Highway 11 when I heard what sounded like three rifle shots fired in rapid succession accompanied by a thunking sound on the truck. I stomped the gas pedal. Once parked in front of the store, I examined the truck and found a bullet hole in the driver's side wall of the bed and an exit hole in the other. The person with the rifle was either a bad shot or was sending a warning. I could only believe it had something to do with my testimony, previous and forthcoming, regarding the Victorio Peak incident.

After that I saw no sign of the Cadillac. I did hear rifle shots again on a subsequent trip to town but the truck was not hit. When I arrived back in Ysleta several days later, a front window of my house sported a bullet hole. Over the next four days I received anonymous death threats by phone, a muffled voice trying hard to sound sinister. I got an unlisted number.

In Albuquerque I testified before a panel of six men—lawyers and military officers—for one half-hour in a meeting room. We sat around a large table. When they were finished with me, I was escorted into the hallway. There, I encountered the officer who threatened me at Victorio Peak in the company of a man I assumed was his lawyer. When he saw me, the officer raised his right hand, pointed his index finger toward me, cocked his thumb, and fired an imaginary round into my head.

During the ensuing months, I kept an eye out for the blue Cadillac. I often spotted unfamiliar vehicles I thought might be following me, but it always turned out to be nothing but my imagination. Time passed, and I learned that the officer had died of cancer.

Ova Noss has been dead now for many years, but her descendants continue to try to regain the right to enter the cavern inside Victorio Peak. They have had no success. Some are convinced that members of the military removed the treasure and nothing remains inside the great chamber. I know for certain that the military, with or without formal sanction, removed some of it. Subsequent research suggests that the gold ingots we watched being carried from the shaft did not come from inside the large chamber, but from where they had been stored in a passageway. I am convinced there was no access to the chamber found by Doc Noss from that particular shaft, or if there was, it was sealed off either by man or by some natural cause such as a collapse or earthquake.

While there is a possibility that some of the treasure from the chamber was removed by someone other than Doc Noss, I am inclined to believe that much of it, if not most, still lies within.

People have asked me what keeps me from going after the treasure. The answer is simple: the U.S. government. They continue to maintain tight control over the region, including regular patrols around and through Hembrillo Basin. I have approached White Sands Missile Range public relations personnel on several occasions, and they are quick to point out they are not permitted to discuss the matter of searching for treasure at Victorio Peak. I am given ten minutes of their time before they order me from the range.

During the 1970s, White Sands Missile Range officials allowed a research crew into Hembrillo Basin. A high-technology imaging program revealed that a huge cavern does indeed exist deep inside Victorio Peak, just like Doc Noss said. It also revealed at least two tunnels leading to the chamber from outside the peak, but they were both clogged with rock and debris. More attempts were made during the following years, but due to the severe and incomprehensible restrictions placed on the searchers by the U.S. Army, as well as the unreasonably short time limits, the cavern was never breached.

Whatever treasure remains inside Victorio Peak cavern appears to be secure for the time being.

3

STRAP SILVER

There are many shades in the danger of adventure.

—Joseph Conrad

The month of March is windy in the northern part of the Mexican state of Chihuahua, but the one of 1966 was the worst I'd seen in several years of exploring and working in that country. The blowing, gusting, warm air irritated and itched, making all of us wish we were somewhere else. Instead, we were outdoors in the vast ranch empire of the Palomas Land and Cattle Company digging postholes, stringing barbed wire fence, rounding up stray cattle, and keeping an eye out for Mexican lobos, mountain lions, and squatters that had been killing calves for food.

I was working with a crew of five men, all Mexican save for me, and we were camped in a rugged and remote foothills section of the ranch for days, sometimes weeks, at a time and miles from headquarters. We dined on canned goods, dried meat and fruit, flour, corn meal, coffee, sugar, and other staples carried with us on the backs of two mountain-bred mules. Two goats provided milk. Occasionally, one of us would bring down a deer or bag some quail, dove, turkey, or javelina for a bit of variety in the diet. Except for the constant wind and the annoyance of irritable rattlesnakes emerging from their winter hibernation, the work was alternately invigorating, tiring, and satisfying. The one hundred dollars per month wages plus feed and found was low but about what we expected. Life was simple, pleasant, and seldom dull.

One evening, we sat around the campfire resting from a full day of fencing and cutting cedar posts. We sipped dark, rich Mexican coffee heavily laced with sugar and goat's milk as we digested our meal of venison and canned peaches. Priciliano Samaniego had risen to prepare a second pot of coffee when he spotted a rider approaching the camp. The stranger called out while he was still about fifty yards away. The foreman, Luciano Baca, rose, peered into the darkness beyond, and then issued an invitation to the newcomer to ride on in. A man astride a roan mare and leading a pack mule halted several feet away, tied off his animals to a low bush, and joined us at the fire.

Sweeping his large felt sombrero from his head and executing a slight, mannerly bow, he introduced himself as Gilberto Reyes—hunter, trapper, and sometime trader of precious stones he dug out of the mountains. Reyes was directed toward what remained of our dinner and invited to fill a plate. He helped himself to venison and peaches while Baca poured fresh coffee into a spare cup. Smiling in gratitude, Reyes seated himself by the campfire and ate.

During the course of the evening we learned that Reyes often traveled along the foothills of the Sierra Madres from near Ciudad Chihuahua northward to the U.S. border and back. Along the way, he dug into rock outcrops for agate and turquoise and searched for opals, all of which he sold to a brother who lived in El Paso. The brother, in turn, marketed the stones to lapidarists who cut and polished them and affixed them to bolo ties, bracelets, earrings, and watchbands. Reyes also peddled the tanned hides of fox, coyote, wolf, mountain lion, jaguar, ocelot, and sometimes black bear. Now and then he killed rattlesnakes, peeled them, and used their patterned skins to fashion unique belts and hatbands. In addition, Reyes found buyers for ornamental feathers taken from birds that lived in the deep, verdant canyons of

the Sierra Madres. During his forays into the mountains and his
journeys to the border, Reyes kept himself fed by shooting game
and bartering for corn, beans, squash, and peaches with residents
of small pueblos he encountered along the way.

As the campfire conversation progressed, Antonio Mata
poured Reyes another cup of coffee and told him to help himself
to more *carne de venado* and a couple of *tortillas de maiz*. Reyes gave
his thanks and offered to trade a coyote pelt for the meal, a gesture
politely refused by foreman Baca.

Reyes looked to be about fifty years of age and in fine physical condition from his life in the outdoors. His face, deeply chiseled with lines caused by sun, wind, and smiling, was handsome
and squarish, looking somewhat Indian. His broad shoulders ta-
pered to a narrow waist belted by a handmade leather girth that
held up the baggy cotton pants favored by *campesinos*.

Following some exchanges of news and gossip and more
coffee, my companions spoke of the coming day and the work
it would bring, then crawled into their bedrolls and fell asleep.
Reyes and I were left seated by the glowing embers of the dying
fire.

As we conversed, Reyes walked over to his horse and mule,
removed the saddles and bridles, hobbled them, and turned them
loose to graze on the swath of nearby grass. From one of the packs
he withdrew a bullet mold, a long strip of soft metal, and two or
three small implements. Reseating himself next to me, he stoked
the fire and added two forearm-sized mesquite logs. As the blaze
grew, he took his skinning knife and began shaving pieces of the
soft metal from the thin strap into an eight-inch cast-iron skillet.

Sensing my curiosity, he looked up and said, "*Plomo, por las
balas.*" Lead, for bullets.

When the metal had melted, he carefully poured it into a
set of molds, making two-dozen loads for .30-.06 caliber bullets. As Reyes worked, I picked up the metal strap and examined
it. "Strap" is a term used to refer to a long, thin bar of bullion,

often of gold, silver, or lead, fashioned by Spanish and Mexican miners two and three centuries earlier. For molds, the workers would sometimes employ pieces of cane found near streams and cut lengthwise into equal halves and into twelve- to fifteen-inch pieces. Into these thin, shallow molds the melted silver would be poured and allowed to cool, thus fashioning a crude but effective ingot. Until the Spanish miners began carrying premade molds with them into the mining areas, many of the first Spanish silver ingots were formed in this manner. Sometimes, the natural joints of the cane were easily discernible on the metal bars.

The strap produced by Reyes had been fashioned in this manner, suggesting it was very old, perhaps two hundred years or more. It was about fourteen inches long, no more than one inch wide, a half-inch thick, and rounded on the bottom. It was heavy for its small size. Near one end of the strap I noted the figure of a small Christian cross topped with a tiny caret, both of which had been hammered into the soft metal.

I asked Reyes where he had obtained his lead.

"I found a great quantity of it," he said, "in an old abandoned mine deep in a canyon far to the south in the Sierra Madres. The nearest settlement is miles away, and the *campesinos* who live there tell me that the mine was worked many generations ago by the Spanish padres who enlisted the labor of the Indians."

Reyes paused a moment to regard his bullet-making progress, then continued. "The Indians, it is said, soon tired of the enslavement and revolted, killing or driving out the *catolicos* and abandoning the mine. Since that time, all of the lead that had been molded into bars such as this one has lain stacked inside the mine. There are hundreds of them."

As Reyes spoke, I sliced off a shaving of the soft metal with my pocket knife and examined it closely in the light of the fire. The metal was so soft that the thin sliver could be rolled into a ball with small effort.

"Is it hard to get to this mine? I asked.

"Not at all. I visit it several times a year for the lead. Why do you wish to know? Do you need some lead for your own bullets? There is plenty."

"This is not lead," I told him. "This is almost pure silver."

He showed little emotion at the comment as he stared into the skillet. "Even so," he said, "it makes good bullets."

Reyes and I visited well into the next morning. We talked about the possibility of the two of us traveling to the old mine shaft and retrieving a quantity of the silver bars. Elated less at the prospect of becoming wealthy and more at the prospect of having some company on his journey, he agreed to rendezvous with me at the same spot in two weeks on his return trip from the border. From there, we agreed, we would travel to the abandoned mine, assess the richness of the stacked silver straps within, and then make plans to retrieve it and sell it.

Two weeks later to the day, Reyes rode in from the north up to the same stone ring that held the comforting fire during his earlier visit, his pack mule trailing along behind him. I was on a borrowed horse, one loaned to me by the head wrangler, Lalo Gutierrez, with blessings from Tom Cruz, the ranch manager. In the saddlebags were *tortillas de maiz* made fresh that morning, a sack of dried pinto beans, and some jerked beef and venison. My bedroll and a light denim jacket were tied behind the saddle.

Since most of the new fence construction and the old fence repairs were completed, Cruz was cutting back on hands for a few weeks, so it had been easy to deal for some time off to ride south with Reyes.

Reyes and I exchanged greetings and small talk while his animals rested and grazed on the nearby grass. When they had their fill, we mounted up and rode south, the animals following a well-traveled trail into the folded and canyoned foothills of the Sierra Madres.

For days we rode, skirting the maze of canyons and ridges of the range that lay to the west. Once, during a still, warm morning, a large rattlesnake struck wildly at the right foreleg of Reyes's roan from the side of the trail, missing by a half-inch. The snake gave only a second's warning, and it took several minutes for Reyes to calm the horse.

"*Las viboras* are cranky and dangerous from their long winter sleep," he said. "There will be more of them and we must be careful."

We continued on, watching more intently for snakes than before. Early on the morning of the fourth day, we left the main trail and rode along a much less traveled, narrower path that led into the dark, shadowy foothills. The days had been warm and the nights cool. The evenings seated around a campfire were welcome after weary hours of riding. In the distance, wolves howled and the large cats screamed as we sought sleep, edging closer to the blaze.

Late on the afternoon of the tenth day, Reyes guided us into the mouth of a wide canyon with high vertical walls of igneous rock, the crystals in the granite matrix sparkling in the light of the descending sun. A narrow, slow-flowing stream of clear, cool water wound its way in lazy meanders along the floor. At one point we stopped to drink and water the horses and counted twelve large rattlesnakes lurking in the low-growing greenery along the bank. Languid in the cool of the canyon, the snakes posed little threat. From the great maw of the largest of *las viboras* extended the long legs of a half-swallowed bullfrog, the amphibian being slowly peristalted into the snake's digestive system, its legs moving feebly.

When we finished watering the animals, we continued winding our way up the seldom-used trail that wound around the pine trees, willows, and cottonwoods spaced along the valley floor. Another hour of riding brought us to a widening of the canyon. Here, the walls graded from the earlier verticality to a gradual slope. Along the north wall I spotted the tailings from ancient mines, the small shaft openings perched above them looming dark and forbidding. Reyes led the way to a flat, grassy sward and said, "Here is where we camp tonight."

It was a good place—plenty of dead limbs for firewood and ample water and forage for *los caballos*. As Reyes hobbled the animals, I gathered several armloads of dry wood.

"Sundown in this canyon will not be long in coming," said Reyes. "We rest tonight. In the morning we will climb to the shaft and I will show you the straps."

Following a meal of beans, jerky, and tortillas, we sipped coffee and watched shooting stars streak across the night sky visible between the ridges. Tired, we climbed into our bedrolls for a good night's sleep, hoping the rattlesnakes would not join us.

In the middle of the night, the screams of a mountain lion woke us. The cat was not far away, only a few hundred yards farther up in the canyon. The horses and mule stomped and snorted, nervously flicking their tails, and Reyes spent many minutes calming them.

By the time it was light enough to see in the morning, Reyes and I were already drinking coffee and tending to the stock. Anxious to have a look at the old mine, we decided to skip breakfast. Carrying only a canteen apiece, we climbed a steep slope of loose gravel, the product of millions of years of weathering from the granite walls. Once above the talus and onto the bedrock of the mountain, our boots crunched into the more recent scree, the tailings from the old mine that had been dumped down the slope generations ago.

At the top of the loose rubble, we paused for several minutes to catch our breath. Reyes pointed to the opening, a low, dark mouth in the side of the mountain. The light from the outside penetrated only a few feet into the opening.

"We'll need torches," I said to Reyes.

"They will not be necessary," he replied. Then he turned and entered.

The opening was low, only about four feet high, and only wide enough for one man to pass through at a time. Reyes, no more than 5'6" tall, bent low and entered. At 6'1", I was forced to crawl through the opening and proceed either dramatically stooped over or on my hands and knees.

After twenty feet, the ceiling of the shaft was barely five feet high. At this distance from the entrance, barely enough light trickled in so we were not in complete darkness. I was concerned, however, that if we proceeded any farther into the shaft we would need torches.

"How are we going see?" I asked.

"Do not be concerned," replied Reyes. "We wait a moment so our eyes grow accustomed to the dim light. Be patient. Soon you will look upon what you have come for."

As my eyes accommodated the darkness, I saw the walls of the shaft and the figure of Reyes seated on the floor of the shaft three feet away. Even in the Cimmerian gloom of the tunnel, I could see he was smiling.

"Behold," he said, and pointed behind him.

There, against the opposite wall of the narrow shaft, were hundreds of the silver straps, all arranged in the criss-cross pattern of stacked cordwood. Each stack was three feet tall, and they extended deeper into the shaft and out of sight in the blackness beyond. They were covered with a thick layer of dust, and I estimated well over two thousand straps were stored in the cave.

As I became more accustomed to seeing in the dimness, I spotted several rotted leather sacks on the floor. A quick inspection revealed they were all empty and what they might have contained we would never know. Here and there among the sacks were odd pieces of metal fittings, a single spur, a bit, some buckles, and perhaps two dozen large nails, all very old.

I eased over to the stacks of silver straps, picked up and examined several, and saw that each was marked with the same Christian cross topped with a caret I had noticed by the campfire more than three weeks earlier. Each strap weighed, I estimated, around eight pounds.

We decided that each of us would carry five of the straps back down the slope to the camp, and then make another trip. We would load as much as practicable into our saddle packs and carry them out horse- and mule-back. Our plan was to sell the first load to a mineral broker I had done business with in Texas and use the money to obtain more mules to pack out the rest. Given the weight of each bar and the number I believed to be stored in the cave, I estimated the value of this cache of silver at well over one million dollars, assuming that each bar had at least 75 percent silver content. The remaining 25 percent would likely consist of lead and zinc. We managed to carry forty straps back to our camp before we tired of the labor.

That evening as we curled up into our sleeping bags, the desert air turned cool and a slight breeze rattled the leaves on the willows. From somewhere in the canyon, we again heard the unmistakable scream of a mountain lion, unnervingly close. At the sound, the two horses and mule directed their gazes into the dark, ears pricked forward, braced to flee. Reyes picketed them closer to camp for the night. The gurgle of the narrow stream tumbling over rocks soon lulled us to sleep.

At first light, Reyes stirred the embers of the fire into a small blaze and began preparing coffee. I rubbed the sleep out of my eyes, brushed my hair back with my fingers, put on my boots and hat, and went to check the animals only to discover they were missing. Believing they had not gone far, I struck out down-canyon in search of them.

I found Reyes's roan three hundred yards away. It was dead, the throat ripped open and barely scabbed over from a great spilling of blood. The large opening in the stomach allowed the contents to be spilled onto the ground, most of which had been eaten. As I approached the dead horse, a vixen that had been lapping at the entrails scurried away. Here and there in the dirt, I could see the tracks of a large mountain lion. I looked around, but could find no sign of the other horse or the mule.

We were afoot.

I returned to the camp and informed Reyes of our situation. Together, we searched for another four hours but could find no trace of the missing animals save for their tracks out of the canyon.

We got back to the camp around the middle of the afternoon, exhausted from the search. We decided to cache the forty silver straps we had removed from the shaft, walk to the nearest pueblo, and try to borrow some horses. We dug a shallow trench several yards from the grassy area and placed all of the straps within save one, which I stuck in my belt. It might come in handy when arranging for the loan of horses. Then we covered the cache over with large rocks. Since the weather was growing warm, Reyes and I decided to hike out of the canyon as the sun was setting and travel during the cool hours of night.

For several hours we retraced our route along the old narrow trail, constantly keeping an eye out for the lost horse and mule. The rough, rocky ground made walking difficult, and we were often forced to sidestep rattlesnakes every few yards. A large rattler struck at Reyes's leg. He was lucky—the fangs penetrated only a loose fold of his *pantalones*. The incident, along with the growing abundance of the poisonous vipers, made us more nervous and cautious.

In the bright moonlight, I noticed several of the snakes were impressively long and thick-bodied. One of them, crossing the trail a few feet in front of us, was at least seven-and-a-half feet in length and as big around as my thigh. I recalled reading somewhere that the record for a diamondback rattlesnake was just under seven feet, though I had seen a few in West Texas that were longer. Reyes told me he had spotted many rattlesnakes in this valley at least eight or nine feet and more. He said his uncle told him once some rider for a ranch he worked on encountered a rattler that was twelve feet long.

About two hours before dawn, the soles of Reyes's boots had parted. He was forced to discard them and proceed barefoot.

Within thirty minutes, however, he was limping badly. When he stopped to examine his feet, I could see they were bleeding.

Just as it was growing light, we spotted a rock overhang about thirty yards off the trail and headed toward it. Our water was used up, we were exhausted, and Reyes's feet were a bloody mess. It was obvious he would be unable to continue.

We checked the space under the overhang for snakes. Satisfied there were none, we stretched out to try to get some rest. I removed the silver strap from my belt and placed it between us.

We surprised ourselves by sleeping almost until noon. The insides of our mouths were dry and cottony and it was difficult to make spit. Just as we were beginning to stir awake, we heard the sound of hoof beats on the trail beyond. I started out of the low shelter to wave the riders over when Reyes hissed at me, warning me to lie down and remain out of sight.

"Robbers," he said. "*Pinche bandidos* who will kill you merely for your boots and hat."

We waited, quiet and still in the shade of the overhang, until the five riders were well out of sight. When the sounds of their passage faded into the distance, I left the shelter and assessed our situation. It wasn't good. We were out of water, and Reyes was in no condition to travel. He told me there was a small pueblo about twelve miles to the southeast, one we skirted on the way to the canyon. There, said Reyes, water would be found and perhaps a couple of horses to borrow.

We decided I could carry Reyes piggyback and, with any luck, reach the pueblo before nightfall. I replaced the silver strap in my belt. Though Reyes was not a heavy man, the hike was made difficult by the rough, rocky trail, Reyes's weight, the constant vigilance for rattlesnakes, and thirst.

We had covered only four miles when I was forced to stop. It was mid-afternoon and our progress was slower than anticipated. After a brief discussion, Reyes and I decided that I should continue on alone, secure a pair of mounts, and return.

We found protection from the sun where a stream had cut a low, shallow niche into a soft limestone cliff at the outside of a bend. Unfortunately, there was no water in the stream. Here we napped in the relative coolness, disturbed now and again by the comings and goings of packrats.

Late in the afternoon, I awoke from a sensation of something crawling across my forearm, which was lying across my chest. Opening my eyes, I spied a large brown scorpion making its way slowly up my arm toward my elbow. Reyes spotted the arachnid at the same instant. When he saw me about to move, he motioned me to lay still. Taking a cigarette from a shirt pocket, he used it to flick the creature away.

Looking around, we discovered that the recess in which we napped was thick with the poisonous arachnids. Shaken, we moved to another location, this one under the shade of an ancient cottonwood tree near the dry stream bank. The slight breeze we caught in this outside location was pleasant. We slept again.

Sundown revealed a waxing, almost full, moon and a clear sky. Visibility was good and the heat rapidly dissipated. I decided I would proceed toward the pueblo in the cool of the night and, with any luck, return for Reyes by noon the following day. I left the silver strap with him.

I walked without stopping until two hours before dawn when I topped a low rise and saw spread out before me the tilled fields of the pueblo residents, the newly formed rows being readied for planting visible in the moonlight.

Light was breaking in the east when I entered the tiny village and encountered a number of dogs that, in turn, alerted the residents. Several men exited their adobes and approached me with suspicion, one of them armed with an ax, another with a hoe. When I explained my predicament, they redirected their efforts toward seeing that I was fed and made comfortable.

While I was eating a breakfast of *frijoles*, *tortillas*, *pollo*, and *café con leche*, I asked about horses. I was told there were none in the village.

I steeled myself for the long walk back to the Palomas Land and Cattle Company ranch where I would be certain to obtain a couple of good mounts and return for Reyes. Even so, it amounted to many days of hard travel. By then, it could be too late for Reyes, who had no food or water. An old man approached me and explained that there was a large *rancho* approximately one day's walk to the southeast.

"There," he said, "You will find many horses. When you tell the *patron* your dilemma, I am certain he will lend you what you need."

I was given precise directions to the *rancho*, thanked all of the fine *gente* who fed and watered me, and left the pueblo at a brisk walk. A sense of urgency relative to returning to Reyes coaxed a pace that ate up the miles and I reached the Rancho Guerrero early in the afternoon. After explaining to the foreman the immediate need to return to Reyes, he provided me with a good horse—a stout, spirited buckskin. He had saddlebags stocked with water and food and gave me a spare mount. He also instructed two of his *vaqueros* to return with me because, as he explained, "that trail is dangerous, often traveled by *bandidos*." The vaqueros carried .44-caliber revolvers in holsters and carbines in saddle scabbards. We left at dawn following a quick breakfast of scrambled eggs, *chorizo*, *tortillas*, and coffee.

Midmorning of the second day found us riding single-file along the trail that would lead us past the dry stream and the cottonwood tree where I left Reyes. The slight breeze at our backs barely offset the growing heat. We were less than two miles away from the tree when one of the *vaqueros*, Gilberto Torres, pointed skyward. Ahead of us and about four hundred feet above the ground, a trio of vultures was gliding on the new day's thermals rising from the desert floor. They were searching for something to eat.

As we watched *los zopilotes*, one of them broke from its glide, lazily flapping its great wings into the wind. There is only one reason a buzzard would fly against a current—it spotted carrion.

In a moment, the other two followed. Then, as we passed around a low bluff, we lost sight of them.

A half-hour later we found Reyes's body on the trail, two of the buzzards tearing at his face and stomach. A pistol shot from one of the vaqueros sent the birds skyward as we loped the horses toward the still form.

Reyes was less than one hundred yards from the cottonwood where I left him. His *pantalones*, shredded at the knees, gave evidence that he crawled to this spot. His thickly swollen, purplish right arm with the two puncture wounds in the tricep showed he had been struck by a rattlesnake, a large one given the space between the holes made by the fangs. Reyes had been dead less than twelve hours. I guessed he must have been struck while he was taking shade underneath the tree and crawled away in an attempt to seek help when he succumbed to the poison.

With the help of the two riders, I buried Reyes under a mesquite tree several yards off the trail, covering the shallow hole with heavy rocks to discourage coyotes and foxes. We rode over to the cottonwood where I found the silver strap lying next to the base of the tree.

I returned to the headquarters of the Palomas Land and Cattle Company nine days later on the borrowed buckskin. After explaining the loss of the horse I borrowed earlier, as well as the death of Reyes, I was offered sympathy, then immediately put back to work on another fencing crew, one that took me several miles to the northwest. I did not tell anyone about the huge cache of silver in the old mine shaft. The cost of the lost horse was to be deducted from my pay. While I dug postholes and stapled wire, I made plans to travel back to the canyon and retrieve the cache of strap silver.

Weeks later, with the work completed, I returned to Texas. Low on discretionary funds, I took a series of jobs, trying without success to set some of the money aside for a return trip to Reyes's canyon. Fate intruded, however, with a series of obligations that kept me occupied: family, jobs, and enrollment in classes at Texas Western College in El Paso. All the while, I maintained my hopes of mounting another expedition to the canyon in the Sierra Madres.

Three years later in March 1969, I took some time away from family and school and returned to the Palomas Land and Cattle Company ranch. Here, I renewed old acquaintances, borrowed a horse, and rode south toward Reyes's canyon to assess the logistics relative to retrieving the strap silver.

Much of the country I passed through was unrecognizable: new fences had been strung, new roads had been laid out and bladed, and old roads and trails rerouted or abandoned. Large herds of cattle now grazed on irrigated fields where three years earlier there was only sand, rock, and desert scrub. The trail I followed, the one Reyes and I rode long ago, had been mostly obliterated by recent expanded farming and ranching activities and I found myself on a road heading in a southeasterly direction, taking me away from the mountains. When the opportunity arose, I passed through gates onto private property in hopes of finding the old trail again but was unsuccessful.

I finally managed to find a route to the higher elevations of the foothills, but it was not the same road Reyes and I traveled earlier. This one was more difficult to follow, having been washed out in places by flash floods roaring down from the slopes and obscured in others by landslides.

I passed by the mouths of several canyons, but none of them looked like the one into which Reyes and I ventured. I spent six days searching on horseback and found nothing.

When I returned again to Texas, I summoned my new partners—James Poet, Mungo Slade, and Dr. Trenton Stanley. Months earlier we had joined forces to search for treasure. Though we seemed an unlikely quartet, we had many common interests. Poet was a native of Great Britain and maintained his citizenship there, but was fascinated with searching for lost and buried treasure in the western United States and Mexico. Slade was a former Marine, experienced in combat, unshakeable, and fearless. Stanley recently left a position teaching history at a large midwestern university to concentrate on researching and searching for treasure and artifacts. He conducted antique and artifact sales out of his home. The four of us were dedicated, tireless researchers, competent and reliable in the field, and got along well. And we had all found treasure.

We met over dinner and drinks at an old hotel with a comfortable bar in downtown El Paso. During post-steak margaritas, I explained the circumstances leading to the discovery of the strap silver and described the canyon, the mine shaft, and its contents, along with the difficulties encountered during the return trip. I suggested a systematic search of the countryside until we located Reyes's canyon. When we found it, we would then determine the best way to retrieve the ingots and transport them into the United States. I brought the strap I carried with me from the canyon and passed it around.

I told Poet, Slade, and Stanley, "I'm guessing, conservatively, there is at least a million dollars worth of silver stashed in that mine shaft."

Stanley, ever the practical one, said, "Yes, but given the current price of silver, we would have to load several tons of it to realize any kind of money to make it all worthwhile."

We agreed.

"The reward is wealth," said Poet, "but we need to discuss the obstacles in the way of obtaining it, as well as the difficulties in bringing it back to the United States. The most prominent obstacle is that you don't know exactly where the canyon is located. What are some others?"

"Other than the fact that we would be starting out on this expedition with only a vague notion of where we are going," I replied, "the other obstacles include the *bandidos* who roam the region, rattlesnakes everywhere you look between the months of March and October, and the difficulty of bringing out that much silver and transporting it to the U.S. border undetected. A large mule train, which is what it would take, would only attract attention, even if we took the back roads to the border. I'm thinking we can't accomplish it without a truck."

"The problem with trucks," said Slade, "is that the crossing guards and everyone else want to look into them to see what you are carrying."

"We don't cross in a truck. We unload the straps to a location a few miles west of the Palomas crossing, get rid of the truck, cross on foot as *touristas*, then go retrieve the bars and sell them through Marquez. He will pay us the going rate for silver."

"What have we got to lose?" I asked.

"Plenty," said Slade. "If we get caught, we lose the silver and spend the rest of our lives in a smelly Mexican prison for trying to smuggle artifacts out of the country."

Slade's accurate observation was met with silence as we pondered the truth of it.

Stanley said, "I've got a better idea."

We all leaned forward on our elbows to hear what he had to say.

"I returned last month from the libraries in Mexico City," he said. "While examining some old religious archives, I found a journal that relates the caching of twenty-two burro loads of silver in another remote canyon in the Sierra Madres, one I suspect lies somewhere to the south of the one you describe."

Stanley regarded each of us, awaiting a response. Our eyes and body language invited him to continue. Looking at me he said, "It may not amount to any more than what you found, but it might be easier to recover."

"How do you know?" I asked.

"Because, unlike you, I know exactly where this one is."

Stanley waited a few moments for his comment to sink in, then continued. "I have obtained written descriptions of the canyon, its location, and a route leading to it from the north. The information was dictated to church authorities in 1728 by two men, two packers, who hid the silver and fled from an Indian massacre that killed all of their companions."

"Who besides you knows about this treasure cache?" I asked.

"As far as I can tell, no one," replied Stanley. "The container in which I found the documents had not been opened since it was sealed in 1754."

"Let's do it," said Slade.

"I'm in," said Poet.

"I'm already counting my fortune," said Stanley, grinning.

"Let's leave in a month," I said. "That will give us time to make arrangements, plan our route, gather and check equipment, and make excuses to our wives."

Today, lying in Reyes's long-abandoned mine shaft somewhere in the eastern foothills of Mexico's Sierra Madres are hundreds of twelve- to fifteen-inch-long, one-inch-by-one-half-inch bars of silver. I know this to be true for I have seen them, held them in my hands, and carried several of them out. One sits before me on my desk as I type, serving as my favorite paperweight for the past forty years.

4

LOST SPANISH GOLD
IN THE PALOMAS SAND DUNES

An object, lost and hidden, waits and whispers.

—Anonymous

Gold is where you find it," opined some anonymous observer a couple of hundred years ago. Based on my experience in searching for and finding gold, there always seems to be some kind of fate involved. Some people refer to it as luck; others call it coincidence. I don't believe that luck just happens; I am convinced you make your own. The better prepared I am, the luckier I seem to be. And I don't believe in coincidence. And then sometimes things happen when you least expect them.

I've found this to be particularly true when it comes to searching for lost treasure. We might labor for months, even years, in search of a legendary or little-known cache of gold or jewels or a lost mine only to return empty-handed. Other times, significant discoveries have fallen into my lap with hardly any planning, and often without any knowledge of the facts at all. When that happened, the most difficult job was sometimes keeping it from getting away from me.

One of these accidental discoveries of an uncountable fortune in gold happened to me in 1968. Due to unanticipated circumstances, the chance at recovering the treasure got away and I've been trying to relocate it ever since.

This story has its origins in the seventeenth century, and the gold involved has lain in the same spot for around three hundred years. It was found once and then lost. It is waiting for me, or someone, to find it again.

From the waning years of the sixteenth century until the first two decades of the 1800s, Spaniards and Mexicans searched for, found, and extracted tons of gold, silver, and other precious metals from dozens of locations throughout the western United States. From sites as far north as Colorado, gold- and silver-laden pack trains carried millions of dollars worth of the valuable ore and bullion to government and church headquarters in Mexico City, as well as to port locations along the east coast of Mexico where it was loaded onto ships and transported across the Atlantic to fill the treasury of the Spanish government or add to the already vast wealth of the Catholic Church.

Stories handed down during previous generations have suggested that not all of the gold and silver arrived at their destinations. Many times, the cargo became lost and disappeared en route. Greedy soldiers, miners, or priests diverted other pack trains. Indians and outlaws attacked several more. One such tale concerned a pack train of some forty burros, each one loaded down with gold that was mined, smelted, and formed into ingots at some remote location somewhere in southern Colorado. The pack train, carrying millions of dollars worth of bullion, was attacked in 1710 by Apache Indians as it crossed the sandy wastes south of today's United States-Mexico border not far from the northern Chihuahuan town of Las Palomas.

The account of the skirmish with the Apaches and the subsequent loss of the gold was recorded and filed in church archives where it lay untouched for over two-and-a-half centuries. During the 1960s, the document was discovered by my treasure hunting partner and intrepid researcher, Dr. Trenton Stanley. Here is the story:

Captain Antonio Garza was the commander of the contingent of Spanish soldiers assigned to escort the long pack train as it wound its way southward through the mountains and onto the wide stretches of desert plain in present-day southern New Mexico. Garza's mission—to oversee the delivery of the gold from the Colorado mines to Mexico City—was his third such assignment in the past three years. Previous trips had been uneventful, but since riding away from the narrow Colorado canyon where the gold had been loaded onto the burros weeks earlier, Garza could not rid himself of the sense of foreboding that gnawed at him. Ever cautious, the seasoned military officer stationed soldiers at the front, rear, and along the flanks of the long, strung-out column as the experienced drivers herded it through deep passes, high mountain ridges, and over endless sandy flats.

After the train had advanced about five miles onto the open, gravelly, windy desert floor just south of Cooke's Range in southwestern New Mexico, Garza began to relax a little, believing the worst of the trip was over. The captain had little time to savor the feeling, however, for within the hour one of his soldiers rode up from the rear of the column and reported sighting a dust cloud several miles behind them. Riders, he reported, and they were gaining rapidly. Garza spotted the dust kicked up in the distance and deduced it came from an Indian war party, probably Apaches and no doubt intent on overtaking the pack train.

After alerting the others, Garza encouraged the drivers to increase the speed of the burros, but the heavily laden animals were already straining under the weight and were weary from the long day's march.

For the rest of the afternoon, the soldiers cast fearful glances to the rear of the column at the approaching cloud of dust. Presently, one of the rear guards could see the advancing riders in the distance and alerted the captain that they were indeed Apaches.

Garza's worst fears were confirmed. Apaches were the scourge of the desert mountain country where they reigned unchallenged, and few travelers, no matter how well-armed and mounted, escaped the horrors of capture and torture that would be so expertly inflicted by these seasoned raiders.

Garza could do little more than continue southward at the agonizingly slow pace and pray that the Apaches might lose interest. The Indians, however, were likely in need of horses, and the well-bred mounts in the possession of the Spanish soldiers were especially attractive to them. Apaches, like most Indians, cared nothing for gold except to fashion ornaments, and they did little of that, but Garza did not know this.

It was still two hours before sundown when the pack train entered the sandy wastes of what is known today as the Palomas Sand Dunes, a short distance across the present-day international border and several miles southwest of the New Mexican border community of Columbus. The wind, which had been blowing all day, was more noticeable as it picked up dust and saltated the heavier grains of sand along the ground. Visibility was reduced to less than one hundred yards.

From the rear of the column, Garza heard a shout of alarm. Turning in his saddle, he watched as several dozen mounted warriors rode into view through the airborne veil of windblown dust. In the short distance that now separated the pack train from the Apaches, Garza could see the paint-streaked features of the ferocious desert dwellers. Mesmerized by the sudden appearance of these frightening raiders, Garza sat his saddle and tried to sort out his feelings of fear and wonderment.

The captain was shocked back into reality at the sound of a shrill cry from the leader of the Apaches. With the scream, the Indians dug their heels into their ponies and surged into the midst of the pack train. The soldiers, terrified and disorganized, milled in confusion as the burros scattered. Garza's shouted commands to his men to stand and fight were lost, carried away by the strong winds, and as he watched, the Apaches slaughtered soldiers, drivers, and pack animals alike. As Garza tried to control his own panicked mount, he was pierced by a dozen arrows. He was dead when he fell from the saddle.

Within minutes all was quiet in the dunes save for the silica hiss of the blowing grains of sand and the grunts of the Apaches as they scalped the victims. As the Indians took boots and clothing from the bodies, mutilated the remains, and rounded up the horses, the blowing sand was already accumulating along the windward sides of the dead animals and men.

The Apaches ignored the gold ingots packed into the leather containers attached to wooden saddles strapped to the dead burros. Once they had loaded their battle trophies onto their newly acquired mounts, they rode out of the sand hills toward the north from whence they came, leaving the slaughter behind them.

That night, the light from the pale moon barely penetrated the dense layer of dust hovering above the landscape. A number of the dead burros, along with their loads, were already half buried by the ever-shifting sands. Nothing moved in the darkness for several hours, and then, as if erupting from a sandy grave, one of the soldiers slowly, painfully rose from the floor of the desert, shaking sand from his uniform. In the middle of the bleak and dreary landscape, he stood with his back to the wind and surveyed the scene before him.

Lieutenant Cristoval Olguin, one of Garza's flank riders, was one of the first to go down during the initial seconds of the attack, felled by an arrow that passed completely through the fleshy part of his side. Too frightened to rise and continue to fight, Olguin feigned death and, because he was more than forty yards from the heart of the battle, was overlooked and forgotten by the time the Apaches began scalping their victims. Dazed and still bleeding, Olguin looked around and determined he was the only survivor. A dedicated soldier, he retrieved a canteen full of water and continued southward on foot, determined to reach Mexico City, report to his superiors, and tell them what had occurred.

Months later, Olguin, following a terrible trek across rugged desert and mountains, enduring heat, thirst, hunger, and hiding from Indian hunting parties, arrived in Mexico City. After relating the details of the attack on the pack train at Palomas Sand Dunes, he was regarded as a hero and awarded a higher rank. When officials wished to place him in command of an expedition to return to northern Chihuahua to retrieve the gold, Olguin pointed out the dangers of the hostile Indians and convinced his superiors such a mission was foolhardy. Eventually the matter was set aside, and soon the gold in the Palomas Sand Dunes was forgotten.

As time passed, settlement along the U.S.-Mexico border increased, ranches were established, and towns were founded. As these developments gradually unfolded, the great fortune in gold ingots lay buried not far away in the Palomas Sand Dunes, unknown to all. Then, in the spring of 1966, this incredible treasure, at least a portion of it, along with several skeletons of men and burros, was accidentally discovered.

Between the ages of twenty-one and twenty-six, I worked at a number of different jobs while taking college classes: ranch hand, dockworker, disc jockey, and hay bucker. I also created freelance art and played some music. In addition, I worked part time for my father on his ranch located near the Mexican border outside of Columbus, New Mexico. For several years, the principal activity of this ranch was the acquisition, raising, boarding, and training of horses for use in Western movies. Because I was fond of ranch work, when I was not taking college classes or searching for lost treasure, my father employed me. I was not aware at the time that all of the horses were stolen.

I learned years later that my father was one of the last big-time horse rustlers in the country. He stole stock from ranches throughout West Texas, southern New Mexico, and southeastern Arizona. With the help of a rancher who lived four miles north, he trained these animals to do stunts required at the time by Hollywood moviemakers. Many of the Western movies made during the 1960s used horses from my father's ranch, all of them stolen. Things started unraveling for him when moviegoing horse ranchers began recognizing their own stock in the films.

Columbus was a fascinating place to live and work because of its strong connection to history. The opportunities to explore and search for silver and semiprecious stones in that region and in northern Mexico were limitless. Abandoned silver mines in the nearby Tres Hermanas Mountains offered unique opportunities for adventure, and the volcanic makeup of the area mountain ranges yielded turquoise and other precious stones by the bucket load.

This border area lay along what was once a major migration route for certain Apache tribes, and artifacts from these Indians, as well as from pre-Columbian settlements, were plentiful. In 1916, a band of Mexican revolutionaries under the leadership of Pancho Villa raided Columbus and a nearby military encampment, burned some buildings, and killed a number of citizens and soldiers. Prior to leading the pursuit of Villa and his small army into the mountains and canyons of Chihuahua, General John J. "Black Jack" Pershing and his troops bivouacked nearby. One segment of his vast encampment extended onto a significant portion of what, by this time, was my father's ranch.

It was a cool March morning in 1966 when my father received a call from Bart Kuykendall, an employee of the Palomas Land and Cattle Company (PLCC), which consisted of several sections of ranch land across the border in Chihuahua. I cooked a breakfast of chorizo, eggs, and chiles and sipped dark Mexican coffee while they talked. Bart and my father had been friends for years and often helped one another with branding, fence building, trading equipment such as backhoes and graders, and other ranch-related chores. On this occasion, some PLCC cattle were missing, and all of the ranch hands save for one were involved with shipping several truckloads of yearlings to the market in Ciudad Chihuahua, some 250 miles to the southeast. Bart asked my dad if he could spare any men to help search for the lost livestock. Dad could spare only one—me.

We finished breakfast, and an hour later I drove through the port of entry at the Mexican town of Palomas and on to PLCC headquarters located several miles to the south and west. As I steered the pickup along the rutted dirt road, I noticed a darkening of the sky and a gradual increase in the speed of the west wind. It was beginning to look like we were in for a strong blow and an accompanying sandstorm before sundown, common for that time of year.

I had been to the PLCC spread several times before so I had no trouble finding it. As I drove up to the headquarters building, a Mexican ranch hand came out to greet me. I remembered him from previous visits but had never met him. He introduced himself in Spanish as Crispin Ortiz, the only cow hand left to oversee things on the ranch. Ortiz was in his forties, his skin darkened and wrinkled by decades laboring in the desert sun and wind. Wasting no time, he led me into the barn where two saddled horses were waiting. His was a stout gray mustang-looking animal with muscle that fairly burst from the skin. The one loaned to me was a long-legged roan with thoroughbred features. With a minimum of small talk, we set out in search of the missing cattle.

As we circled a portion of the vast ranch looking for sign of the strays, I recalled a tale of lost Spanish treasure I once heard from an old man who lived in Palomas and echoed by others in the region. Somewhere near here, a forty-burro pack train carrying what must have been millions of dollars worth of gold ingots was attacked by Apaches. After killing the Spaniards and taking their horses, the Indians rode away, leaving the gold lying on the desert floor. I asked Ortiz if he had ever heard the story. He had not.

Riding in the creosote bush–choked desert floor, we finally encountered the tracks of the missing cattle. Ortiz estimated we were following eleven of the animals, their trail leading toward a section of the desert called the Palomas Sand Dunes. When we arrived at the edge of the dunes, I marveled at the abrupt change in the landscape from the low brush and gravelly desert to the smooth, red and khaki-colored sand hillocks. Ortiz explained that sometimes when cattle grazed onto this part of the ranch, they often entered the dunes and traveled to a fresh water spring deep within this island of sand. The spring, he said, rarely went dry, and he and others had recovered cattle from the site in the past. The tracks we were following led into the sandy expanse, disappearing over the nearest rise.

Since we still had a few hours until sundown, we followed the trail at a leisurely pace, hopeful of locating the cattle and returning them to the main herd. As the desert scrub disappeared behind us, the sky darkened even more and the wind picked up significantly. Soon, it was strong enough for us to have to tie down our hats with bandannas.

We walked our mounts through the extensive array of dunes, following the tracks. As the wind grew in velocity, however, it became more difficult to find them in the shifting sands. Visibility was reduced such that we could not see more than forty yards ahead. The wind was so strong that Ortiz and I had to shout in order to be heard above the din of the whistling gale.

As the storm increased in intensity, the sand grains were lifted higher, saltating along the dune surfaces nearly to stirrup height. The lighter dust, lifted up from the desert floor, filled the air with a choking thickness that made breathing difficult. Sometimes I was unable to see Ortiz even though he was never more than thirty feet away. What small amount of light the sky offered was obscured by the dust cloud. No horizons were visible and it was difficult to maintain our bearings. The tracks, by now, were impossible to follow because of the shifting sand.

Riding close, Ortiz motioned for me to follow him and he led the way to the lee side of a tall dune. Dismounting, we scooped out a hollow in the sand at its base and sat in it, seeking some relief from the dust and sand. A few feet away, our horses stood ground-hitched side by side, unmoving, heads lowered, rumps turned to the wind.

We sat in the hollow for an hour listening to the drone of the moving air and observing the blowing sand and dust, feeling the airborne grains as they struck our clothes and flesh. If any-thing, the wind grew in intensity. I covered my face with my hat. Oddly, I found myself falling asleep.

Later the wind lessened a bit and visibility increased. Ortiz shook me awake and pointed to an object lying in the sand about forty feet to the left of our position. There, through the veil of blowing dust, I could barely discern a whitish feature, just a lump on the ground sticking up above the desert floor, its shape and identity obscured by distance and haze. It was apparent, however, that the winds were gradually shifting the surface layer of sand, slowly uncovering the object. After watching the feature become more exposed with each passing minute, Ortiz decided to go examine it. He scrambled through the blowing dust over to the object and brushed more of the sand away. He pulled it from the ground and carried it back to where I sat. In his hands he held the bleached and badly weathered skull of a burro.

We looked over the object with only mild interest. The remains of equines, bovines, and other animals were not uncom-mon in the desert. When Ortiz finally set the object aside, he looked back at the place where he first saw it and pointed. By now, bits of the skeleton were exposed, the cage of weathered and broken ribs pointing toward the sky.

Another half hour passed, and four more partial skeletons were uncovered by the wind. While skeletons of burros were not rare in the desert, five of them all lying within six feet of one another was curious. Just as I was beginning to wonder about this odd circumstance, Ortiz made an excited noise, jumped from his position, and ran once again out into the wind. A moment later he was back, this time with a human skull in his hands.

As Ortiz and I pondered the significance of this discovery, the Mexican rose once again and walked out into the dust of the storm and poked around. While I sat in the shelter of the sand hill grateful for the relief from the abrasive winds, I watched Ortiz in the distance digging into the loose dirt and tugging at an object. Presently, he walked back to the shelter and tossed a weathered wooden packsaddle onto our growing pile of curious objects.

"There is more," he said, almost solemnly, and returned to the spot where he had been digging.

In another few minutes he was back, cradling a heavy load in his arms. After dropping it into the sand next to the skulls, I stared in amazement at two gold ingots.

As I examined the crudely smelted bars of gold, Ortiz cried out loud enough to be heard over the howling wind, "There are dozens more scattered across the ground over there by the skeletons."

Unable to contain myself, I stood up and rubbed the stiffness out of my legs, cramped from sitting so long in one spot. With my companion, I walked through the wind and airborne sand to the place where he had found the ingots. There, lying partially exposed in the transient floor of this small sandy basin were dozens of bars of gold. As we gazed in awe, the wind continued to shift the loosely consolidated sand, uncovering even more.

Dropping to our knees, Ortiz and I sifted through the sand and found the remains of old leather packs; more packsaddles; more bones, both burro and human; and several pieces of dried belt, strap, bridle, and other tack. The leather, which had lain in the arid sands for over two-and-a-half centuries, was brittle and broke easily. But mostly, we found gold ingots.

As we knelt in the sand, eyes tearing from the wind-borne debris, I quietly acknowledged that we had likely found the lost gold of the Palomas Sand Dunes. We dug and scratched into the sandy floor of the desert, finding more gold ingots and artifacts, delirious with our newfound wealth. Our hearts thudded in our chests, notions of what this gold would buy us intruding into all other thoughts. We forgot about the lost cattle.

After we retrieved and stacked approximately two hundred gold ingots into a low, wide pile in the lee side of the dune where we sat, we decided it would be necessary to ride back to the ranch, procure a couple of wagons, and return to recover our riches.

Ortiz picked two gold bars off the top of the pile. Together, we staggered through the strong wind to our horses. As I climbed into the saddle, I watched the Mexican place an ingot into each of his saddlebags. In another moment, we were riding away. The sky was dark with dust and the approach of sundown. Following the brief lull, the sandstorm grew in intensity. Acting on a hunch, we rode in a direction we believed would return us to the place where we entered the sand hills. Heads down and eyes squinted against the blowing dust, we rode slowly and deliberately, our thoughts on the gold lying in the sand behind us.

The wind raged more violently than before. Even the horses were straining to keep their balance against the fury of the gale as we, crouched low in the saddles, held tightly to the pommels. It was now dark as pitch. I remembered from the night before that there was only a sliver of a waning moon, so even if the storm lessened we would still be riding in near-total blackness.

We rode on, and it soon became clear that we were lost. We could only hope that the storm would abate and that Ortiz would recognize some pertinent landmark that would facilitate our return to the ranch, but we could see nothing.

All night long we sat our saddles as our weary horses plodded through the storm. Occasionally we dismounted and, holding tightly to the reins, led the mounts across the dunes. We had been gone much longer than we planned, and with no water or feed, the animals weakened.

Finally, the wind began letting up slowly, and then with a strange suddenness it stopped altogether. Dawn was minutes away from breaking above the eastern horizon as we looked around trying to determine where we were.

Somehow we had arrived at the southeastern margin of the dunes, several miles from where we entered. Pausing at two isolated ranches in the region, we rested, watered, and grained our horses. We made it back to PLCC headquarters nearly two full days from the time we initially set out. We were exhausted and weak, but eager to return to the sand hills to retrieve our gold.

The following morning we breakfasted on corn tortillas, hominy, chiles, and strong coffee. Afterward, we determined that the only horse-drawn wagon on the ranch was not stout enough to transport any significant weight. Instead, we fitted five spare horses with jerry-rigged packs with which we intended to carry back some of the gold. Around mid-morning, we left to ride back to the point where we first entered the dunes.

Even as we spurred our mounts onto the sandy wastes of the dunes we were filled with a sense of foreboding. Though neither of us said a word, Ortiz and I were keenly aware that the mighty winds had markedly changed and shifted the topography of the dunes such that it bore little resemblance to what we had observed and experienced earlier. The ever-shifting sands had migrated once again. Entire dunes composed of tons of silica particles had been dismantled by the winds and blown grain by grain across a landscape unimpeded by trees or rocks to be deposited in some new shape a quarter of a mile away. After two hundred yards into the dunes, we were lost and disoriented.

Still we rode, scanning the terrain for the exposed bones of burros and men, for our pile of gold ingots. I wondered to myself how many times the gold had been exposed and reburied by the winds over the past three hundred years.

How different it was this day. The air was still, the sky clear, the sand still and quiet. The only sound that penetrated the desert air was the occasional blowing of the horses.

All afternoon we rode in ever-widening circles in search of the treasure. Every now and then we would spot a dune that looked familiar and rode over to it only to be disappointed, to discover we had made a mistake. Once, I spotted a setting that resembled the one where we crouched to wait out the storm, but it turned out to be another. Later, we rode up to a partially exposed skull. Excited, we dismounted and dug it out of the dirt only to find it had belonged to a calf. By the time the sun was only minutes away from descending below the western horizon, we turned the pack train and headed back to the ranch. On the way, we encountered the eleven cows that had wandered away days earlier. They were making their way back to the main herd on their own.

Hours later, Ortiz and I were feeding and currying the horses and returning the equipment to its proper place. Neither of us spoke, but it was clear where our thoughts were. Later, seated wearily at the headquarters kitchen table in the bunkhouse drinking beer and sharing a can of cold beans, we relived our experience.

"The desert," said Ortiz, shaking his head, "it tricks you. It never stays the same. It takes and hides from you what you want the most. It fools you with its changing light, the strong winds, the ever-shifting shapes."

I nodded, admitting we had been outwitted by nature.

Ortiz continued. "The desert meets you on its own terms, not yours, and it always wins. This is the way of the desert, my friend."

Following a few minutes of contemplative silence, I said, "Sometimes I think the whole thing was a dream, that we really didn't see what we thought we saw, that the gold was only the result of a sandstorm-induced delirium. Maybe that gold wasn't really there."

Ortiz finished off his beer, rose, and walked outside. In a moment he was back, his saddlebags slung over one shoulder. He lowered the bags to the table, untied the strings on one side, and opened the flap. He reached inside with a dark brown hand and withdrew a large gold ingot. The hand reentered the second bag and pulled out the other one. Lying before me on the wooden table was the evidence of our discovery, the two gold ingots, each weighing about twenty-five pounds. I caressed them.

"It was real, amigo," said Ortiz. He slid one of the ingots across the table. "This one is yours."

I have been back to the Palomas Sand Dunes several times during the past four decades. It never looks the same. Each time I enter these sand hills, I feel I am arriving at a place I have never been before. During some of those visits, I rode with Ortiz, other times alone. Each time, I came away with nothing.

Ortiz is gone now. He lived a good life for a man who liked to work hard all day long, a man who was born to the desert range. He was sixty-five years old when he died in his little cabin on the Palomas Land and Cattle Company ranch. He died penniless, but I was told he had a smile on his face when they found him one morning. I like to believe he passed away delighting in his dreams. I learned he gave his gold ingot to a daughter. I used my ingot as a doorstop for years, and then converted it to cash when I needed some money to pay for my college tuition.

Someday the blowing winds will once again uncover the lost Spanish treasure of gold ingots somewhere within the complex of the Palomas Sand Dunes. Perhaps someone will be there to witness this event and lay eyes on the uncountable fortune seen by Ortiz and me so long ago. Perhaps the desert may again decide to keep it for herself as she has for so long.

The gold is there. I saw it, held it in my hands. I even kissed my ingot once. Because of the gold Ortiz and I found in the sands, I never stop dreaming. And I continue to search.

5

A MAN RETURNED
FROM THE DEAD

Nothing is exciting if you know what the outcome
is going to be.

—Joseph Campbell

It was one of the strangest telephone calls I ever received. I was
living in Ysleta, Texas, and lost deep in the process of studying
geologic and topographic maps of the Jarilla Mountains in New
Mexico's Otero County in preparation for an exploration of the
long-abandoned and extremely dangerous Tiffany Turquoise
Mines when the ringing phone jarred me back to reality.

The caller was a woman named Helen Pitcock who lived
in Toccoa, Georgia. She had read a recent syndicated newspaper
article describing a treasure-hunting expedition I had led into
Arizona's Dos Cabezas Mountains in search of a lost Spanish silver mine. The expedition, though filled with nonstop adventure,
failed in the sense that no mine was located. Pitcock seized my
attention at the outset of the conversation by telling me she was in
possession of a map that showed the precise location of the mine
we had been looking for.

After spending more than half an hour on the phone with
Mrs. Pitcock and asking dozens of questions, I decided she was
telling the truth about possessing the map. This foundation established, she then told me the rest of her story.

Seven years earlier, Mrs. Pitcock's husband, Herman, took an extended leave from his job at a textile mill and traveled to southeastern Arizona in search of the same mine. He had been researching and collecting information on the mine for years and believed he was ready to try and locate it. After three months in the harsh desert and mountain country, he returned to Toccoa with seven Spanish ingots of almost pure silver. Pitcock told his wife that not only did the mine contain a seam of silver, but there were also hundreds of silver bars stacked along one wall of the shaft. Because the ingots each weighed approximately twenty-five pounds and Pitcock had to hike a distance several miles from the mine to where he parked his vehicle, the seven bars represented all he was able to carry out at the time.

A week after returning home, Herman Pitcock resigned from his job and made preparations for a return trip to Arizona to retrieve more of the silver. Before leaving, he sketched a map of the location and gave it to his wife for safekeeping. He left with the promise that he would return in a month with "a trunk load of silver." Helen Pitcock never saw her husband again. When he failed to return in a reasonable amount of time, Mrs. Pitcock alerted the Cochise County, Arizona, sheriff's department and reported her husband missing. The authorities recorded her concerns, conducted a cursory search with no success, and informed her they had little time and manpower to devote to an ongoing investigation. At the time of her call, seven years had passed since the disappearance of her husband.

Mrs. Pitcock wanted me to take her map, locate the mine, and split with her anything I might find. I informed her I had three partners who accompanied me on every expedition and our collective portion needed to be 80 percent, since we were taking all the risks. In a sweet way, she bargained me down to 60 percent. I told her I would have to discuss it with my partners.

She also wanted me to try to find her husband's remains, for she was convinced he met his death while trying to retrieve the silver. I agreed. Two days later, I called her back and told her my partners and I were fine with the 60 percent share and would do our best to find the mine. Two days after that, I received a package from Mrs. Pitcock via private express courier. It was the map. A week later, Poet, Slade, Stanley, and I departed for Cochise County, Arizona.

Leaving Stanley's International Harvester truck near the little community of Dos Cabezas, we consulted our maps, hoisted our packs, and undertook the long and strenuous hike along a winding, rocky trail into the heart of the mountain range, all the time climbing in altitude. The day was warm, a light breeze blowing, and birds serenaded us across the arid foothills. I had been fascinated for a long time by this special and unique environment. Though I had never spotted any sign of them, area ranchers had reported seeing jaguars in the range over the years, During previous visits, I had encountered artifacts indicating the former presence of ancient Indians as well as early Spanish.

It was late afternoon when we entered a sparsely wooded canyon that contained a narrow, shallow stream of fresh water located in a section of the range I had not previously visited. Deer sign was abundant, as was that of black bear. Rattlesnakes were everywhere. The shadowy, protected environment seemed like paradise compared to the long trek across the dusty foothills. As we took a well-earned break at creek side, Stanley noticed what appeared to be a very old trail paralleling the stream. It was, he surmised, the one used by the Spanish pack trains generations ago to transport the silver from the mine down into Mexico. According to Stanley's research, the mine we were looking for was worked by the Spaniards during the mid-seventeenth century. Every three months or so, they would lead a silver-laden mule caravan to church and governmental headquarters in Mexico City, fifteen hundred miles away to the southeast. A series of Indian attacks finally drove the miners from the area, and according to church documents, no one ever returned to resume the

operation. According to Stanley's notes, acquired from researching the history of the Spanish here in a long-ignored archive in
Mexico City, there should be around four hundred silver ingots
stacked inside the mine.

Since sundown was only an hour away, we decided to make
camp by the stream. That night as we chatted around the fire, we
heard noises in the distance toward the head of the canyon, as if
someone were walking around and watching us. From time to
time, it sounded like footsteps crunching on the loose rock and
gravel that made up much of the floor of the gorge.

"Probably an animal," muttered Slade, "but there's something about it that bothers me." He checked the loads in his pistol
clip. Poet and Stanley pulled their rifles closer. Without a word,
Slade, carrying the nine-millimeter in his right hand, slipped away
into the darkness.

Slade returned an hour later and explained he had found a
secluded position about sixty yards away where he sat and listened
to the sounds. He was certain something or someone was watching the camp but felt the unknown observer knew he was being
stalked and left.

Following breakfast the next morning, Stanley examined the
map and again determined the mine would be found near the
head of the canyon and about one-third of the way up the steep
north slope. As we proceeded up the trail, Slade, who was in the
lead, stopped and pointed to a fresh footprint in a patch of soft
earth. It was the track of a boot, and a well-worn one at that.

"We've got company," he said.

Curious about whom else might be in the range and why,
we pushed on, eyes scanning the woods ahead and the slopes
alongside.

Just before noon, Poet called out and directed our attention
up ahead and toward one side of the canyon. Following his point,
we spotted a large accumulation of tailings on the slope. At the
top of the tailings was a low, narrow entrance to the mine. Con-

vinced we had found what we were searching for, we dropped our packs and hurried forward. Stanley and Poet left their rifles with their packs; Slade and I carried ours.

After scrambling forty yards up the rocky slope, we came to the tailings. The loose rock was difficult to negotiate, and it seemed we slid down slope almost as much as we climbed up-ward. After several yards, we stopped to catch our breath. At this point, Stanley laughed and pointed to an old dim trail that led from the entrance to the mine across the top of the tailings and down a gentle slope several dozen yards from where we stood.

"Haste makes—" Stanley was interrupted by a rifle shot ring-ing out from the wooded gradient opposite from where we stood, the bullet spattering loose rock just to the left of Slade.

"Get out of the open!" yelled Slade.

In less than a heartbeat, the four of us were racing down the tailings toward the shelter of the trees below. Two more shots followed, the bullets missing us by several feet.

Seconds later we were behind a screen of pines and junipers and peering up at the opposite side of the canyon, trying to ascer-tain the location of our ambusher. Slade offered to sneak around, climb the grade, and come at the shooter from above, but we voted him down. We wanted better odds.

One by one, we slipped from cover and retreated back down the canyon, retrieving our packs along the way. After rounding a slight bend in the trail and getting out of sight of whoever might be watching us from higher ground, we found a suitable place to set up camp among some large rocks and fallen trees, one that could be easily defended.

For the rest of the day we cleaned and checked our weapons and discussed our next move. Slade, the oft-decorated Marine with four years of Vietnam experience behind him, suggested he climb to the top of the ridge and commando his way down toward the shooter. We continued to discourage him, insisting it was just as likely the shooter would see Slade before Slade spotted him. Stanley suggested we should just get out of the canyon and go home, a notion we discarded as too easy. Poet offered to approach the shooter and try to discuss the matter with him, but we decided he might be crazy enough to gun him down without benefit of conversation. I thought the best idea was to try to reach the mine under cover of night, but nobody else cared for my suggestion.

Finally, we decided to sleep on it. Slade took first watch. When he woke me two hours later, he said he could hear someone walking around in the darkness. He lay down and went straight to sleep as I pulled on my boots. During my shift, I also heard sounds, but couldn't tell for sure what they were. They never got closer.

The next morning, we headed back up the trail, fully armed but sans our packs that we left in camp. During the hike toward the mine, we agreed on a plan, which I thought wasn't much of a plan at all. We reached the place behind the trees where we had taken shelter the previous day and scanned the opposite slope. Between the thick cover of pines, brush, and rock, it was hard to see much of anything. An Apache war party could have been hiding up there and we would not have been able to spot them.

Following a long silence, Stanley, facing the wooded slope, called out to the gunman, requesting an opportunity to talk with him. He said we wanted to enter the mine, but if someone else had a legitimate prior claim to it, we would turn around and leave. Stanley called and talked for twenty minutes to no response.

Finally, he took a deep breath and said, "This is it." He left his rifle and revolver behind and stepped out in front of the tree, arms extended out to his sides and exclaiming loudly that he was unarmed. He walked forward several paces.

As Stanley continued to talk, I whispered to Slade, "Maybe the shooter's not here today."

"He's here," he whispered back. "He's playing with us." Slade held his rifle as if it were part of his arm.

Stanley continued up the old trail as it wound toward the mine entrance, all the time facing the opposite slope, holding his arms out to show he was not carrying a weapon, and talking. As he backed up the trail, he entreated the would-be ambusher to speak with him. More minutes passed. Stanley arrived at the top of the tailings and was standing in front of the mine adit. He looked down at us, shrugged, and then dropped his arms.

As he did, a shot rang out and Stanley dropped like a lead weight. My heart pounded with this unexpected development. Adrenaline coursed through my system as I pulled my revolver from the holster.

Slade cursed. "That son of a bitch. I'm going after him."

Poet yelled and pointed to the mine entrance where Stanley fell. "He's not dead."

Stanley writhed on the ground as if in great pain. Another shot boomed, and pieces of rock whanged from the side of the opening. Given the direction the rock splinters flew, I knew where the shots were coming from.

I turned to tell Slade but he was gone. I spotted him dashing from tree to tree, rock to rock, as he sought a route up the opposite slope. I turned back to Poet, but he cut me off with "I've got to go help him," and then he dashed from cover, scrambling toward the mine entrance, trying to get to Stanley

"Hold up, goddamnit!" I yelled to both of them. "The shooter is *inside* the mine shaft. He's shooting from inside the mine."

Slade stopped and looked up at the entrance, nodded, and started running back. Poet continued on up the tailings with me closing in behind him and Slade coming fast on my heels. When we reached the top, we saw that Stanley had crawled away to the opposite side of the entrance and was leaning back against the granite rock. He was breathing heavily and his right pant leg was soaked in blood.

"How bad is it?" asked Poet.

"I got punctured by about a hundred rock splinters from where his bullet hit the side of the adit. It's ugly, I think."

Without hesitating, Poet dashed across the front of the entrance, knelt beside Stanley, and slit open his pant leg with his folding knife. Stanley bled from dozens of tiny cuts. Poet cut the legs of Stanley's khakis into strips and began binding the wounds.

I had left my rifle back at the tree and asked Slade if I could borrow his. He handed it to me and I tied my white handkerchief to it and waved it in front of the adit. The gesture was answered with a shot from within, and I handed the weapon back to Slade.

Acting on a hunch, I yelled into the shaft. "Herman Pitcock!"

Silence.

I yelled again. "Herman Pitcock. We've come with a message from your wife."

More silence, then a raspy voice echoed from within the shaft. "I'm Herman Pitcock."

Behind me, Slade muttered, "I'll be goddamned. He's alive."

Poet paused in bandaging Stanley's wounds as he listened.

Calling into the shaft, I explained to Pitcock that his wife, Helen, sent us to look for him, that she missed him and wanted him back home.

Another few seconds of silence, and then Pitcock responded. "I can't go home. I can't leave this place. If I do, someone will steal my treasure. I think you people are here to steal my treasure. It's not yours, it's mine, you thieving sons of bitches." Pitcock's voice reverberated with anger and tearful anguish.

"We can help you get the silver out and back to Georgia," I said. "It's all part of the agreement we made with your wife."

Pitcock talked on, giving me reasons why he could not leave the mine. He had clearly grown deranged during the seven years he lived out in this canyon, guarding the fortune he found and subsisting on god-knows-what.

"I'm curious. Are there silver ingots stacked inside this shaft?" I asked.

"I'm standing behind them now," he answered.

"How many are there?"

"More than a thousand."

At this, Stanley looked up, eyes wide, and silently mouthed, *one thousand!*

"Pitcock, listen to me, I said. "If we work together, we can have the silver carried from here, loaded into a transport, and be back in Georgia within three weeks. Your wife is anxious and worried about you."

In response, Pitcock accused me of trying to steal his treasure. "I'll die first," he screamed, then fired three more shots from his rifle. He would have fired a fourth, but the hammer of his rifle clicked on an empty chamber.

Slade took a step forward and said, "He's mine now."

"Wait," I cautioned. "I have a bad feeling about this. Hang tight for a second."

"And give him time to reload?"

"Trust me. This man is crazy. He's got more than a rifle in there."

As if he could hear our conversation, Pitcock yelled, "I've got four barrels of powder stacked next to me and a bunch of sticks of dynamite. I'll blow this goddamn mine to kingdom come and nobody will get my silver."

"He's not bluffing," I said. Poet could tell also, because as soon as he heard Pitcock's threat, he started dragging Stanley down the trail.

I turned to Slade. "He means it. Let's get out of here. That crazy man has the black powder equivalent of a large bomb in there."

Without hesitating, we leaped to the opposite side of the adit. Slade went to help Poet carry Stanley while I paused near the opening.

"Pitcock," I yelled. "What do you want us to tell your wife?"

"Tell her . . . tell her . . . " He was crying, great sobs reverberating from the walls of the shaft.

Then, silence.

I took a chance and leaned a few inches from the protective rock and peered into the gloom of the shaft's interior. At that moment, Pitcock struck a large wooden kitchen match. In the brief second of the flash of light that illuminated the darkness within, I saw him. His face was pale and twisted into a grimace, the white hair on his head sticking out in all directions. His clothes were little more than rags that hung from an emaciated, skeletal frame. Pitcock looked like a madman.

During that second of light, I also saw the kegs of powder and the bound bundles of dynamite at his feet. As I watched, he lowered the match toward the dynamite fuses.

"Shit," I muttered, and turned to run toward the others who were now at the point where the trail turned downslope toward the canyon floor near an adjacent slope.

"Climb that slope! Climb that slope!" I screamed as I ran toward them. "He's going to blow the mine and we need to be up, not down."

Poet and Slade responded by clawing their way up the steep incline, dragging the bloody Stanley behind them. Then I was with them, taking a turn at pulling our partner through the brush and over the rocks.

I turned to say something to Poet, but my words were lost in the sound of the explosion. The entire canyon vibrated. Slade lost his balance and toppled several yards downhill. A horizontal stream of dark smoke and powdered rock debris shot straight out of the shaft opening for sixty yards or more, filling the canyon and reducing visibility to only a few feet. As the ground trembled, rocks and boulders were shaken loose from the steep walls and tumbled and rolled down, crashing into the canyon floor. I looked up the slope on which we sat but spotted no large boulders that posed a threat. Still, we were pelted with small rocks loosened from the perches, some as large as golf balls. Slade scrambled back up to where we were seated on the slope and the four of us huddled together, arms over our heads to protect ourselves from the falling debris.

Moments later it was over, save for an occasional boulder, loosened from its age-old moorings, falling to the canyon floor. In the distance, where we could not see through the thick dust, we heard the sound of more rockslides.

Coughing and spitting from the heavy dense smoke and aerosols that enclosed us, we sat in silence and tried to recover some composure. A thick cloud of dust covered the canyon floor to a depth of dozens of feet. As we watched, an almost imperceptible breeze began coaxing the mass down-canyon toward the mouth. Several minutes later, Poet looked over at Stanley and said, "How are you feeling?"

"Let's get the hell out of here," Stanley said, forcing a smile.

I don't remember the trip back to the campsite. I recall we waited for at least another hour for the dust to dissipate before setting out. I recall arriving at our campsite and building a fire to make coffee and helping tend to Stanley's cuts, not only the ones from the flying rock shards but also from us dragging him across rocks and cactus as we pulled him up the slope just before the blast. From a small first-aid kit we retrieved some antiseptic, clean bandages, and aspirin. The bleeding had finally stopped and we could see that only a few of the cuts warranted some serious attention. With Stanley taken care of, I downed a half a cup of coffee and fell asleep leaning against a tree.

I awoke to birds singing. I was stiff and hurting as a result of my unchanged position during the night. A large scab covered my elbow, but I didn't remember getting injured. Slade was squatted Mexican-style in front of the campfire making coffee. Poet walked up carrying some firewood. Stanley was awake and trying to work the stiffness out of his leg but having little success.

After a brief breakfast of coffee, nuts, and peaches, we left Stanley in camp and walked back to the head of the canyon. Now and again a loosened rock or boulder rolled and bounced down the mountainside, joining the hundreds of others strewn about the canyon floor.

When we arrived at the former location of the mine shaft, we were stunned at the change in the landscape. Instead of the adit and the tailings, we saw only a huge concave scar on the mountainside, about half the size of a football field. Tons of solid rock that had once been part of the mountain were gone, pulverized into fine dust and rubble. We looked over the maze of rocks and boulders, large and small, that filled the canyon floor and wondered how we ever managed to negotiate our way through them and back to camp the previous day. We returned to the camp in silence, slowly picking our way through the rock debris back toward camp.

"What are you going to tell Mrs. Pitcock?" Poet asked me.

I thought for a moment and then said, "Nothing. I'll just tell her the canyon doesn't look anything like the map depicted it. I can't bring myself to tell her about her husband."

Slade, who was several yards ahead of us, stopped and began kicking into the dust at his feet, raising small plumes around him. He bent down and retrieved something. When the dust cleared, we saw him holding a silver ingot. It had been blown one hundred yards from the mine.

"I bet if we poked around in this stuff, we'd find more of 'em," offered Slade.

"You're probably right," said Poet, "but I'm for getting Stanley out of here and properly tended."

We took turns carrying the heavy ingot back to camp. We had a long way to go, and it was going to be a difficult hike for Stanley along that winding, rocky trail back to the truck. The silver ingots would have to wait, and as we made our way out of the canyon, we began making plans for a return trip.

6

LOST TREASURE AND HIGH WATER

> Adventure is nothing but a romantic name for trouble.
>
> —Louis L'Amour

It was a typical West Texas summer morning, warm and dry with a slight breeze, when Dr. Trenton Stanley drove up to my house with a proposal for a new adventure. After receiving no response to his knock on my front door, he walked around to the rear of the house and found me perched on a fence overlooking a small herd of cattle containing some newborn calves. I had a Winchester Model 94 aimed at something in the distance. As he was about to speak, the rifle barked. A second later, a pack of dogs broke from the middle of the milling cows and calves, fleeing for safety. One of their number lay dead on the ground a few feet from the calf he was stalking, a bullet through the head.

"Jesus," said Stanley, staring out into the field. "Did you have to do that?"

"It's my job," I said. "Keeping predators off these cattle for the owner, among other things, is how I pay my rent here."

"You just shot a dog, probably somebody's pet."

"Contrary to what people believe, the most common predators on livestock are not wolves, bear, and mountain lions. The culprits are mostly dogs. A lot of them are feral, but that dead one out there used to belong to a welder who lives about a mile over yonder. I warned him twice. Now I don't have to do it again."

"Christ," muttered Stanley. "Seems like a shitty job to me."

"My wife is not too crazy about it either," I said, "but it saves us a little money. It's good this happened while she was teaching at the elementary school today."

I welcomed Stanley and asked him, "What brings you to this part of town?"

Stanley lived on the other side of El Paso's Mount Franklin in a spacious house from which he did his research and writing and sold what he called collectibles: artifacts such as pots; obsidian and flint knives, points, and scrapers; and other items found at ancient sites in Mexico and the southwestern United States. Because of his many contacts, he was also the one we turned to when looking for a market for the gold and silver we recovered from buried caches and lost mines.

Stanley was a good man to have on the hunt. Serious and dedicated, he came up with ideas that led to most of our quests. As a result, many of the expeditions took place in Mexico where he spent a lot of his time.

In the kitchen I poured coffee as Stanley sat at the table, pulling some items from his backpack, all of them clearly very old. He frequented flea markets all over the Mexican states of Chihuahua, Coahuila, Sonora, and Durango, generally returning from his trips with old books, Bibles, documents, photographs, handmade tools, and other odds and ends, most of which he sold at a huge profit.

As we visited, I threw together a lunch of warmed-over *tamales, frijoles, tortillas de maiz*, and peaches. As we ate, Stanley said, "I recently returned from the town of Buenaventura. There, I spent most of my time at a large flea market, one that covered more than two acres outside of town. I bought this."

With a smile, he held up a faded and worn hardcover book on some aspect of Mexican history and said, "The publication date is 1876."

I looked it over, thumbed through the pages, and handed it back, waiting.

"And," he said, as he tapped out a poor imitation of a drum roll on the kitchen table, "tucked into the middle pages of this little book was this." He held up a folded and crinkly parchment, stiff and brittle with age.

Stanley, in his professional antique and artifact dealer manner, carefully unfolded the parchment on the table. It was a map, with Spanish writing in the margins.

"This cartograph," he said, "shows the location of several hundred gold ingots which were stacked in a shallow cave in Chihuahua, not far across the border over yonder." He pointed southward out my kitchen window toward the Rio Grande, which flowed less than four hundred yards away.

Turning back to the old book, Stanley paraphrased a short paragraph. "In 1771, a pack train transporting hundreds of gold ingots from a mine located somewhere in Texas was attacked by Indians," he said.

"Probably Apaches," he added. "The attack occurred shortly after crossing the Rio Bravo, now called the Rio Grande, and entering a range of low mountains. The Spaniards repelled the onslaught, but suffered casualties. While the Indians regrouped, the soldiers and herders lashed the pack animals into a faster pace and steered them along a trail that passed through a canyon. The Indians followed a hundred yards behind. Fearing that the indigenes were after the gold, the leader of the pack train ordered it cached in a small cave he spotted in the canyon wall."

The Spaniards continued southward. About an hour later, the Indians struck again, picking off the stragglers at the rear of the column. This went on for the next two days until there were only a few men left. As the Spaniards searched for a place from which to mount a defense, the Indians turned and retreated to the north.

The journey back to Mexico City was long and arduous, and only one man survived. There, he related the story of the attack and pursuit by the Indians and the caching of the gold ingots. From memory, the survivor sketched a map of the location of the cache. It was the one Stanley found in the old book that was now flattened out on my kitchen table. How the map came to be in the volume Stanley purchased is anybody's guess.

Following a careful examination of the crudely drawn cartograph, it became clear that the gold was hidden somewhere in a portion of an unnamed, low range of mountains south of a crossing on the Rio Grande at Indian Hot Springs in Hudspeth County, Texas, some one hundred miles downriver from where I lived.

"I know the crossing well," I said. "I have used it several times in the past. There used to be a primitive swinging bridge made from tree limbs and rope that spanned the stream, but when it was washed away by floodwaters, I waded the river at the ford."

"It's the same crossing used by cattle rustlers," said Stanley. "Historically, some Texas ranchers would ride into Mexico, rustle cattle from the large herds found there, and drive them back into Hudspeth County at that point. In contemporary times, the crossing was used by modern-day cattle thieves to herd stolen livestock into Mexico where it was sold. Some of that is believed to be still going on."

Several days later, Stanley and I rounded up Slade and Poet. At my house, over a dinner of grilled steaks and asparagus, roasted peppers and squash, baked potatoes topped with a homemade *pico de gallo*, along with a flavorful cabernet from one of California's better wineries, the historian explained to the others what he had found.

During a dessert of Mexican flan and a tasty port, Stanley proposed we cross the river into Mexico and try to locate the hidden gold ingots. Slade, always ready to embark on another expedition, nodded.

Poet brought up a logistical problem. Since the alleged location was several miles south of the river, and since gold was heavy, it precluded us making a successful recovery on foot. If we found the treasure, the sheer weight of the ingots would limit how much we could transport back across the border. Taking riding and packing stock into the area to make the crossing and the journey was also fraught with difficulty. The roads into Indian Hot Springs were in such bad shape that it would be difficult to impossible to haul a horse trailer to the location. There was a chance of renting some horses at the small Mexican town of Ojo Caliente across the river from Indian Hot Springs, but we didn't want to raise the curiosity of the residents any more than necessary.

Ultimately, we decided to employ trail bikes. Each of us owned a rugged, durable, trail-tested dirt cycle, and we often raced each other over self-designed obstacle courses, honing our skills. The bikes would be efficient, save time, and optimize our chances for an effective search. With saddlebags, each of the bikes was capable of transporting several ingots, depending on the weight, in addition to the rider.

We left Ysleta an hour before dawn one April morning, the four of us crammed into the front seat of Poet's long-bed, high-clearance, four-wheel-drive pickup truck, the four trail bikes secured in the back. An hour and a half later, we turned off the paved highway at Sierra Blanca and followed a seldom bladed dirt road south to the Rio Grande. It was slow going, and we were forced to stop several times to rebuild the road at crossings where it had been washed out by flash floods. Though it was less than thirty miles as the crow flies, it took over two hours. We finally arrived at the low ridge overlooking the crossing. We stopped and surveyed the scene.

Below us lay the remains of the old Hot Springs resort, once the grand scheme of a Chicago entrepreneur who was convinced people from the north and east would pay high prices for a visit to the healing waters he advertised as being a cure for arthritis, consumption, cancer, migraine, impotence—even venereal disease. The resort was in operation for only a few years during the

1930s and 1940s before it was abandoned. Visitors had difficulty traveling the rough, sometimes impassable roads over which we had just come. One trip to the springs seemed to be enough for a client, for there were rarely any repeat customers. Eventually, the business dried up and the owners went elsewhere. The resort was abandoned and left to the weathering and erosional whims of nature.

From where we stood on the ridge, we could see five of the hot springs below, each one supplying the so-called healing waters to tubs inside the spa. To the east about a quarter of a mile was a tiny cemetery with only seven graves. Here, black U.S. Army cavalrymen were buried following their murder by a band of Victorio's Apaches in the 1880s. The Indians had escaped a massacre at the hands of the Mexican army in the Tres Castillos Mountains many miles to the south and had been attempting to join relatives living in the Guadalupe Mountains about one hundred miles to the northwest.

Across the river, behind the trees, and perched on the terrace rising above the floodplain, the small, squat adobe buildings of the tiny Mexican village of Ojo Caliente shone in the morning sun. Near the riverbank, two men hoed dark soil that was the village garden. After sipping from our canteens, we climbed back into the truck and drove down to the crumbling resort.

Poet parked the pickup in the shade of a large, spreading cottonwood tree about seventy-five yards from the river. We unloaded the bikes and checked that each had plenty of gas, that the saddlebags were secure, and that we carried sufficient water and trail food. Since this was to be an exploratory trip and we didn't expect to be gone more than two days, we carried only granola bars, dried apricots, and some pecans we harvested from my backyard. In addition, we each carried an extra gallon of gasoline strapped to the back of each bike.

While Slade and Poet checked tire pressures, Stanley and I walked along the river to locate the crossing. As expected, it lay directly in line with the trail to Ojo Caliente, a shallow water route that had obviously been used thousands of times. It consisted of a thick, extensive deposit of gravel that lined the river bed. I estimated the depth of the water in the middle of the channel at eighteen inches, an easy passage for our bikes. I noted that the river was lower than I had seen it in years.

Deciding to have a bite to eat before making the crossing, we sat in the shade of one of the resort's old ramadas. Slade pointed at the western sky. Large, dark, ominous clouds that threatened a lot of rain were building. If a substantial amount fell upstream in the catchment area, it portended the likelihood of some serious downstream flooding.

"I suggest we get moving and cross before the water rises," said Slade.

As we started the bikes and let them warm up, Poet asked, "What if the river is in flood when we return? Maybe we should have an alternate plan."

Slade shrugged and smiled, saying, "We've never had an expedition yet where there wasn't some kind of obstacle or challenge. It seems to me that we resort to alternate plans more often than we follow the original."

"We'll just make it up as we go," I offered. "It's more fun that way."

After a brief examination of a copy of the map, Stanley mounted his bike and led the way across the river and up the bank on the Mexican side. Several of the Ojo Caliente residents walked out to the edge of the floodplain to observe us. We waved at them as we rode by. They smiled and waved back. Behind us in the west, the dark clouds thickened and rose, bulging out wider and higher. We could hear distant thunder above the whine of the cycle engines.

Just beyond Ojo Caliente, we found a game trail that led in the general direction of our predetermined destination. The rough trail wound away from the river and toward the foothills of the small mountain range we identified as the location for the cached gold ingots.

The trail bikes, tuned and serviced before we departed, performed well, carrying us across several miles of Chihuahuan Desert scrub and foothills that would have taken us hours to hike. As we climbed higher, the game trail disappeared, and we had to negotiate the machines around the rocks and boulders that littered the ever-steepening slope. In places, we were forced to dismount and lift the vehicles over large rocks and fallen trees.

After hours of riding, we arrived at a point where the bikes could go no farther. Slade, Poet, and I checked our handguns for loads and cleaned the desert sand and grit from the barrels and mechanisms. After slinging the saddlebags over our shoulders, we proceeded on foot.

Stanley unfolded the map, alternately examining it and the surrounding terrain. Pointing southwest, he identified the opening to a particular canyon and said, "This might be the one we're looking for."

"This seems too easy," said Slade. "I've got one of those feelings that tell me something is getting ready to go wrong."

The expedition pessimist, Slade invariably pointed out real and potential obstacles and hazards and muttered a litany of misgivings. His uncanny sixth sense, however, was usually on target. Thunder erupted behind us as the sky turned blue-black.

"Let's get moving," said Stanley.

We had hiked a mile into the shallow, unnamed canyon, sidestepping rattlesnakes, when we decided to take a break. Lifting canteens to our lips, we spotted a small herd of mule deer up ahead. In the dirt beneath the same tree under which we relaxed, Stanley pointed out the print of a mountain lion.

After we holstered our canteens, Poet pointed toward the northwest wall of canyon, less than a quarter mile ahead.

"Look there," he said. "Caves."

We followed his finger and saw a number of small openings lined up side by side in the limestone, eight in all, and no more than ten feet between each of them and the next. Below the caves was a natural slope of loose talus.

"This is too easy," repeated Slade, as he felt for his revolver.

"Shut up, Slade," said Stanley.

We shouldered our saddlebags and began making our way up the steep slope. The talus, composed of finely weathered, sharp-edged limestone, made the climb to the caves difficult. With every step we sank into the scree up to our boot tops. With every foot we gained, we slid backward eight inches. By the time we reached the junction between the solid rock of the canyon wall and the top of the talus, we were exhausted.

After pausing in the relative coolness of the first cave to catch our breath, we examined it. It was shallow, less than twenty feet deep, the ceiling close to four feet high. Inside each we found pack rat nests and large spiderwebs occupied by arachnids of a huge species none of us had ever seen before. They were dark blue, which Stanley said was unusual.

A layer of very fine blow sand eight inches deep covered the floor of the cave. When we entered, the dust we kicked up swirled throughout the confined space, obscuring vision and filling our nostrils. After exploring the second cave, we donned bandannas across our faces to repel the light, dense aerosols.

In the fourth cave, the deepest so far, Stanley pointed to the blackened ceiling.

"Smoke from cooking fires," he said.

After scraping away some of the blow sand, he uncovered a rock-lined fire pit. In the middle of and adjacent to the pit were bones, probably the remains of a long ago meal. Nearby, Poet found a hand-sized piece of worked flint that Stanley identified as a primitive knife, no doubt used to cut meat.

While we searched for more artifacts, Slade wandered over to the next cave, the fifth one. As Poet, Stanley, and I crawled around in the dense atmosphere of airborne dust of cave number four, making one artifact or bone discovery after another, we heard Slade yell, "Bingo!"

Stanley, Poet, and I looked at one another with big grins on our dirty faces, knowing that only something like a cache of Spanish gold ingots could elicit a "bingo" from our stoic companion. We scrambled outside to find Slade standing at the entrance to the next cave, thumbs hooked into his belt, head nodding toward the opening. It was starting to rain, heavy drops spaced far apart.

Peering into the small cave, we beheld a sight that greets only a few men on this planet. Piled haphazardly against the back wall were gold ingots, each about eighteen inches long, three inches wide, and an inch-and-a-half thick.

Breathless, we plopped down on the ground in front of the cave, letting the raindrops fall on us. Stanley's eyes mirrored the joy of the discovery. He jammed his forefinger at the map, saying, "I told you! I told you it would be here!"

"Are we rich?" asked Poet.

We all began laughing as the rain, denser now, fell on us, soaking our clothes.

We counted the gold bars and restacked them against the rear wall of the cave. There were 541. When we finished, Stanley scratched some calculations into the soft sand of the cave floor. Estimating the value of gold at the time at thirty-two dollars an ounce and providing an average twenty-five pounds for each ingot, he said we were looking at nearly seven million dollars worth of gold.

"Christ!" muttered Poet. "This is the biggest one yet in all the years we've been doing this."

"It's the best payday ever," said Stanley.

Slade, who was kneeling inside the opening of the cave, looked out at the pouring rain. Turning toward us, he said, "Men, we have a problem."

"Leave it to Slade to find a problem with finding seven million bucks worth of gold," said Poet.

Knowing Slade's instincts were generally good, Stanley asked, "What is it?"

"I figure we might be able to carry four to six ingots each in these saddlebags. That's a weight of between one hundred and one-hundred-and-fifty pounds apiece that we have to haul down that treacherous talus slope. Any more than that would be troublesome."

Slade paused a moment, then continued. "But here's the worst part. After every trip down, we've got to climb back up this goddamn talus for another load."

He paused again. Then he said, "We need burros. Those Spaniards herded burros up this slope to dump the gold into the cave. They sure as hell didn't carry 541 gold ingots weighing twenty-five pounds apiece up here on foot. I figure we've got over thirteen thousand pounds of gold sitting here, probably more, which represents yet another recovery problem. If we can acquire some burros, we can bring 'em up here and load 'em up, we can get it all out a lot easier than us doing it ourselves."

Doing some quick calculations in my head, I said, "Assuming a maximum load of one hundred and fifty pounds, which is pushing it, it would take about ninety burros to haul all of this stuff out of here."

"Ninety?" said Slade

"In the first place," I responded, "I don't know where we're going to find that many burros. In the second place, how are we going to drive them across the river without being noticed? Not only will the people in Ojo Caliente wonder what in the hell we're up to, but I assure you ninety burros is going to attract the attention of the Border Patrol who make a habit of riding or driving up and down this section of river several times a day."

"Let's don't cross here," said Slade. "Let's lead the burros to a point downstream and cross the river at the Crabbe Ranch. That's a good crossing."

"I'd rather face the Border Patrol than the Crabbes," I replied.

"Who are the Crabbes?" asked Stanley.

"Two of the three Crabbe brothers served time in prison for rustling cattle," I said. "They were known to be ruthless, unforgiving neighbors in this rugged border country. Over the years, rumors have filtered throughout West Texas attributing a number of killings to the brothers. Nothing proven, mind you, but a lot of interesting tales. It was also claimed by many that anyone who entered Crabbe property uninvited was never seen again. The crossing Slade referred to was the one the law enforcement people believe they used to run stolen cattle into Mexico."

"I vote against using the Crabbe crossing," said Stanley.

"I vote against bringing that many burros in here," said Poet. "It'll be too obvious that we're up to something. We're asking for trouble."

Stanley's coolness intruded. "OK. We're facing some logistical problems, all of which can be discussed, ironed out, and agreed upon at some later date. For now, I suggest we load up what we can, carry it back across the river, then decide what we want to do."

"We're not going anywhere until this rain lets up," said Slade.

Stanley looked at his watch. "Let's spend the night here in one of these caves, load up what we can carry in the morning, and head out."

"Works for me," I said. Poet and Slade nodded.

We broke out the dried fruit, granola bars, and nuts and had a quiet supper as we watched and listened to the rainfall pounding the slope outside the cave.

I awoke during that crepuscular time before dawn. There was just enough light to see a brown scorpion perched on my chest. To my left, Stanley was snoring. To my right, Poet was beginning to stir, his left arm bumping me in the ribs. I feared the poking would arouse the nocturnal arachnid. I could not see Slade and wondered where he might have gone. The rain had stopped and the air was cool and fresh, but it was still cloudy.

Keeping as still as possible, I felt in the blow sand next to me with my left hand for some kind of implement. Finally, I found four-inch length of twig, probably dropped by a pack rat. Slowly, I brought my hand up behind the scorpion and, using the twig, flicked it off my shirt. It landed in the narrow space between Poet and me and scurried toward my slumbering companion.

I shoved Poet, rolling him onto his belly and away from the scorpion. At the same time, I leaped to a crouch because of the low ceiling and stomped the creature with my booted foot.

"What the hell . . . ?" Poet said, groggy from being aroused from a deep sleep.

"Sorry," I said. "Just controlling some of the local wildlife."

I picked up the scorpion by one of its claws and dangled it in front of Poet's eyes.

Now wide awake, he jerked to a sitting position, his eyes scanning the cave in search of more of the creatures. We found eighteen, one of which was crawling up Stanley's pant leg. I dispatched it like the other. Stanley, roused, rolled over and regarded us with sleepy eyes.

"I encourage you to move out of the cave with all possible haste," I said.

Once outside, we spotted Slade looking into an adjacent cave.

"Where'd you go? I asked.

"Had to get out of that cave. Too many scorpions."

"Thanks for warning us," said Poet.

"Looky at what I found," said Slade, gesturing into the second to the last cave.

We stepped over and saw three skeletons, mostly covered with blow sand.

Stanley bent to the task of brushing away the sand and searched for evidence of the identities of the remains. He lifted up what was left of a rotted leather belt. To the belt was attached a metal scabbard which held a dirk.

"Three dead Spaniards would be my guess," he said.

After a light breakfast from our food stores, we started packing ingots into our saddlebags. Slade, the stoutest of the four, loaded three ingots into each of the paired bags and swung the 150 pounds up over his right shoulder. Stanley, the oldest by several years, packed 75 pounds into his bags but had difficulty lifting them. I helped him place them on his shoulder and he staggered a bit under the load. Poet, at 5'8" and weighing about 155 pounds, went with two ingots. He refused help and wrestled the bags up on his own.

I decided if Slade could carry 150 pounds, then so could I. After loading my bags, I swung and leveraged them up over my left shoulder, finally getting them where I wanted after three attempts. I felt top-heavy and close to toppling over.

Slade started straight down the slope.

"Hey," I called out. "If you zigzag your way down, it'll be easier on the knees and provide less of an opportunity to fall face forward. It's slow going but safer."

Slade, who seldom listened to advice from anyone, ignored me and proceeded another ten steps before the heavy bags and insecure footing forced him into a tumble. He and the bags slid another twenty feet before stopping.

I led Poet and Stanley in quartering the slope, taking short, mincing steps. We passed Slade seated on the talus, examining the scrapes on his arms. Giving us a dirty look, he grabbed his bags and dragged them down the rest of the way.

At the bottom, we dropped our packs and drank some water as we caught our breath. The weight of the ingots had torn the stitching of one of my bags, and it was in danger of ripping open. After a brief rest, we loaded up again and hiked to the point where we had left the trail bikes.

"I hate to bring this up again," said Slade, "but I still have a bad feeling that something is going to go wrong before we get back. It's just a hunch."

No one said anything.

After topping off the gas tanks and strapping the bags onto the back of the cycles, we cranked the engines and made our slow way out of the canyon. At one point, I stopped to wrap some cord around my bag to prevent the tear from expanding any further.

Because of the additional weight, my cycle was unstable, as was Slade's. The clouds associated with the tail end of the storm of the previous night were breaking up, allowing a few rays of sunshine to pass through. We traveled single file to a point about a quarter of a mile from Ojo Caliente. Slade, in the lead, slowed his bike and signaled for us to stop.

"Listen," he said, as he shut off his engine and cocked his ear toward the river.

We did likewise and were greeted by the sound of a muffled roar. At first we couldn't place the source of the noise, then Slade said, "River's up."

We restarted the bikes and continued. A few minutes later, we stopped at the edge of the river terrace about fifty yards from Ojo Caliente. The waters of the surging Rio Grande, gravid with storm runoff, lapped at the edge of the low bank only yards from where we sat astride the bikes. About one foot of water covered the floodplain and we estimated the depth in the middle of the channel at four feet or better. The current appeared strong enough to float a boxcar.

Yelling above the noise of the river and the idling engines, Stanley said, "We're going to have to wait and let the river go down before crossing. It might be a couple of hours or it could be all night."

I agreed and Poet nodded. Slade, however, had other ideas.

Pointing, he said, "The water's only a couple of feet deep on the plain. That's not a problem for the bikes. If we get a good running start, we can push through that current and be on the other side in time for a late lunch."

Stanley shook his head. "Absolutely not. With your weight along with the ingots, you'll never get that bike across. That's about 350 pounds altogether, not counting the bike. That current will stop you like a brick wall."

"Bullshit!" yelled Slade as he revved his engine, popped the clutch, and shot down the terrace and into the water like an enduro contestant.

Stanley mouthed the word "numbskull."

Slade's bike cut through the sheet of water covering the floodplain. The front tire threw up feathers of the liquid as he sped toward the channel forty yards away.

Passing over the submerged stream bank, the bike, Slade, and his load of gold dropped out of sight. He surfaced in the middle of the raging stream, stroking desperately for the far shore. He was making little progress as the high velocity current swept him downstream and out of sight around a bend.

"Idiot," muttered Stanley.

My first impulse was to try to save Slade, but there was no clear way of doing so without jeopardizing my own life. Sensing my inclination, Stanley said, "There's nothing we can do."

Without knowing whether Slade was alive or dead, we steered the bikes back toward a rock outcrop, shut them off, and waited.

Stanley tried to nap but was too restless. Poet killed some time poking around in the jumble of granite rocks. He had an uncanny ability to spot things like arrowheads, spear points, and pottery shards.

I pulled out my Schrade Uncle Henry lock-blade and whittled on a piece of dry mesquite. The tiny vulture head sculpture I intended didn't materialize, so I made some toothpicks and stuck them into my hatband.

From time to time I walked to the edge of the terrace and scanned the river bank on the far side, searching for some sign of Slade. Nothing. I turned to find Stanley staring into the wooded groves across the river. He shook his head and returned to the shady spot near the rocks.

I walked over to the little village and was greeted by the same two men we saw hoeing the garden patch the previous day. They *buenos dias*'d me, pointed to where the cycles were parked, and asked what we were about. I provided our usual explanation. I told them we were trying to get photographs of a rare warbler, *un pájaro raro*, that lived in a canyon back in the mountains. Satisfied, they moved on.

I wandered around the village of thirty people who lived with no electricity or plumbing. Potable water was drawn from hand-dug wells. I walked into the Catholic church, a building only slightly larger than most of the adobe dwellings. A trio of handmade pews, a couple of salvaged metal folding chairs, and some tree stumps served to seat the churchgoers, yet the building was immaculate. Across a flea market kind of table that served as an altar was stretched a colorful *serape* upon which was placed a number of Jesus and Virgin Mary icons along with a stuffed teddy bear. I was told that a priest had not visited this tiny village in more than twenty years.

Somewhere outside, meat was broiling. Hungry, I returned to Stanley and Poet and fetched a snack of dried fruit from my pack.

Before sundown the three of us walked over to the edge of the terrace to check on the water level. It had dropped six to eight inches, not much but enough to be encouraging.

"There is nothing to do but wait until morning," said Stanley. "We'll evaluate the situation then." The three of us continued to search the other side for Slade but to no avail.

We spent a restless night. Poet couldn't sleep at all. Stanley tossed and turned as if experiencing bad dreams. I rose and, in the moonlight, looked out across the river, hoping to see movement on the other side.

At the first hint of dawn, we stood at the edge of the terrace surveying the condition of the river. The water had receded from the floodplain, but was still running swift in the channel.

"There's no way we can cross that," said Stanley. "No sense in even trying until it goes down more. Our bikes would be packing too much weight for us to have any control over them in that current."

Poet nodded, but I could tell he was thinking about trying anyway.

As though reading his mind, Stanley said, "Don't even think about it. One idiot on this team is one too many, and Slade has that honor."

Three hours later, the river was considerably lower. We estimated the depth at the crossing to be about two-and-a-half feet deep but still with significant velocity.

Standing between me and Stanley, Poet said, "I'm going for it."

"Don't be stupid," responded Stanley. "Let's give it more time."

"It can be crossed," said Poet, gazing intently at the water. "I'm going to dump my load of ingots over here and make a run for it unencumbered. I'm tired of sitting on my ass when I could be looking for Slade. He might be hurt somewhere downstream."

I stood rooted to my spot as Poet broke away and walked toward his bike. He cranked the engine and let it warm up while he unhitched his saddlebags. Looking around to make certain no one from the village was watching, he walked over to a thin grove of juniper trees, scooped out a shallow hole, pulled the ingots from the bags, and buried them.

As we watched, hands on hips, Poet pointed the bike toward the crossing, revved up the RPMs, popped the hand clutch, and shot away. Leaving the edge of the terrace, he was airborne for a second before hitting the floodplain. Though the muddy texture of the ground slowed him down a bit, his bike maintained impressive speed as he raced toward the river.

The cycle slowed dramatically as it knifed into the current, but it kept going. Above the sound of the river, Stanley and I heard the whine of the little Japanese engine as it powered the bike forward. Poet had passed through the middle of the channel where the current was the strongest. Stanley and I were about to erupt in a cheer when the engine died and the cycle came to an abrupt halt.

Struggling to remain upright, Poet scrambled off the bike, grabbed the handlebars, and, fighting the current, began pulling the machine through the water toward the far shore. He was making progress an inch at a time. From where we stood, Stanley and I were caught up in the struggle, making pushing and pulling motions with our hands and arms as though it would somehow help our friend.

I yelled across the expanse of water, "Forget the bike and save yourself!" I could not be heard above the roar of the current.

Poet finally pulled his bike onto the bank on the Texas side of the river and then collapsed next to it, his chest heaving.

"Hell's bells and shotgun shells," exclaimed Stanley. He looked over at me and said, "What do you think?"

I shrugged and said, "Let's go for it."

After burying our ingots alongside Poet's, we started our bikes and made ready. As I looked to see that everything was in order with my bike, Stanley punched me on the shoulder, pointed to the sky, and said, "Look!"

To the northwest, another huge storm cumulus was building, the type of cloud that delivers hail and huge rainfall.

"Let's get the hell out of here!" Stanley cried and shot out on the same path taken by Poet. By the time Stanley made it through the main channel surge, Poet, standing thigh-deep in swirling water, was waiting for him. Together the two men pulled the cycle to shore with little difficulty.

I stared up at the sky while I revved the engine. Unbelievably, the cloud was twice as large, twice as dark, and much closer than the last time I had looked. An earth-shaking crack of thunder drowned out the sound of my engine as a jagged streak of lightning shot across the horizon. On the opposite bank, Stanley and Poet were waving me on.

Ready, I popped the clutch, the cycle jolted forward, and the engine died.

"Shit!" I hissed as I turned the key.

The only response was a whining, grinding noise. I had flooded the damn thing. I counted to five and tried again. Same result. The cloud was less than a mile away, dropping tons of rain. The river was already rising, the current stronger.

I turned the key again and for the second time was greeted with the annoying sound of a flooded engine. I shot the kickstand, dismounted, and walked around the bike, gritting my teeth. I wasn't crazy about the notion of spending another night on the Mexican side of the river.

Stanley and Poet had their hands extended outward and upward and shoulders shrugged in the universal what-the-hell-is-going-on gesture. A deafening peal of thunder shook the ground again. Lightning struck the ridge where we had stopped in the pickup truck the previous day.

I stared at the bike, willing it to cooperate. I counted to thirty. Another clap of thunder pounded. The rain started to fall, large drops, slowly at first, and then it turned into a downpour accompanied by hail.

I climbed onto the bike, took a deep breath, and turned the key. The engine surged to life. I revved it a couple of times, let the clutch out slower this time, dropped off the terrace, and raced across the muddy plain, hailstones pelting me and splashing into the shallow water that had gathered on the floodplain.

Staying in the barely discernible tracks made by Poet and Stanley, I aimed the bike toward the crossing. My two companions waded into the river to meet me, now hip-deep in water.

I hit the channel and felt the force of the current. Fighting the handlebars to keep the machine on a straight course, I felt myself being shoved downstream. I gave it more gas and at the same time prepared to ditch the bike if necessary and try my luck at swimming for the opposite shore. The engine didn't die. I passed the thalweg where the current was strongest and continued moving forward. Stanley and Poet sensed success and moved aside as I fed gas to the straining engine while at the same time fighting for balance.

Then I broke free from the pull of the current. The bike and I fought our way up the north bank, RPMs high and tires spinning on the loose gravel, but gripping enough to propel me onward. Shooting out of the water, I was airborne for a second, and then made a two-point landing as though I had practiced this kind of stunt for hours each day.

I spun around to face Stanley and Poet, put the kickstand down, and turned the key to off. The engine wouldn't stop running. I turned it on then off again several times, but it never quit. I dismounted to congratulations and embraces as rain and hail pounded us.

More thunder broke up the celebration, and another bolt of lightning hit a big cottonwood over in Ojo Caliente. The heavy rain plastered our hair down over our heads and faces. Visibility was about twenty yards, and the wind was howling.

"Let's get the hell out of here," yelled Stanley, pointing to the river. It was already out of the bank, the overflow moving toward us. I rode my cycle to Poet's pickup while the other two were forced to push theirs because they wouldn't restart. God knew where Slade's bike wound up. For that matter, only God knew where Slade was. I stopped the engine by putting the cycle into gear and popping the clutch like I had on the Mexican side of the river.

I looked up and saw Slade sitting in the dry cab, watching us from the window. He didn't bother to help us load the bikes in the downpour, and the sudden relief of seeing him alive gave way to minor annoyance.

After strapping the cycles down, we scrambled into the cab and saw why Slade hadn't moved. His shirt had been torn away, and his torso and face were a mass of bruises and scabbed-over cuts. His Levis were in shreds. He held up his right hand and one finger was badly broken, angled out in a grotesque, abnormal direction.

"Jesus!" said Stanley.

"That river dribbled me like a basketball along the rocks and submerged logs and then spit me out about two miles downstream."

"Anything else broken?" asked Poet.

"Some ribs, I think." Slade pointed to his feet. "I lost my boots and had to walk back barefooted. Goddamn, I think I stepped on every sharp rock and cactus between there and here." Blood soaked the floor mat under his feet.

Poet started the truck, stating, "I'll warm up the engine and get the heater going." More thunder accompanied his comment.

Stanley, staring out the window, said, "You better get going right now! Look at that water."

Through the curtain of falling rain and hail, we saw the rising floodwaters moving toward us. In the distance, during the illumination from lightning strikes, we could make out whitecaps on the stream surface. A tree trunk at least two feet in diameter bounced along in the current as though it were no more than a toy boat.

Poet slammed the truck into four-wheel drive and drove away as the water lapped at the tires.

During the drive home, we tuned in to a weather report. The announcer stated it was the biggest storm to hit that part of West Texas in eighty years. Flood warnings were issued for all of Hudspeth and adjoining counties. There were reports of flooded ranches, lost livestock, and at least three human deaths. Residents of communities located near the Rio Grande were being told to evacuate.

Poet, Slade, Stanley, and I decided to wait at least two weeks before returning to Ojo Caliente and retrieving the ten gold ingots we had left buried near the town. Stanley placed a value of nearly $128,000 on the smaller cache. We couldn't wait.

Weeks passed before we were able to coordinate our schedules for a return to Ojo Caliente. Besides waiting for Slade to recover from his injuries, the intrusions of jobs, families, and college classes kept us from getting together. Because we were confident that returning to the site and recovering the ingots would be a simple matter, we were in no particular hurry.

When we finally arrived at the ridge overlooking the shallow valley before us with Ojo Caliente on the other side, everything was changed. When the flood waters had ripped through the area, they carried away entire groves of trees, a portion of one of the resort buildings, and at least two of the abandoned corrals on the other side. Nothing looked familiar.

We drove to the crossing and stared toward the place where we had buried the ingots in the juniper grove. Not only were the trees gone, several square yards of the ground under them had been washed away. Our cache of gold ingots was likely deposited at the bottom of the Rio Grande some significant distance downstream.

The river was low enough to wade across, so we did, and headed to the point where we thought the grove used to be. We searched, but found nothing.

"Not a problem," said Slade. "We've still got five hundred and twenty-five bars of gold lying in the cave."

"True enough," said Stanley. "But we still have to figure out a recovery process that doesn't draw any attention to us. I don't think the idea of using ninety burros is workable."

Poet spoke up. "I know where we can get a helicopter. I'm thinking a few trips with a whirlybird may be the most efficient way of retrieving those ingots."

"How big is it?" asked Slade.

"It's a two-seater."

"Shit," said Slade. "That means only one of us and the pilot can get in the damn thing, and we don't need some helicopter jockey wise to this venture. The fewer people who know about our discovery, the better. I say we keep it to ourselves. Besides, there wasn't a decent place to land a helicopter anywhere near the cave."

In the end, we decided to retrieve the ingots a few at a time as we did on the first trip to the caves. Over the years, the ingots provided a steady source of income for the four of us in between other expeditions and jobs. Stanley used his share to purchase expensive artworks. Poet bought a big sailboat. Slade and I purchased homes.

With the passage of time, it became more difficult to retrieve the gold. We were never bothered on the Mexican side of the river, but in Texas the U.S. Border Patrol was closely monitoring traffic at the Ojo Caliente crossing via high-technological sensing equipment in blimps tethered hundreds of feet above the region.

During a recovery trip to the area, we encountered two truckloads of Border Patrolmen who stopped us in order to check our IDs and search Poet's truck. After accepting our explanation that we were bird hobbyists, and apparently having nothing better to do, they engaged us in conversation. During the visit, we learned that because of an increase in the smuggling of immigrants and drugs through the Ojo Caliente crossing, they were stopping all vehicles they encountered.

"What do you do with the stuff you seize from vehicles?" asked Stanley.

"It's confiscated," said one of the patrolmen, "and the smugglers are arrested."

"Have you ever confiscated any artifacts?" I asked. "Stuff like Indian pottery or statuary or, say, Spanish artifacts?"

"All the time," he responded. "In fact, the smuggling of artifacts and precious metals is currently regarded as a major problem, and we are working with the Mexican government on apprehending the perpetrators and returning the items. It amounts to millions of dollars worth each year."

We bade the Border Patrol officers good-bye and proceeded on to Indian Hot Springs. During the trip, we decided not to cross and retrieve any ingots for fear of being caught with smuggled goods. It was a good decision because we were stopped by the same patrolmen during the return trip. In spite of the pleasantries we had exchanged earlier, Poet's truck was searched again.

"Procedure," one of them explained.

Four hundred and seventy-seven gold ingots remain in one of the caves several miles south of the international boundary. Given the price of gold at this writing, the cache is worth around eighty million dollars. With the growing problem of illegal immigration and drug smuggling, the surveillance of the border near Indian Hot Springs is continuous, twenty-four hours a day, 365 days a year; burro trains and helicopters are out of the question. Sensing equipment used by the Border Patrol can detect an individual, even an animal as small as a fox, immediately, even at night.

We had worked on a plan to enter the canyon from Mexico, remove the treasure, and carry it to some prescribed location in that country and convert it to cash, but the roadless desert and mountain ranges we would have to traverse made it impracticable.

I am still trying to figure out a solution.

POSTSCRIPT

The cache of gold ingots served as a bank for us for many years. From time to time we would cross the river, make withdrawals of two to four ingots each, return, and convert them to cash. As the U.S. Border Patrol installed more sophisticated aerial surveillance and assigned more men and women to cover this region, crossing over into Mexico and back became problematic. In time, we abandoned our expeditions into the area.

In the months prior to writing this account, I was imbued with the desire to make another attempt to reach the cache of gold in the tiny cave in those unnamed mountains. Since my longtime partners are either dead or inactive, it appeared as though I would go by myself. Because of the increased attention to the border and the movement of items back and forth, I decided to make a reconnaissance trip to gather information relative to geography and logistics.

Imagine my surprise when I discovered a small U.S. Border Patrol station had been constructed near the location of the old crossing. At first I was disappointed and decided to retreat for a time to make other plans. Then it occurred to me that oftentimes the easiest way to smuggle anything is right under the noses of those responsible for preventing such things. The Mexicans have been doing so for generations.

I'm still making plans.

7

PICTURES DON'T LIE

Adventure is the champagne of life!

—Anonymous

For most normal people, one hair-raising encounter with a life-threatening flash flood would be one too many. Poet, Slade, Stanley, and I, however, seemed to attract such hazards with nearly every expedition. Maybe it's our lot in life, maybe it was our collective karma, but the truth was we were challenged and tested almost every step of the way.

Most of our treasure-hunting expeditions into Mexico came about as a result of intense research conducted by the indomitable and unrelenting Dr. Trenton Stanley. Stanley spent as long as three months at a time in Mexico City churches and environs, going from library to library, monastery to monastery, to examine old documents; seeking out private collections; and immersing himself in archival material from the Spanish colonial period. Much of the information he derived relating to lost Spanish treasure pinpointed caches and mines in Mexico, mostly in the Sierra Madres. On a couple of occasions, however, he had encountered references to Spanish mining activity in what is now the United States.

One mine in particular attracted his attention. At one time it was quite rich and productive and supplied silver bullion to destinations in Mexico City. It had to be abandoned because of continued Indian raids. When the Spaniards fled the area, the mine was sealed up. Though it was their intention to resume operations when the threat of Indian depredation was over, circumstances were such that the Spanish never returned.

The directions Stanley found to a long-abandoned silver mine in southern Arizona were imprecise and confusing, but we settled on a location not far from the border town of Douglas in Cochise County, Arizona. According to the documents, the entrance to the mine shaft had been filled in with rocks by the Spaniards prior to abandoning the site. This was a common response to Indian threat, the rationale being that by covering the mines, they would keep the indigenes from entering and removing the ore. What the Spanish did not understand was that the Indians could not have cared less about silver and gold. They merely wanted the trespassing foreigners out of their territory.

When the mine was first opened, the engineers had carved into the granite canyon wall just above the adit a Christian cross topped by a caret, an inverted V. This was a common symbol employed by the Spanish miners during that time. We were convinced there was a good chance of finding this mine.

Late one afternoon during the spring, Poet drove his Land Rover stuffed with camping and caving gear, along with me, Slade, and Stanley, into the rocky desert near the Pedregoza Mountains in southeastern Arizona. After hours of negotiating narrow, almost impassable dirt roads, we topped a low rise overlooking a broad drainage channel. There was no water in the channel, and on the sands and gravels at its edge, we spotted a military surplus canvas tent and a pickup truck. Seated in a folding chair next to a campfire was an older man, probably in his mid- to late sixties, who was worrying over a coffeepot that he kept resetting on the coals as if trying to find a better spot. We drove down to visit him.

After introductions, the old man poured us each a half-cup of coffee and made a fresh pot. Poet asked him what he was doing out there in the desert so far from a town. He surprised us by saying he was searching for a lost Spanish silver mine. Stanley pressed the old man for details.

"Years ago," he said, "I bought an old wooden trunk at an auction down in Florida. It was battered and stained with a few of the metal fittings loose or missing. I decided to refurbish the trunk and use it for a table. As I worked on it, I discovered it had been designed with a narrow, concealed space in the bottom."

"I've seen similar trunks," said Stanley. "The false bottom was a common tactic of years past for travelers who wished to hide secret or valuable documents or money."

"After I found the secret space," continued the old man, "I withdrew an account, written in Spanish, of a silver mine abandoned in the desert. The document was dated 1659. In addition to this, there was a map."

Stanley pressed for more details.

"It took me almost three years to locate someone who could translate the document as well as all the cryptic notations on the map," he said. "When I realized it was a treasure map, and that the document told of a mine that had been abandoned and apparently never reopened, I decided to come here and search for it."

None of us could believe what we were hearing. Completely by accident, the stranger had encountered a reference and a map to the same treasure we were searching for, only his information appeared to be more precise than the documents Stanley had found and studied for weeks.

Rather than reveal why we were in the mountain range, Stanley asked, "Have you had any luck looking for the mine?"

"I found it," said the old man, chuckling.

"You found it?" asked Stanley, incredulous.

"Yep. This is my sixth trip out here, and I finally located the damn thing. Now all I have to do is find a way to remove all the rocks piled in the entrance to the shaft."

By common agreement, we never tell anybody what we do, that we are treasure hunters, and we saw no immediate reason to

inform this man. Stanley explained to him we were nature pho-
tographers and were trying to get photos of a rare bird that lived
in these mountains. Fortunately, the old man didn't ask to see our
cameras, for we weren't carrying any.

After a few more minutes of small talk, Stanley said, "We'd
better be moving on. It's getting late and we need to set up
camp."

As we turned to go, Poet addressed the old man, saying,
"You know, it's not a good idea to be camping in a wash such as
this one. When there are thunderstorms higher in the range, the
runoff, which gathers in the gullies, arroyos, and washes, can swell
to an impressive volume, carrying away everything in its path."

Poet pointed to a lone cottonwood on the bank about forty
yards downstream. In the branches approximately ten feet off the
ground could be seen the accumulated debris of a previous flash
flood.

The old man chuckled again and said, "I've camped in this
wash every time I come to these mountains and never had any
trouble."

"It only takes one time," said Poet.

"I'll be fine," the old man assured us.

We drove back to the rise, then turned east and traveled
about two miles from the wash before setting up our own camp.
During dinner, we discussed the situation and decided to pursue
our search of the lost mine based on the documents we possessed
simply to see how accurate they were. Since the old man claimed
to have found it first, we would yield to his prior discovery. We
discussed the possibility of approaching him with the notion of
combining our efforts and sharing whatever might be found inside
the mine. In the end, we rejected the notion. For one thing, we
did not want other people to know what we did. For another, we
didn't know the old man well enough to make such a proposal.
We knew of other treasure hunters who carelessly spoke of their
expeditions and recoveries to men who turned out to be law en-

forcement agents, government investigators, or Internal Revenue Service employees.

The next morning, we followed the directions from the account as interpreted by Stanley, wandering over and across the foothills and up and down canyons. Here and there we were able to make associations with certain landmarks indicated on the map, but time and again we came to dead ends with zero results.

The second night in camp we heard thunder in the distance as we washed the dishes and stowed equipment. As we conversed, the wind picked up and we could smell rain. Moments later, a loud peal of thunder was accompanied by a lightning strike on a ridge a few miles away. Slade was about to say something else, when another crash of thunder drowned out his words and the rain started falling. In the moments we dashed from the fire ring into our tents, we were soaked, the rain coming down in torrents. All night long it fell, and the rain and strong winds, along with the falling temperatures, forced us deeper into our sleeping bags. Hours later when the storm abated, I finally fell asleep.

We rose to a cool, wet morning. As Slade made coffee, the rest of us scrounged around for more dry firewood but had little luck. Poet and I walked together and our search took us to an overlook where we could see into an arroyo about two hundred yards away. Flowing full, the roiling, red, rushing water sounded very loud, even at this distance.

"I hope that old guy didn't get water like that," said Poet. "We ought to go check on him."

When we got back to the campsite, Stanley asked, "Did you see any high water in the arroyos?"

When we said we did, he, like Poet, voiced a concern about the old man. During breakfast, Poet suggested we take the time to drive over to the wash and see how the old camper had fared.

We arrived at the top of the rise overlooking the camp. The wash ran full, the swift current foamy and thick with the residue of sand and brush. The spot where the old man's tent had been pitched was under two-and-a-half feet of water, his pickup truck partially buried in mud. We looked around hoping to spot where he might have retreated to higher ground, but could find no sign.

Fearing the worst, we decided to search downstream to see what we could find. After a mile, Poet found the old man's tent caught in the branches of a low tree. Poet waded out into the water that still covered the floodplain and retrieved it. He pulled it to higher ground, opened the flap, and found several items inside: a change of clothes, one sneaker, a butane lighter, the remains of a paperback book, and mud. Feeling around in the muck, he retrieved a camera.

We spent the entire day searching for the old man, hoping he had been able to make his way to safety before the flash flood struck.

"He's probably walking out of these mountains right now while we're tromping around in the mud," said Slade.

"I don't think so," said Stanley. "I fear the worst."

We camped that night on the rise overlooking the wash. The next morning we drove into Douglas for breakfast and afterward stopped at the sheriff's office to report our observations and conclusions. We hung around town for two days and nights while deputies and search-and-rescue teams combed the mountain range. The old man was never found. Using the license plate from the truck, the sheriff learned his name and that he lived in Tucson. By the time we decided we needed to leave, authorities were trying to find relatives to notify.

When we arrived back in El Paso, Poet was still in possession of the camera he found in the old man's tent. He cleaned it up and realized it was still in decent working order. He also discovered it contained a partially exposed roll of film. On a hunch, he rewound it, removed it from the camera, and dropped it off to be developed.

Several days later, Poet was driving Slade and me to a green chile and *asadero* lunch at the Pine Knot, Jr. in El Paso when he remembered the film. Since it was on the way, he stopped to pick it up. As he drove out of the photo shop parking lot, he handed the unopened package of prints to Slade. I was reading the morning paper.

Slade examined the prints one by one. The first nine or ten were landscape shots, many of them of locations we had encountered during our search for the lost Spanish mine. There was a picture of the old man's pickup truck and another of his campsite, his tent pitched and his coffeepot resting atop the campfire coals.

Then Slade gave a low whistle and said, "Would you look at this!" He held up a print. I gasped, dropped the paper, and grabbed the photograph. There, in color, was an image of a rock-filled entrance to a mine shaft. In the solid granite above the partially concealed entrance was a barely discernible Christian cross topped with a caret symbol chiseled into the rock.

"That old man wasn't lying," said Slade. "He found it. He found the mine."

The old camper, inexperienced but in possession of a detailed description of the long-abandoned silver mine and its location, found what we were unable to. Standing in front of the old mine shaft to take that picture, he was within a few feet of a fortune, but never lived to recover it.

Poet pulled his truck into a parking space near the café and cut the engine, and together the three of us examined the photograph. Slade found three more images of the mine entrance in the package and passed them around. We searched the photos in vain for some landmark that might indicate the location. Unfortunately for us, none revealed the surrounding environment.

Poet, Slade, Stanley, and I returned to the Pedregoza Mountains several months later. We resumed our search for the mine but remained unsuccessful. One clear night we pitched our tents on the ridge overlooking the place where the old man had camped in the wash and tried to imagine which direction he might have taken to look for the mine. We had no luck and, frustrated, gave up.

As we packed up to leave, menacing clouds appeared in the northwest and we heard thunder. As we drove out of the range on the poor road, it started raining. Each ravine we drove across had a shallow stream of water running through it, runoff from farther up in the drainage basin. By the time we crossed the fifth ravine, the water was up to the hubcaps on the truck.

As a result of the storm-generated flash floods, it took two days to drive out of the range. Other goals and other expeditions took us in different directions over the years, but we always had a yen to return to the Pedregoza Mountains to search for the lost Spanish silver mine. We never did, and to the best of my knowledge, it is still waiting to be found.

8

THE CURSE

What people speak of as adventure is something nobody in his right mind would seek out, and it becomes romantic only when one is safely at home.

—Anonymous

I have never believed in curses. I have never been superstitious. In 1971, however, something happened to cause me to rethink my position. A centuries-old lost mine located deep in the Datil Mountains of west-central New Mexico contained stacks of gold bars and sacks of gold nuggets and was said to be jinxed by an ages-old curse that may have been responsible for the deaths of the three young men who found it, as well as others.

The three friends had known each other since the sixth grade. They shared the same enthusiasm for cars, baseball, girls, and searching for lost treasure. Together, they undertook an expedition one weekend in 1966 to try to find a lost mine as well as a hidden cache of Spanish gold in a range of mountains in Catron County in western New Mexico. Against all odds, the three young and inexperienced men found the mine and cache of gold on the first attempt. But each, according to family and friends, was destroyed by a mysterious curse alleged to be associated with the hidden fortune.

Arnie Acosta, Rudy Gallegos, and Florentino Gomez grew up in a poor section of Albuquerque. Poverty and hard times permeated their small Mexican neighborhood, and finding work was always difficult for their fathers and uncles. When jobs were found, they often paid little. The three boys appeared to be unaware of the difficult times facing their families as they pursued life and all it had to offer with smiles and energy.

While having no money never created the depression in the boys that their parents and relatives were saddled with, they did aspire to a life of secure income, of fine homes and cars, of rewarding careers. Like many young men from low-income environments, they often dreamed and talked about what having wealth would bring them. They were especially attentive to the tales of lost mines and buried treasures related by the elderly Armando Gomez, grandfather of Florentino.

One of the tales most often told by Armando was that of a lost Spanish cache of gold bars and saddlebags filled with gold nuggets lying in an ancient abandoned mine shaft somewhere in a remote section of the Datil Mountains, about one hundred miles southwest of Albuquerque.

The gold, according to Armando, was dug from the shaft by Indian slaves, and the mining was supervised by monks who were ordered to deliver the wealth to the Catholic Church. The Indians were recruited from area tribes and promised great gifts if they would dig the gold. Once they arrived at the mine, however, they were placed in chains and fed barely enough to keep them alive. When they faltered, they were punished, whipped until flesh hung from their backs. Sometimes they worked until they died from exhaustion or hunger. Other times, they were killed by their cruel Spanish masters. Tiring of the enslavement and brutal treatment of tribal members, the Indians from the surrounding area rose up and drove the Spaniards away. Once the intruders were gone, according to the tale, a powerful medicine man placed a curse on the treasure, stating that any who tried to remove the gold stored in the shaft would die a horrible death.

Acosta, Gallegos, and Gomez were thrilled by the story of the gold ingots stacked along one wall of the mineshaft. Even before they were old enough to drive, they began making plans to travel to the Datil Mountains and search for the treasure.

Two years after graduating from high school, Acosta, Gallegos, and Gomez were each working at tedious and unsatisfying jobs that paid little and offered no satisfaction. Wanting much more out of life, they decided to take a few days off to search for the lost Spanish cache.

After piling camping gear into Acosta's 1960 Chevrolet Impala one spring morning, the young men drove south on Interstate 25, turned west at Socorro on State Highway 60, and proceeded across the San Agustin Plain toward the small town of Datil. From there they followed a series of rough ranch roads until they found a suitable campsite in the foothills. On the second morning, the trio breakfasted, then backpacked into the mountains with enough supplies to last for several days. Following the somewhat vague directions provided by Gomez's grandfather, the three proceeded with the confidence of most novice treasure hunters: they had no doubt they would locate the gold and become wealthy.

After four days of exploring a number of canyons in the Datil Mountain backcountry, they were growing convinced they had made a mistake. They were tired, hot, hungry, and had run out of water. They decided to explore one more canyon before abandoning the search altogether and returning to Albuquerque.

As sometimes happens, the three men were the beneficiaries of beginner's luck, something that occasionally occurs in the treasure-hunting business just like in fishing and marriage. In a relatively short time, they stumbled onto what some believe may be one of the largest caches of Spanish gold on the continent.

While hiking in the canyon, Gallegos discovered the ruins of a very old stone dwelling, little more than a roughly rectangular pattern of tumbled-down rocks. Excited at finding an indication that this remote canyon was once occupied, they searched the area. A few feet away they found several metal tools half-buried in the ground, all very old and rusted.

Midway into the canyon, Acosta spotted the low opening to a mine shaft partially hidden by trees and brush. Given the size of the junipers growing in front of the entrance and on the scree that spilled down the low slope, the place had not seen human activity for hundreds of years. After selecting a more or less level campsite forty yards away, the youths dropped their packs, retrieved flashlights, and returned to the shaft entrance. Burning with anticipation, they made their way through the brush and crawled into the mine.

Initially, movement through the shaft was very difficult owing to the jumble of rock debris scattered across the length of the floor, the result of past cave-ins. After some difficulty negotiating passage between the fallen rocks, a few as big as file cabinets, along with some scraped knees and elbows, the three succeeded in penetrating fifty feet of the shaft.

As they proceeded into the dark tunnel, Acosta, Gallegos, and Gomez became aware of the presence of a strange, gray-beige dust that floated in the air. The farther they crawled into the shaft, the thicker the dust.

Acosta and Gomez complained of breathing difficulties and watering eyes and were forced to stop. Gallegos was not affected by the dust as were his friends and he continued onward. After crawling another sixty feet and rounding a gradual turn in the shaft, Gallegos came face to face with the treasure. When the glare of his flashlight struck the stacks of dust-covered gold ingots, he sat back on his haunches, breathless from the sudden rush of adrenaline, and tried to recover his composure.

When he finally caught his breath, Gallegos crawled over to the stacks and ran his hands across the top bars, wiping away a dense cover of the fine, light dust that hovered in the thick air of the mine shaft.

The bars of gold were fashioned from a crude smelting process, each of them an irregular, uneven, and elongated rectangle. Each also bore the mark of the Christian cross. With his thumbnail, Gallegos opened his pocketknife, scratched the ingot, and found it to be quite soft, suggesting a significant percentage of gold. Due to the somewhat primitive smelting of ore practiced by the Spaniards, most of the processed ingots we have encountered over the years contained only between 60 to 75 percent gold, the rest being copper and other impurities.

After crawling several feet farther into shaft, Gallegos discovered dozens of leather sacks piled nearly two feet high at the end of the row of ingots. The sacks were rotted, and some fell apart in his hands, spilling their contents of gold nuggets onto the floor.

As he moved about, Gallegos stirred up more of the strange gray-beige dust. Visibility was reduced to the point that he could see no more than four feet ahead. Even the flashlight beam had difficulty penetrating the dense aerosols. The dust began to interfere with his breathing, and after placing a handful of gold nuggets into a hip pocket, he returned to his companions to tell them of his discovery.

When Gallegos caught up with his friends, Gomez was attempting to drag an unconscious Acosta along the floor of the shaft toward the exit and fresh air. Gomez's breathing was labored and he kept losing his grip on his friend and falling down. He had trouble maintaining his balance. The gray dust was so thick Gallegos felt rather than saw his companions. He helped Gomez pull Acosta outside, the task made more difficult by having to negotiate the maze of large rocks.

Once outside, Gallegos related his discovery of the gold bars and nuggets. Acosta was unconscious and Gomez much too disoriented to comprehend. With great difficulty, Gallegos helped the two men over to the campsite. Both Gomez and Acosta lapsed into a semiconscious state.

Early the following morning, Acosta appeared near death, his breathing labored and his eyes rolled back. Gomez was little better, barely conscious. Gallegos explained to him that they needed to get Acosta out of the mountains and into a hospital as quickly as possible. After gathering a supply of food and water, he and Gomez, abandoning their camping equipment, alternately carried and walked their weakened friend out of the canyon. Exhausted, hungry, and thirsty, they arrived at the vehicle four days later. During that time, Acosta was unable to eat and drank very little water. He retched, convulsed, and passed out. Gomez fared little better, stopping often to rest and vomit.

As Gallegos and Gomez sat with Acosta in his hospital room, the two discussed the treasure they had found and vowed that as soon as their friend regained consciousness, they would return to the shaft and the treasure.

Acosta, Gallegos, and Gomez never returned to the lost Spanish gold cache. Arnie Acosta, twenty-one years of age, died in the hospital three days after being admitted. His death was listed as resulting from undetermined causes.

Florentino Gomez, always a quiet, studious, industrious, and pleasant young man, had taken to manifesting bouts of deep depression. A few weeks after Acosta's death, Gomez did not show up for work at his place of employment one morning. Since Gomez was regarded by his employer and coworkers as reliable to a fault, they became concerned. When a friend went to his apartment to check on his whereabouts, he found it empty. Another friend drove to the home of Gomez's family and made a grisly discovery. His mother, father, and two sisters were found dead inside, all shot through the head. Two weeks later, Gomez was located in Los Angeles, California, and arrested for murder. Following a series of court appearances, he was judged mentally incompetent and sent to an institution where he was to undergo extensive psychological tests. One week after he was admitted, Gomez committed suicide by hanging himself from an overhead water pipe by a noose made from his shoelaces.

Rudy Gallegos eventually married, took a job in Albuquerque at an auto-parts franchise, and fathered three sons. He had no desire to return to the Datil Mountains to retrieve the great treasure he found in the mineshaft because he was convinced his two friends had died as a result of the curse placed on the gold as related by Gomez's grandfather.

On a day in June in 1971, Gallegos learned about me from a friend who had read an article in the *Albuquerque Journal* about a treasure-recovery expedition my partners and I were involved with in Mexico. The story detailed the discovery of a cave filled with silver ingots of Spanish origin and the difficulties involved in retrieving them. The article was derived from an interview with a relative of Dr. Trenton Stanley. Stanley made a casual, and careless, remark about our expedition, and the relative expanded on it, making the adventure appear more glamorous than it was. Since we tried to avoid publicity at all costs, none of us—Poet, Slade, Stanley, and I—was happy to see the publication.

Fascinated with the story, Gallegos spent the next month tracking me down and finally obtained my phone number. I was living in Norman, Oklahoma, at the time and attending graduate classes at the university. He called long distance and for an hour related the story of his discovery and the loss of his two close friends. In talking about the treasure cache, Gallegos mentioned the mysterious gray-beige dust he and his friends had encountered in the shaft, a type and color of dust he had never seen before or since. He related the tale he heard from Gomez's grandfather, and he told me about the curse.

Gallegos and I made arrangements to meet in Albuquerque two weeks later. I arrived by vehicle, checked into a motel, and called him. For the next two days, Gallegos and I visited. He went into great detail about the cache of gold and the old mine shaft.

He sketched a rough map showing the route he and his friends had taken from the first campsite to the mine. He drew another map of the mine's interior, including twists and turns in the passageway and the location of the gold. Gallegos revisited the subject of the curse time and again and was clearly frightened.

"Is there any way you and your team, knowing about the curse, could enter the shaft and retrieve the gold?" he asked.

"I don't believe in curses," I said. "I've been confronted with and cautioned about them several times in the past, and in my opinion, they inevitably wound up being the product of overactive imaginations."

"This one is real," he said.

"Furthermore," I continued, "none of the members of my team believe in curses. In the business of professional treasure recovery, one cannot be concerned with superstition."

"Perhaps you would do well to adopt a new respect for them should you undertake to enter this mine shaft," said Gallegos, clearly agitated at my response.

"I am concerned about the dust," I said. "I've known professional treasure hunters and cave explorers who came down with severe pulmonary disorders following an extended period in a cave or mine shaft, generally ones associated with bats. The condition was sometimes diagnosed as coccidiomycosis, a disease caused by inhaling the dust from certain fungi that might grow on bat guano. A number of researchers claim the pathogen is fatal only to animals and not humans, though there is some disagreement about this."

"There were no bats in this mine shaft," said Gallegos.

"I'm determined that, given certain precautions, there is a good chance we might retrieve some or all of the gold," I said.

I told Gallegos I would go to El Paso, meet with the members of my recovery team, explain the site and situation logistics, discuss an operational plan, determine a fair division of whatever was recovered, and select a time to undertake the expedition.

"We'll keep you informed of our decisions and plans," I told him.

Within a week, I had apprised Poet, Slade, and Stanley of the situation. I explained Gallegos's concerns about the curse and the dust and his conviction related to its role in the deaths of his friends. We agreed to make Gallegos an equal partner in the division of anything that might be recovered. Gallegos would not be allowed to accompany the team on the recovery quest, or even to the campsite, a policy we instituted early in our partnership and from which we never wavered. We made arrangements, gathered and double-checked our equipment—ropes, lights, packs, and camping gear—and made plans to depart for the Datil Mountains. Before leaving, I obtained four surplus chemical warfare masks from a mail-order military supply company.

Following Gallegos's maps and descriptions, Poet, Slade, Stanley, and I arrived at the first campsite. The next morning, following a light breakfast of fruit and coffee, we set out in search of the canyon that contained the old mine shaft. It turned out Gallegos's map was not precise; his distances and directions were way off. After three days, however, we eventually located what we were certain was the correct canyon. Not long after entering, we found the ruins of the old rock structure and the temporary camp established by the three young men. The remains of their gear were still there, apparently untouched since the time they fled years earlier. According to Gallegos, the opening to the shaft was less than fifty yards from the camp. Dropping our packs, we undertook a search of the area and found the mine within ten minutes.

After examining the opening and the first few feet of the shaft, we decided to return to the campsite, rest up from the long hike, enjoy some lunch, and then investigate.

We returned to the mine opening with flashlights, carbide lamps, and the gas masks. As was our practice, one member of the team would remain at the opening. It was Poet's turn for this duty. Slade, Stanley, and I secured our gas masks to belts, checked flashlights and headlamps, and entered. Stanley led the way, I followed, and Slade brought up the rear.

The shaft was low, less than five-and-a-half feet in height and only five feet or less in width. The granite rock into which the mine had been excavated was very old, highly fractured from eons of earthquakes, and clearly unstable. The rocks that had fallen from the ceiling made passage difficult, and at times we could barely squeeze between them and the wall. The old timbers used for shoring were thick and had experienced little decay, but they were spaced too far apart to be effective. I imagined the difficulties encountered in dragging Acosta's limp, unconscious body through these narrow spaces and voiced the hope that we would not be faced with the same predicament.

We noticed the dust within minutes after we entered. Just as Gallegos described it, it was gray-beige and very light and hovered in the shaft in a kind of translucent mass. The slightest movement from any of us agitated more of it into the ambient air. The dust was of a color unlike any I had seen before. And it was luminescent, a detail Gallegos had omitted. Extracting an empty baby food jar, I filled it with a quantity of the dust and replaced it in my shirt pocket.

The dust grew quite dense as a result of being stirred up by our movements. We were unable to see beyond arm's length. Within minutes, Stanley began sneezing violently, then complained of some breathing difficulties. We donned the masks and spent several minutes assuring a tight, protective fit. Stanley signaled he was ready to continue and resumed crawling. He continued coughing in his mask, stopping often to take deep breaths before going on. We proceeded another few feet, but Stanley, now shaking, turned and gestured that he needed fresh air and was returning to the outside. As he squeezed past, he was unsteady on his feet.

I led the way farther into the shaft on hands and knees. Visibility was reduced to almost nothing and I could barely see my hand in front of my face. I wiped the dust from the plastic goggles of the mask in hopes that it would help but it didn't. My vision was beginning to blur and, like Stanley, I was having difficulty breathing; the masks seemed ineffective. Slade, who could see no better than I, kept crawling up the backs of my calves.

Struck by a fit of violent coughing, I sat down, trying to take deep breathes but unable to draw any air into my lungs. I signaled Slade to head back to the entrance. He nodded and led the way.

With great difficulty, we reached the opening of the shaft and fresh air and sunlight. We ripped off our masks and inhaled great gulps of clean, juniper-scented, mountain air. Too weak to stand, we collapsed on the ground. Though clearly affected, Slade was not as bad off as I. In the near distance, Stanley was on his hands and knees vomiting into a shallow ravine, Poet holding onto his heaving shoulders. Hearing us cough, Poet looked in our direction, brushed some of the dust off of Stanley's shirt, and asked, "What in the bloody hell is this stuff?"

We remained outside the shaft, trying desperately to clear our breathing passages and inhale enough oxygen to keep from passing out. I cataloged our symptoms: dramatically restricted breathing, violent coughing, watering eyes, weakness, nausea, and disorientation. I pulled out the little jar of dust I had collected and examined it, struck by its unusual color, and recalled the faint luminescence.

Stanley and Poet returned to where Slade and I were sprawled on the ground and sat down. Poet queried us about the symptoms and shook his head in bewilderment. In all our years of treasure-hunting expeditions and cave crawling, we had never come up against anything like this before.

"What now?" asked Slade.

"The answer to that is easy," I said. "Less than two hundred feet inside that shaft lies millions of dollars in gold. We go get it and bring it out."

"Good plan. How do we do it?"

"Here's what I'm thinking," I said. "We took a long time crawling up to the point we reached, a long time for each of us to breathe in a bunch of that contaminated air. This time, we move quickly, double-time it through the shaft to the cache, grab a few bars each, and high-tail it back out. Once out, we assess."

Slade nodded. Poet said, "I'm going in this time."

Stanley waved a tired arm and said, "I'm not going in. There's something evil in there. It may be the dust, or it may be that medicine man's curse, but something is definitely strange about that shaft."

"Well, let's go find out," said Slade.

"Not yet," I said. "First we rest, then eat, and get a fresh start in the morning." Stanley agreed.

By dawn, Slade, Stanley, and I were feeling better, but Stanley's breathing was coming in ragged, forced gasps. A peculiar tightness gripped my chest, but not enough to hold me back. Slade appeared as though nothing had happened to him at all.

Following a breakfast of hominy, green chiles, flour tortillas, and coffee, we hiked to the mine entrance. Stanley remained at the opening as the rest of us entered the shaft. I led the way, Slade behind me, and Poet behind him. We wore the gas masks and we moved with as much speed as possible through the rock-clogged shaft. By the time we had gone twenty yards, our movements had stirred the dust into an airborne thickness that impeded our progress. Slowed and rendered nearly blind by its indescribable density, we barked our shins on boulders and ran into walls and each other. At one point we paused long enough to take a few deep breaths. I heard Poet exclaim through his mask, "Jesus Christ! The dust is glowing!"

The thick dust pulsed an ebbing and flowing luminescence. I thought I could actually *hear* the dust and wondered if I was hallucinating. My eyes watered and my chest tightened, but I still felt strong. I continued forward, my companions immediately behind me, but I could hear their breathing growing heavy and raspy through their masks.

At one point in the shaft, the floor was clear of rocks and boulders and I hastened onward. I was halted by Slade, who had grabbed a handful of the back of my denim shirt. When I turned, I could see he was grinning behind his mask. He pointed to his right. There, less than two feet away, were hundreds of gold bars stacked up against the wall and extending as far as I could see. For some reason, the dust was not as thick in this part of the shaft.

Poet passed between us and the stacks, his right hand sliding along the tops. He paused. "I started at that end," he said, pointing back toward the way we had come, "and I'm counting the stacks." He continued down the shaft until he disappeared in the dust three seconds later.

I stood stunned, staring at the quantity of gold before me. Slade's fist still clutched the back of my shirt. The stacks were uneven, but averaged about three-and-a-half feet tall.

Poet returned, grinning. "Sixty-seven stacks. And guess what? At the end is a pile of gold nuggets and some old rotten leather sacks." He held out his open hand and revealed at least twenty impressive nuggets.

I started coughing and my eyes poured water. "Let's grab some of these bars and get out of here," I said.

We each stuffed two of the heavy gold bars into our belts and started retracing our way toward the exit, the movement made more difficult by the extra weight. By the time we saw sunlight ahead of us, we were all choking and sneezing violently. Slade, complaining his mask was clogged, yanked it off. It was a mistake. After the first lungful of dust-choked air, his eyes bulged, his face turned red, and he collapsed. One of the gold bars slid out of his belt. Though Poet and I were also having difficulty, we took turns helping Slade out of the shaft. With still a dozen feet to go, Stanley took a deep breath, dashed into the shaft, pulled Slade from our grasp, and hauled him the rest of the way.

Over a lunch of bean, onion, and green chile burritos, we took stock of our situation. We had retrieved five gold ingots. Slade, Poet, and I were all for going back into the shaft and hauling out more in spite of the sickness we experienced. Stanley, the oldest, most enlightened, and most logical of the group, cautioned us.

"There is something wrong here," he said. "Something terribly wrong and out of sync. We've all been in the cave, and we've all gotten sick from it, Poet less than the rest of us. The masks are useless. Is it the dust that is making us sick? I suspect so. Perhaps there is also some kind of poisonous gas in there, but the point is we don't know. I assure you, something is wrong, and until we figure it out, I believe there is a good chance one of us could get hurt. Someone could die."

A long silence followed, and then Slade said, "I agree with him."

Poet nodded, as did I.

I pulled the sample jar containing the strange dust from my pocket and said, "Let's get this analyzed, see what the results say, and then go from there?"

The next morning, we began our trek out of the Datil Mountains and toward home. At the first opportunity, I shipped the jar of dust to a contact at the University of Texas at Austin for analysis. I received a report a few weeks later and a bill for $25. The report stated nothing out of the ordinary was found in the dust, nothing infective, nothing organic. The analyst offered no comment on the luminescence I described and even suggested I simply misinterpreted what I saw. The analyst was unable to identify the source of the dust.

For weeks after the experience in the Datil Mountain cave, each of us suffered respiratory problems and general malaise, with Stanley having the worst of it. In time the symptoms passed, and none of us ever reported any permanent effects from our adventure in the shaft. Slade had blurred vision for ten days, but it gradually cleared up. Other than some weakness and a few coughing fits, Poet had no problems whatsoever. I suffered an odd queasiness in my stomach along with some coughing, but eventually recuperated.

Gallegos appeared to have survived the curse. We remained in contact during the next two years, and I visited with him and his family on occasion as I traveled to other recovery sites in New Mexico. We discussed the probability of a return trip to the mine shaft just as soon as we could figure out a way to overcome the problem of the dust.

"It's not the dust," he said. "It's the curse."

In 1974, Gallegos was diagnosed with lymphoma, a type of cancer. His physicians were stunned at the unprecedented rapidity with which the disease spread throughout his body.

Gallegos insisted he was a victim of the curse and expressed concern for me and my team. He said he was having recurring nightmares, all of them related to his visit to the mine and the dust.

Four months following his diagnosis for lymphoma, Gallegos, in excruciating pain, weakened by the treatments, and troubled by sleepless, frightful nights, awoke and rose from his bed. Clad only in light cotton pajamas, he walked quietly through his house, careful not to wake his wife and children. Entering his car parked in the driveway, he started it up and drove away toward the Manzano Mountains southeast of town. Once out of the city limits and as the sun was barely rising in the east, Gallegos increased his speed—authorities said he was traveling in excess of one hundred miles per hour—and left the road, tumbling several hundred feet into a deep, narrow ravine. On impact, the car exploded and the subsequent fire spread throughout canyon. It burned for days. When rescuers finally reached the car, little was left of Gallegos save for a few charred bones.

Were Acosta, Gomez, and Gallegos victims of a curse, the so-called legendary imprecation placed on the Spanish gold cache by an Indian medicine man long ago? The families of these men are convinced it is true.

What of the mysterious gray-beige dust found in the shaft? Did it have anything to do with the three deaths? We may never know. One death was from unknown causes; two others were suicides following bizarre circumstances.

And what of the hundreds of gold ingots stacked against one wall of the old shaft? And the rotting leather pouches filled with gold nuggets? They are still there. Until someone can determine a way to enter the shaft without suffering the ill effects, they will remain there, protected by the curse.

POSTSCRIPT

Word travels fast in the community of professional treasure hunters. Those who make a living in this strange business often remain in contact with one another, exchanging information, offering assistance, or simply passing news of one kind or another. I was on the faculty at a small Arkansas college in 1980 when I received a phone call from a fellow recovery professional. He related a story to add to the file of the Datil Mountains treasure cache.

About three miles north of the town of Datil, the body of a man was found. He had lain in an unprotected gully for at least three days before he was discovered, and by the time the medical examiner finally arrived, he had been badly scavenged by coyotes, foxes, vultures, and ravens. A dense carpet of ants swarmed about the corpse. There was no evidence of foul play, and the cause of death was listed as "undetermined."

The next day, a pickup truck belonging to the dead man was found deep in the foothills of the range next to a crude campsite. The presence of a small geology pick, shovel, and hand lens for examining ore, along with a few other items, suggested he was a rock hound, prospector, or miner. This was not unusual, for rock hounds and the geologically curious occasionally visit the area in search of semiprecious stones.

What caught my attention, however, was what they found in the front seat of his pickup truck—two gold ingots, both very ancient and crudely smelted, both bearing the mark of a cross.

There was more: his jacket pockets yielded a double handful of gold nuggets. The man was identified from documents found in his wallet. His residence was listed as Holbrook, Arizona.

Catron County, New Mexico, authorities kept most of this information from the inquiring media, explaining they did not want the hills swarming with amateur treasure hunters, the bane of property owners and rescue specialists.

Poet, Slade, Stanley, and I were convinced that the dead man found in the Datils had located the old shaft and the cache of gold. We also believe he encountered the curse.

The author with Mexican youths in a tiny Mexican town.

A common trail hazard.

The author after eighteen hours in a Kentucky treasure cave.

Nighttime trek in Mexican mountains.

Traveling by burro in the Sierra Madres.

James Poet and W.C. Jameson in camp in Mexico's Sierra Madres.

The author relaxing in a Mexican cantina following an expedition to locate a lost silver cache.

9

THE CANYON OF THE DEAD

The more rigorous the way, the more intense the
adventure.

—Gina Comaich

Mexico, an enduring and alluring country, possesses a vibrant
history, one filled with struggle, warfare, bizarre politics,
defense of ancient homelands, art, poetry, and literature. In addition to the descendants of Spanish conquerors, the country is
populated with a wide and diverse variety of Indian tribes that
live from the highest peaks of the Sierra Madre Occidental to the
coastal shores, from the northern border with the United States
south to Guatemala and Belize. A number of these tribes boasted
historical civilizations greater than those of early Europe, Asia,
and Africa. Many are well documented, the results of decades of
research and study by archaeologists and anthropologists. Others
are less well known, and of a few we know nothing.

Mexico contains far more wild and unexplored country than
does the United States. Most of the places I have searched and
explored there are virtually uninhabited, a great advantage to the
professional treasure hunter. Additionally, a number of large and
important treasure caches have been hidden in Mexico, and not
many people know about them. This means less competition from
other treasure-recovery specialists. Furthermore, throughout the

Sierra Madres, there remain a number of lost mines of gold and silver opened during the time of Spanish conquest, subsequently abandoned for a variety of reasons, that have yet to be rediscovered and reworked. More recently, gold, silver, and other metals were mined and processed in Mexico by U.S. companies that were forced out during the Mexican Revolution of the early 1900s.

Over the years, Mexico has provided an abundance of rewards relative to the exploration and search for lost mines and buried treasure. Though successes have been impressive and the adventures unparalleled, the country continues to offer promise of much more, and of the unexpected.

Case in point: In 1980, Poet, Slade, Stanley, and I undertook a search for a cluster of lost silver mines that had been opened and worked by an American mining company and then abandoned in 1915 as a result of hostilities associated with the Mexican Revolution. Our expedition was interrupted by an accidental discovery, one that turned out to be an encounter with a far greater treasure than what we planned for, and one that changed our lives.

At dawn one day during the last week of May, Poet, Slade, Stanley, and I, carrying backpacks, waded the Rio Grande at the Boquillas crossing and entered Mexico. Only an hour earlier we had left our vehicle with a resident of Rio Grande Village, Brewster County, Texas, located inside the borders of Big Bend National Park. The river was low, only thigh-high, and the crossing was uneventful. We hiked the half-mile from the crossing to the Mexican pueblo of Boquillas del Carmen, a sleepy village perched on the first terrace above the floodplain. All of the houses, as well as the cantina and a tiny grocery store, were made from adobe, a few sporting coats of stucco. There was no electricity, no plumbing, and water was dipped from hand-dug communal wells. Burros, chickens, and dogs wandered the dusty streets. During this time, Boquillas boasted about seventy-five residents, a small one-room school, and two churches, one Catholic and the other, oddly, Baptist. Due to the remote and relatively unpopulated location, neither supported a priest or minister.

We met with a man who owned a small cattle ranch nearby and who earlier had agreed to lease us horses and mules for our expedition. The horses were well-fed and muscular and appeared travel-worthy. The four mules, which were to carry provisions into the interior and, hopefully, transport sacks of silver ore out, likewise were durable and seemed anxious to get moving. At our request, the rancher also provided us with a guide; a short, wiry man named Guadalupe Maldonado. Maldonado sported a long Zapata-style mustache and a battered felt cowboy hat. Not only would Maldonado serve as guide, he agreed to cook our meals and care for the riding stock.

Since we planned to be out for three weeks, we made some purchases in the tiny store in town—some tinned goods, freshly made tortillas, dried beans and meat, and Mexican coffee. Once packs and purchases were tied onto three of the mules, Maldonado mounted the fourth, and we rode southeastward out of town.

We followed the occasionally graded dirt road that led to the city of Melchior Musquiz 175 miles to the southeast in the Mexican state of Coahuila. At a point indicated by Maldonado, we left the road and continued toward a distant range of low mountains to the southwest. Pointing, Maldonado told us we would travel around the northern end and continue on to the location of the old mines for which we were searching. The mines lay in another range of mountains a two-day ride beyond. The trail we followed was barely discernible, but our guide appeared to know exactly where he was going.

Inside one or more of the mines, according to mining company reports located by Stanley in a Cincinnati, Ohio, library archive, were thick veins of almost pure silver, with minor quantities of lead and zinc. The mines were first discovered and opened around 1900 and remained productive until 1915, when the violence of the Mexican Revolution and the growing threat of border raiders forced the American owners and workers out. Escape for them back across the border was imperative, and they had little time to pack their belongings. Before departing, according to the documents, the owners ordered thousands of silver ingots carried into the mine shafts and stacked against the walls. Following this, the openings to the mines were closed, either by stacking rocks in front of them or blasting them shut. The miners intended to return after the war was over, but the reduced price of silver made resuming the operations unprofitable. During the 1980s, when the price of silver soared, there was some interest in reopening these mines, but the troubled and muddied waters of Mexican politics made it impossible. If silver existed in sufficient quantity, we intended to mine some of it, smuggle it back across the border, and broker it through men with whom we did business.

If we found the entrances blocked with stacked rocks, we were prepared for the work of removing them. If they had been blasted shut, then we could be facing some serious, backbreaking labor. We hoped for the former, for the latter would likely necessitate earth-moving equipment that would have been difficult to bring to the isolated location undetected. There was no way of knowing until we arrived at our destination.

On the afternoon of the second day of our expedition, Maldonado indicated once again the north-south trending range of mountains he would lead us around.

"When we pass the northern end," he said, "we will see the low granite mountains you seek."

Near the middle of the closer range that loomed before us, I spotted what appeared to be a deep, narrow, and shadowy cleft.

"Tell me about that great slice in the mountains," I asked our guide.

Speaking in a fluid, musical Spanish, Maldonado said, "The canyon passes completely through the range. My grandfather told me it is the result of a massive earthquake that occurred millions of years ago."

"Can we pass through it?" I asked.

"*Sí*. If we traveled through the canyon we would shave two days from our travel time."

"Why don't we do that?"

Maldonado paused for several seconds, then looked directly at me and said, "Because the canyon is cursed, *señor*, haunted. It is called *El Cañon del Muerto*, The Canyon of the Dead."

At this, Slade, Stanley, and Poet reined to a halt, looked at one another, and then at Maldonado. We sat our mounts in silence awaiting further explanation.

Looking uncomfortable, Maldonado coughed, then continued.

"The spirits of the dead live in this canyon, *señores*, and will allow us to pass only if they are in a favorable disposition. Some of the old ones in Boquillas tell of young men entering the canyon and never returning, leaving grieving mothers and wives and orphaned children. One *viejo*, Armando Sanchez, he is about ninety years old now, tells of entering the canyon when he was a young boy with three of his *compañeros*. One of his friends was bitten by a huge *cascabel*, a Mexican rattlesnake, and died before sundown. Another fell to his death while climbing a steep incline to examine a cave. Sanchez and his remaining friend fled from the canyon, but by the time they returned to the village, his friend had gone insane and never spoke another word for the rest of his life."

"Who, or what, in the hell do you think is in that canyon that has your people spooked?" asked Stanley.

"Two things," replied Maldonado. "For one, it is an environment for snakes, thousands of them. During the warm months, the *cascabeles* come out to sun in the mornings, then before the heat reaches the canyon floor, they retreat under the rocks, into burrows, into the caves, under the shade of trees and bushes."

Maldonado looked up at the sun and said, "This is the time of the year they are out in great numbers. Some of the *cascabeles* found here grow thicker than a big man's thigh and long, some more than twelve feet long."

"Twelve feet!" Stanley said in astonishment. "Jesus, man, the world record for a diamondback rattlesnake is less than seven feet long. Are you trying to tell me these snakes here grow longer than that?"

"*Si, señor*," replied Maldonado. "A particularly large one was killed at the entrance to the canyon seven years ago. The hide is in Boquillas in the home of the man who killed and skinned the beast. The skin is seventeen feet long."

"Jesus!" Stanley whistled.

"You mentioned two things," I said. "What is the other?"

"*Las almas perdidas.* The lost souls."

"What does that mean?" asked Slade, fingering the butt of his revolver.

"*Quien sabe, señor*? Who knows? Many say the canyon is cursed."

"How? Why?" asked Stanley.

"I can say no more," said Maldonado, as he made the sign of the cross. "To talk much about it is to bring bad luck."

Looking at the position of the sun in the sky, I said, "Let's ride another couple of miles and then make camp."

The next morning, Slade, Stanley, Poet, and I stood shoulder to shoulder drinking coffee from tin cups near the campfire and staring out at the narrow cleft in the range ahead of us, its flanks illuminated by the rising sun.

"What do you think?" asked Slade.

I took one step forward, as if it would provide me with a better view, turned, and said, "I don't believe in curses. Let's do it."

We stood in silence for another minute, each of us regarding the range. "We can't *not* do it," I said. "It's calling to us."

"I was afraid that's what you would say," Stanley added.

Minutes later, we rode single-file toward *El Cañon del Muerto*. I was in the lead, Maldonado and the mules bringing up the rear.

Five hours later, as we approached the entrance to the canyon, I stared at the narrow cleft, scarcely more than eighty yards wide, and estimated that the sheer walls rose to four hundred feet or more. Along the base of the cliffs were steep slopes of talus, centuries of debris weathered from limestone cliffs and fallen to the bottom to accumulate and extend to the canyon floor.

When we were still a hundred yards from the entrance, I heard a loud buzzing off to my right, the unmistakable resonance of a rattlesnake. I reined up and peered into the nearby bushes. The others halted behind me, also looking for the source of the sound. Slade, pointing, said, "There, in the shade of that creosote bush at two o'clock and twenty feet away."

Wrapped in a tight coil was a diamondback rattlesnake, its triangular-shaped head pointing toward us, the forked tongue flicking in and out, a primitive heat sensor probing the air for intruders. The vibrations of the ground caused by our horses and mules no doubt alerted the rattler. Now, it prepared for defense.

"Probably four-and-a-half feet stretched out," commented Poet.

I looked back at Maldonado and watched him as he stared at the snake, making the sign of the cross over and over. He looked at me, visibly nervous. He stared into the depths of the canyon and made the sign several more times, speaking quietly, saying his prayers.

As we rode into the cleft, shadows covered us like a blanket. The trail paralleled a narrow, winding stream that contained an inch or two of water. Exposed cross sections of the canyon walls showed that the range was made up of uniform horizontal layers of limestone, the thickest being three to four feet, the thinnest just over a foot. In the walls, we spotted narrow, elongated openings that are referred to as slit caves. Here, carbon dioxide–laden water percolating along the bedding planes and joints of the soluble limestone caused some of the rock to erode away along the contact planes, leaving the characteristic openings. The process takes millions of years.

The buzzing of rattlesnakes in the brush that lined the rarely used trail accompanied us as we rode. Sometimes we heard several, perhaps as many as a dozen. Now and then, a *cascabel* slithered across the path in front of us. None was more than six feet long, and I was beginning to think the tales of monster rattlesnakes were a product of imagination. The farther we rode into the canyon, the more nervous Maldonado became. Once along the trail I heard him mutter, "*Madre de Dios, salvaguardarme.*" Mother of God, protect me.

Slade rode point. Without warning, he jerked on the reins, bringing his horse to a sudden stop, and pointed ahead.

"Holy shit!" he said. We followed his point and saw, lying across the sandy trail, a rattlesnake with a body thicker than a football with the head and tail hidden in the grasses growing on both sides of the six-foot-wide passageway.

Stanley eased his mount next to Slade's and stared. "Jesus!" was all he could say.

The large serpent, alert to our presence, began slithering away. As we watched, an additional two feet of tail followed the mass we had already seen.

"Goddamnit!" exclaimed Stanley. "That snake's at least nine or ten feet long!"

"We ought to catch it and bring it back with us," said Poet. "That will surprise the hell out of those prissy university herpetologists who insist these big snakes don't exist."

Maldonado sat his mule, shaking and making the sign of the cross. When Slade spurred his horse forward and we continued, Maldonado said, "*Cuidado!* There will be more of them."

The canyon curved slightly to the right. Pointing, Maldonado said, "Beyond the turn will be found the home of *las almas perdidas*. The lost souls." None of us spoke.

"Perhaps we should turn back," Maldonado said with hope.

In response, Slade spurred his horse forward. We followed.

When I first spotted the graves, I did not recognize them for what they were. Maldonado gestured toward them with a shaking hand. I saw the elongated shapes, perhaps as many as fifty of them. We rode up and dismounted, all except Maldonado, who remained on his mule.

Each of the graves was perched upon a level bedrock layer of limestone above the stream, which over the years had been gradually eroding into the formation. Employing the plentiful thin, rectangular slabs of sedimentary rock found throughout the canyon, a kind of vault had been created for each site, with the sides and ends up to two-and-a-half feet tall. More slabs were laid across the tops, and as we walked among them, we saw that the narrow spaces between the rocks were filled with a primitive mortar. The vaults were arranged somewhat systematically across the exposed bedrock right up to the edge of the stream. Most of them were collapsed or tilting.

Stanley walked from grave to grave, staring in wonder and disbelief. "This is indeed curious. If this is an Indian burial ground, then I assure you nothing like this can be found in the annals of North American anthropology or archaeology," he said.

Maldonado screamed and pointed toward a spot near the stream. "*Madre de Dios!* There is one of them!"

We followed the direction of his point to the edge of the bedrock. At first we were unable to discern the cause for alarm, then we saw it. Walking over to the object of Maldonado's attention, my heart hammered. A portion of the thin layer of limestone had been undermined by stream erosion. A section of the layer had collapsed, impacting one of the tombs perched atop it by collapsing the slabs and exposing the contents within.

There, lying newly exposed before us on the ground, was a remarkably well-preserved mummy partially wrapped in a covering of densely woven grass. In places where the wrapping had come apart, the dark, dried, brittle flesh of an ancient human being could be seen.

We stood side by side, staring in awe at the mummy. Maldonado remained on his mule. He looked first at the remains, and then all around the canyon as if he anticipated a visit from one of the spirits he feared. He appeared as if he was readying himself to turn his mule and bolt back out of the canyon and return to Boquillas del Carmen at any moment.

Stanley knelt and carefully unwrapped a portion of the grass from the mummy, a cautious, deliberate process that took nearly thirty minutes due to the dry, fragile nature of the covering. Before us, a startlingly intact and well-preserved body of a male Indian lay on the ground. The skin was dark, almost black, and the hair had been braided into twin two-foot lengths. He had been just over five feet tall in life.

Around the neck of the mummy was a simple shell necklace made from a species, according to Stanley, that could only be found along the eastern coast of Mexico five hundred miles away. Wrapped around the head was what remained of a rotted cloth band to which was fastened many small blue feathers. Peering closely, Stanley studied the feathers and informed us that they had come from the macaw, a bird that had never lived in this part of Mexico.

On both arms of the mummy were several ornately fashioned bracelets made of gold, each one about three-quarters of an inch wide and hand-etched with simple figures of birds, reptiles, mammals, and humans.

We did not hear Maldonado approach. From behind us, he said, "It is not good for him to lie exposed like this. *Las almas perdidas* will be angered. We must wrap him up now and carry him to the safe place with the others."

"The others?" Slade asked.

In response, Maldonado pointed to a slit cave high in the adjacent canyon wall and said, "More than a dozen lie buried in the small cave you see there."

Maldonado squatted in the sun and worked his tongue to moisten his mouth. Slade handed him a canteen. The Mexican took a long drink and said, "I will tell you the story."

"Eight years ago," Maldonado began, "my father and I were traveling through this canyon a few days after a flash flood had come through, carrying away great portions of rock and dirt and sweeping them downstream. It was our first time here. We had heard stories of the spirits that lived here but did not believe them. As we approached this burial ground, we saw that many of the crude vaults had been torn open by the floodwaters. We were with terror, but my father was curious. I followed him as he walked from one tomb to another, looking at the exposed bodies."

Maldonado stopped to take another swig of water and to collect himself, then continued.

"My father dropped to his knees where *Señor* Stanley is standing right now and began praying out loud to God. He was begging forgiveness for committing some great wrong, for intruding into what must have been a sacred place. He pulled me down to my knees and made me pray too. When we finished, my father rose to his feet and explained what we must do."

Poet, Slade, Stanley, and I stood silent, waiting for the guide to continue.

"With great care," said Maldonado, "we lifted the stiff bodies and carried them, one by one, up the steep rocky slope and laid them into a dry, protected niche. We placed them at the far end of the narrow space. It took us a full day to relocate them all."

We stared at the narrow horizontal opening in the canyon wall above the talus slope.

"That night," continued Maldonado, "we made camp in the canyon. The next morning we bent to the task of making adobe bricks from the mud, grass, and water. We allowed time for them to dry, then carried them to the cave and walled up the front and sealed it with mud, thus protecting the bodies."

More silence, as we pondered what Maldonado said.

Stanley asked, "Were the mummies you reburied wearing gold bracelets like this one?"

"*Si, señor*, they wore many bracelets and other jewelry."

Stanley took his time rewrapping the mummy, careful to arrange the grass blanket so that it covered most of the remains.

While Poet and I watched him work, Slade walked around the area looking at the other graves, bending over every now and then to examine something. When he returned, he said, "We've got six more mummies exposed to the elements, all in varying conditions of decay."

Though the mummy Stanley rewrapped didn't weigh much, the talus slope up to the niche cave was steep and difficult to climb, so we all took turns transporting it to the top. Here, we found the walled-up entrance to the cave just as Maldonado described, the crude masonry offering significant protection from weather and animals. Maldonado loosened several adobe bricks from the entrance and pulled them away, stacking them to one side. Years earlier Maldonado and his father had etched Christian symbols into the bricks while they had been drying.

When the opening was large enough, we peered into the dark interior. As our eyes adjusted to the darkness within, we discerned individual mummies. The cave extended laterally for thirty yards and was close to twelve feet deep. The bodies were arranged with their heads toward the rear of the cave and lined up side by side. We counted thirteen.

At the end of the row of mummies, we arranged the one we had carried up the slope.

"Only six more to go," said Stanley. "It's going to be a long day."

Poet pointed to one of the mummies in the cave. It was only partially wrapped, and a dry, bony hand protruded from the grass covering. "Look!" He pointed to the hand. One of the fingers bore a ring.

Stanley crawled into the cave to examine it. When he backed out, he said, "It's a ring, all right. A simple design but made of gold. Most unusual."

"What's unusual about it?" I asked.

"As a rule," he said, "Indians didn't wear rings."

Stanley pointed down the slope at the graves near the creek and said, "Nor did they bury their dead in this manner."

"Maybe they weren't Indians," said Slade.

"You might be onto something," said Stanley. "There is overwhelming evidence that the Olmecs, a tribe that lived and thrived south and west of here, were direct descendants of Asians, maybe Chinese, who apparently navigated their way across the Pacific Ocean to this continent. There is also some curious evidence that Roman explorers made their way into the Mexican interior. Artifacts and architecture have been found that possess a decidedly Roman influence. There is also abundant evidence that others—Egyptians, Jews, and more—crossed the Atlantic Ocean and explored and settled parts of what became the United States and Mexico."

"Did you see rings on any of the other mummies you laid in the cave?" I asked Maldonado.

"*Si, señor,*" he said. "Not only rings, but necklaces made of gold. Some had pendants of large gold nuggets, and from others dangled green stones. Some of the dead ones wore as many as five rings on the fingers of one hand. Several had earrings, men and women alike, and one or two had golden rings in their noses."

"I think this is going to drive anthropologists crazy," said Stanley. "Everything we've discerned about these people is either rare or unknown. They don't fit into any category I am aware of."

"It will only drive the anthropologists crazy if they find out about it," I said. "I'm for keeping this to ourselves until we decide we have a real good reason to let other people know about it."

"I agree," said Slade.

"I estimate these mummies to be at least a couple of thousand years old," said Stanley. "I also wonder where the gold for the ornaments came from. Though silver has been found in adjacent mountain ranges, the nearest known source of gold is hundreds of miles from here."

When we returned to the ancient cemetery near the stream, Slade, looking pensive, addressed us. "There is enough gold buried with these mummies to make us wealthy."

No one responded. Silent, we pondered his statement. Slade was right. This was the kind of treasure the four of us had searched for many times in the past.

Stanley coughed. Poet stared up at the niche where we'd placed the mummy. Nervous, Maldonado glanced at us, worried at what our decision might be. I placed a hand on his shoulder.

Seeing our reactions, Slade said, "Forget what I said."

Poet, Stanley, and I nodded assent. Relieved, Maldonado managed a weak grin and mumbled a prayer of some sort of Mexican gratitude.

Over the next two days, we carried the remaining mummies to the niche and sealed them within their new sepulcher.

That evening, seated around the campfire, Poet spoke.

"It's funny," he said. "Here we are, treasure hunters leaving a fortune in gold many would kill to possess. Part of me feels good about what we did here, but another part questions the rationale. Did we do this because we wanted to, or because we feared the spirits Maldonado spoke of?"

"We did what we did because it was right," said Stanley. "I feel the spirits too, but I don't have the feeling they are hostile. In fact, I feel the opposite. I think they are grateful for the work we did."

"We came in search of silver," I put in. "That is still our objective. This was unanticipated. The canyon doesn't seem evil; it feels friendly. It feels as if I've been here before, in spirit if not in person. Maybe we were destined to come here; maybe there was a purpose."

Maldonado, saying nothing, poured more coffee.

"So, what about the silver we came on this expedition for?" asked Poet.

"Let's chase it another time," I suggested. "It's not going anywhere."

We decided to spend the rest of our time in The Canyon of the Dead; over the next few days, we found the remains of habitations, and we uncovered dozens of arrowheads, spear points, scrapers, knives, stone axes, pottery shards, and other items. Stanley made sketches of the artifacts in his journal, but we replaced each where we found it.

When we rode out of *El Cañon del Muerto*, we carried no treasure. It wasn't the first time that had happened during one of our expeditions. As with most of our adventures, however, we came away satisfied that we had gained an experience available to few.

POSTSCRIPT

I have returned to *El Cañon del Muerto* three times since that original visit in 1980, once in the company of the others and twice alone. With each visit, I examined the burial ground to assess the condition of the graves. During one visit, two of the vaults had experienced significant disturbance by flash flood runoff washing across the structures. The mummies were removed, with reverence, carried up the talus slope, and placed inside the slit cave with the others.

Poet, Slade, Stanley, Maldonado, and I agreed to serve as *de facto* caretakers of these ancient people and the place, to see to the preservation of the bodies with prayerful care. Stanley continued to study them, to try to learn who they were, where they came from, and why they arrived at that canyon and settled. It remains a mystery, one that has never been solved.

During one return visit, we encountered a frighteningly large rattlesnake. Coiled and prepared to strike, the thick serpent's head was two feet above the ground. Slade tossed a loop over its saucer-sized head and secured it to the trunk of a young oak. Poet and I grabbed the tail and stretched the snake out to its full length while Stanley measured it. The rattler was thirteen feet, seven inches long. At its thickest point, the body was fifteen inches in diameter. I counted fifty-one buttons on the rattle.

During another visit I made alone to the canyon, I sat in the shade of the wall just outside the slit cave one evening, listening to a couple of mourning doves cooing from afar. Behind me, beyond the thick earthen wall, was enough gold in the form of adornments to make many men wealthy. In the ancient cemetery below on the canyon floor lay at least another twenty-five mummies, maybe more, all of them no doubt similarly adorned with the precious metal.

Maldonado, now in his seventies if he still lives, believes the canyon is cursed, but is convinced we are protected when we are there because of the service we render for the dead, *las almas perdidas.*

I still don't believe in curses, but there is something about that canyon I can't quite explain. On approaching the place, I perceive a kind of wispy terror that hovers just beyond rational thought, out of reach beyond my senses. It has to do with the unknown. Once into the canyon, however, the terror vanishes to be replaced by a sense of comfort, of peace.

When I go to the canyon by myself, I don't feel alone. I feel as though I am in the company of those that once lived here, men and women who grew crops of corn and squash and beans near the little stream, lived in shelters, made love, bore children. These spirits don't seem hostile to me. They seem benevolent, even protective. I catch myself speaking to them when I am there, and in recent years, I find myself speaking to them when I am hundreds of miles away from their canyon. And I am certain they hear me. I am coming to know them, whoever they are, or were. Perhaps I am one of them.

10

JESSE JAMES'S TREASURE CAVE

The true adventurer is the one who escapes the tread-
mill of the obvious.

—Chris Bonington

I had heard versions of the tale about the Jesse James treasure
cache for years. In fact, a number of treasure hunters in and
around the Ozark Mountains of Arkansas, Missouri, and Oklahoma had heard the stories, and most of them believed there was
some element of truth in all of them. Several had searched for a
likely cave, but no one possessed any precise information on the
location.

The story goes like this: Following a train-robbery spree, outlaws Jesse and Frank James, accompanied by two gang members,
had accumulated about $60,000 in gold coins. Pursued by law-
men, the gang fled into the Oklahoma Ozarks and allegedly hid
the loot in a remote cave located in a secluded and little-known
and rarely visited hollow. As far as anyone knew, the outlaws
never returned to retrieve the gold and it has remained lost ever
since.

There were two significant problems with this story. First,
there are no less than fifty caves throughout the Ozark Mountains
where area residents claim the James gang hid outlaw loot. Several
are even advertised on billboards and represent local attempts to

attract gullible tourists into town to spend their money. Obviously, these stories can't all be true. Second, though we searched off and on for months, we found no documentation for, or even a decent reference to, the notion that such a thing ever happened. As far as Poet, Slade, Stanley, and I were concerned, it was just a tale.

Then we met Falwell B. Loomis. Loomis, who had lived and worked in the Ozark Mountains all of his fifty-five years and who never graduated from high school, spent the majority of his free time reading about and researching the life and legend of the outlaw Jesse James. Though never formally educated, Loomis was dedicated to his chosen interest and spent hours each day studying everything he could find on the topic. He interviewed not only descendants of the famous outlaw brothers, but also descendants of their victims and of lawmen who pursued the gang. He traveled to locations where James gang robberies occurred and accumulated an impressive library on the outlaws as well as on Arkansas, Missouri, and Oklahoma history. Loomis tried to engage Jesse James scholars and college professors in discussion and debate, but they mostly considered him a hobbyist and crank. In the opinion of many Ozark residents, however, he knew more about Jesse and Frank James than did the so-called experts.

Because of Loomis's unrelenting tenacity in researching Jesse James, he often encountered things that credentialed scholars and researchers never knew existed or just plain overlooked. Among them were the personal effects of an elderly woman living near the Ozark mountain town of Gentry, Arkansas, who claimed to be a "great-grandniece by marriage" to Jesse James. In a wooden chest filled with the accumulated debris of a lifetime of living in a backwoods Ozark community, the great-grandniece had filed a letter written to a long-deceased relative by none other than the famous outlaw. In the letter, James described the circumstances behind the train robberies and the location of the buried coins "in the Territories." During those days, what is now the state of

Oklahoma was designated as Indian Territory. The handwriting has since been examined by a professional analyst and authenticated as being that of Jesse James.

As improbable and unlikely as it seemed, folded into the letter was a detailed map, drawn in pencil, providing directions to the hiding place, which was labeled "January Cave." Within minutes after being shown the map by Loomis, I was convinced the cave could be found in a portion of northeastern Oklahoma. I was somewhat familiar with the area since I had explored a number of caves there. The region was dominated by limestone bedrock that spawned hundreds of caverns, some quite extensive.

Weeks later, when the timing came together for everyone, Stanley, Slade, Poet, and I met at Loomis's mountainside home in northwestern Arkansas, where we reviewed the tale and made copies of the letter and map. Our host prepared a meal of grilled chicken, roasting ears, green beans, onions, radishes, and several different kinds of peppers. Everything was raised on his property. He had a huge garden, a chicken coop, and a hog pen and kept most of his neighbors in vegetables and eggs. During the meal, Loomis, responding to a question from Slade, informed us that his middle initial stood for Bosco, his mother's maiden name.

We agreed that Loomis would be given one-fifth of anything we might recover. Following an evening of pleasant conversation and examining Loomis's extensive library, we camped on his wooden front porch. In the morning after a breakfast of pork chops, eggs, grits, homemade biscuits and gravy, and coffee, we were on our way to Delaware County in the Oklahoma Ozarks in a jeep loaded with camping gear and caving equipment. Because it was in the middle of summer, we also carried snake sticks. This part of the Ozark Mountains was thick with rattlesnakes, water moccasins, and copperheads. In addition, each of us brought a handgun, and Slade and I both packed Winchester Model .94 rifles. With four people and gear, the jeep was quite crowded. In addition to the real and potential danger of poisonous snakes, the hills of the Ozarks, as well as the neighboring Ouachita Mountains to the south, were also home to longtime reclusive residents who more often than not resented intrusion of any kind and often responded to it with violence. We wanted to be prepared.

Following a restful night in a motel in the town of Grove, Oklahoma, we made our way toward our targeted destination. Stanley drove his jeep with Slade in the front passenger seat and Poet and me in the back with most of the gear. After traveling a few miles on the blacktop south out of town, we turned east onto an old forest service road. The road was seldom used except during hunting season. After several miles of twisting, bumpy, rutted, and washed-out trail, we pulled onto another road, this one in worse shape, even to the point of saplings growing up between the deep ruts. From time to time one of us was forced to leave the jeep and remove a sapling with a bow saw. High clearance and four-wheel drive were necessary, and even with those we rarely made over three miles per hour.

The road led into a wide valley ringed with densely foliated ridges. As we started the gradual descent, we encountered a stream that flowed from the north, made a sharp turn, and then paralleled the road to our left.

Brush and briars along the side of the road were thick to impenetrable, and we could only imagine what the snake, tick, and chigger population was only a few feet away. The air was quiet, still, and thick with humidity. Sweat trickled down our chests and backs, soaking our shirts.

We paralleled the stream for almost a mile when, from the front seat, Slade turned, pointed ahead at eleven o'clock, and said, "We've got company."

About fifty yards away and on the opposite side of the stream, I could just make out the figure of a man through the brush. He was seated on the stream bank with a cane fishing pole in his hand. We slowed, nearing a point opposite from where he perched. Completely naked, he regarded us with hard, angry eyes.

We pulled to a stop, with Stanley indicating he wanted to talk to the man, perhaps ask directions, and maybe convince him we were friendly. Stanley exited the jeep and stepped through some roadside brush onto the near stream bank and waved at the man who rose from his crouched position. He stood around 5'8"tall. Judging from his face, he looked to be sixty years old but had the physique of a body builder. His muscles were wiry and well defined, his skin tanned to the color of an acorn. Hair with a hint of gray hung to his shoulders, framing a surprisingly handsome countenance. He looked like he could be Tarzan except for one thing: his earlobes were exceptionally long, dangling an inch and a half or more below his ears.

Stanley introduced himself and was two or three words into his opening sentence when the man dropped his fishing pole, turned, and without a word disappeared into the thick brush behind him. Stanley looked toward us and shrugged. We peered into the woods where the strange man vanished and didn't know what to make of it. Stanley climbed back into the jeep and we proceeded on.

About twenty minutes later, we drove into a clearing about the size of a football field and saw several primitive cabins made from log, rock, and combinations of both. There was also a large barn, several corncribs, and some chicken coops. Seven or eight garden patches were evident, with produce ready for picking. Chickens wandered about clucking and pecking at the ground.

The entire population of this little community, about thirty people, was clustered together in front of the nearest cabin, the naked man we had seen by the stream standing at the very front. We halted the jeep and cut the engine.

While the residents stared at us, Stanley consulted a couple of maps and said, "This place is not indicated on either of these."

As Stanley climbed out of the jeep, Slade whispered, "Keep your handguns where you can get to them easy."

In a row, we approached the cluster when three men, all clothed in ragged and torn overalls and nothing else, stepped forward. Two carried shotguns, one a rifle. The weapons looked to be a hundred years old or more and were pointed at us. We met halfway between the jeep and the crowd of people.

As Stanley greeted them, I looked over the residents of the hollow. All of the men were similar to the one we saw at the stream: good-looking, lean, but heavily muscled. Even the three boys I took to be in their teens were splendidly built as if they worked out in a gym four or five hours a day. There were two youngsters, maybe six and seven years old. All of the males had long earlobes. Several, like the man at the creek, wore no clothes at all.

By contrast, the women were hideous. Those over twenty years of age were heavy. Not fat, but thick and stocky like buffaloes. Their faces were hog-like with wide flat noses and eyes pinched shut, looking almost Mongoloid. As far as I could tell, all of them were cross-eyed. Each woman wore a homemade shift, and all were filthy as if they had just been interrupted cleaning the barn or toiling in the garden.

Stanley introduced each of us, as if it mattered, and said to the men with the weapons, "We are looking for a particular cave in this area, one that might be named January."

The man with the rifle took a step forward and regarded each of us with a look that seemed to be a mixture of annoyance and contempt. He had the whitest, most even teeth of anyone I had ever seen. He spit on the ground, missing Stanley's boots by an inch or two.

"We be January," he said. He spoke as though slightly demented, but his black eyes revealed an evil intelligence and a keen awareness of everything around him.

"What do you mean?" asked Stanley.

"We be January."

"You mean your name is January?"

"We be January." He spit again.

"We're looking for January Cave," said Stanley. "Do you know—?"

The man with the rifle raised it to his shoulder and pointed it straight at Stanley's chest. He said, "You go now."

Slade's hand moved toward his nine-millimeter handgun. In an instant the two shotguns were leveled at him.

Stanley was shaking, whether from fear or anger I couldn't tell. I stepped forward and said, "We're sorry for intruding. We're a little lost. Our mistake. We'll just get back in the jeep and go. Sorry to bother you."

"You go now," commanded the man with the rifle.

"Back to the jeep," I said, leading the way. When we looked back, the weapons were still pointed in our direction.

"Friendly folks out here in these woods," said Poet.

"Bastards," muttered Slade, who looked like he wanted to shoot somebody.

"Let's get the hell out of here," said Stanley.

Stanley was still shaking, so I climbed into the driver's side of the jeep, started the engine, and told him to get in. Slade jumped in the back with Poet, who was more than ready to go. We did a half-circle and drove out of the clearing. Poet turned and waved good-bye at the Januarys on the way out.

We stopped up the trail near where we had seen the naked man earlier. With the engines still running, we got out of the jeep and gathered to assess the situation and discuss our next move.

"That's easy," said Poet. "We leave, the sooner the better. This is like a bad horror movie come true."

Slade checked the clip on his weapon, reholstered it, and stared back down the trail. "I think they're going to follow to make certain we're gone," he said.

"That shouldn't be a problem," said Poet. "Let's oblige them."

As we spoke, Stanley studied the maps. He was examining the copy of the one allegedly sketched by Jesse James himself when he said, "Look here."

Running his finger along some of the lines on the map, he said, "That clearing where those funny people live would be right about here on this map. If that's the case, then the cave we're looking for is up this way." He pointed in the direction we had been heading on the way out and across the stream.

"If this map is correct," he said, "the cave should be at the base of that bluff over there."

The distance looked to be just over a hundred yards from where we were standing. There were a lot of undergrowth and briars between us and Stanley's notion of where the cave might be.

"I vote we go check it out since we're already here," said Stanley.

"I vote we leave," said Poet.

"I vote we go back there and shoot one or two of those bastards," said Slade.

Stanley looked toward the location of the cave, Poet looked up the trail we would take on the way out, and Slade looked back toward the village. After a moment, all three turned to look at me.

"It's a three-way tie, and you have the deciding vote," said Stanley.

I took a deep breath and then said, "We go look for the cave. We check it out. Then we leave."

Slade shot me an angry look.

"In the process," I continued, addressing Slade, "you might get to shoot somebody."

"You ought to be a goddamn politician," growled Slade.

"What a horrible thing to say about somebody," said Stanley.

We steered the jeep along the road for another hundred yards and cut the engine. Because of the winding nature of the road and the stream, as well as the dense foliage, we were well out of sight of the village. At this location, one would have to be within twenty yards of the jeep to spot it, and the only way to do that would be for them to be walking up the road. We decided to take the chance and leave the vehicle there.

We gathered up the headlamps, flashlights, and snake sticks; crossed the stream; and climbed the opposite bank. Each of us packed a holstered weapon, but we left the rifles in the jeep. The water was hip-high. Once on the opposite bank, I was about to plunge into the undergrowth when, thirty feet to my left, Poet said, "Look, here's a trail." We had taken to whispering, not knowing how far our voices would carry in the enclosed valley.

Heading in the direction we wanted to go was a path that had not been used much; there were few tracks, mostly deer and what appeared to be wild hogs. We followed the winding route for several dozen yards when we spotted another trail joining this one. The new one came from the direction of the village. We continued on and came across the confluences of three more trails. As we approached the base of the bluff, the vegetation ahead was beginning to thin out when Stanley, who was in the lead, stopped suddenly and said, "Well, I'll be a sonofabitch."

We bumped up next to him on the narrow trail and looked in the direction he pointed. There was a low, dark opening to a cave, only two-and-a-half feet high and six feet wide. We hurried over, wary of snakes that like to lurk inside of cave openings out of the hot sun. I arrived first and peered into the darkness, searching the interior with the flashlight, but saw no snakes. I stomped the ground, alerting any that might be nearby of our arrival with the vibrations, but the entrance was clear.

"Oh, oh," said Poet. "Look at this." He pointed at the ground and we saw three sets of footprints that weren't ours.

Slade stared and said, "That last trail we passed intersecting this one has gotten a lot of use. Those people are coming to this cave for some reason and they've been here recently."

"Whose turn is it to remain at the entrance?" asked Stanley.

"Yours," said Slade.

"Crap! I was afraid of that," said Stanley.

"I've got an idea," I said. "How about if you perch yourself just inside the opening where you don't make yourself a target for anybody who might happen to drop by with a weapon?"

"Good idea," said Stanley, though it was clear he disliked being left behind.

After lighting the headlamps and grabbing a flashlight in one hand and a snake stick in the other, we crawled on hands and knees for the first thirty yards because the low ceiling prohibited walking upright.

"What's that smell?" asked Poet.

We paused, sniffed the air coming from inside the cave. Slade said, "Wood smoke and ash is what it smells like."

"That, yes. But there's something else, something really pungent, kind of rancid."

Neither of us could identify the odd aroma, but the farther we crawled into the cave, the stronger it became.

Just as I was tiring of the crawling, the tunnel opened up into a chamber large enough to hold a church service in. The ceiling was festooned with dozens of stalactites. The cave, like most of the others in the region, was millions of years old.

But it was not the stalactites and stalagmites that held our attention. There, in the middle of the level floor, was an arrangement of copper pots, tubing, and several porcelain and clay jugs.

"There's the source of that god-awful smell," said Slade.

"Holy Christ!" said Poet. "It's a whiskey still, and a big one."

"No wonder those people wanted us out of here," I said. "This part of the Ozarks is full of tales of folks getting killed as a result of chancing upon illegal stills."

The color drained from Poet's face. "Jesus. Those strange people were about to kill us just for driving into their valley. If they knew we were in here, we'd be catfish bait."

I looked around the large chamber and saw two passageways radiating out from it. Did one of them contain the Jesse James treasure cache? I was tempted to have a look, but instead turned to crawl back through the tunnel.

"Time to go," I said. "The sooner we get out of here, the better."

Without any discussion, we did a double-time crawl back toward the entrance where we found Stanley in the shadows peering intently at something beyond the entrance. As we scooted up next to him, he cautioned us to silence and whispered, "We've got visitors."

"Oh, great," I heard Poet mutter.

"What do you see?" asked Slade.

"Nothing. I just hear stuff like footfalls in the forest, like twigs snapping under somebody's step. A while ago, I thought I heard a cough but couldn't be sure."

"Let me take a look," said Slade.

The former Marine squirmed over to a point where he could peer outside, his body still in the darkness. We sat silent, listening. Slade leaned out to get a look at the forest in the downstream direction. The second his head went from shadow to light, a rifle shot rang out, the bullet striking the limestone rock inches from his face.

Scooting back with the rest of us, Slade murmured, "Bastards!"

We let a few seconds pass while the adrenaline rush leveled out. Slade's face was bleeding from a half-dozen pinprick-size cuts from rock splinters. I handed him my handkerchief, but he waved it off.

"It's nothing," he said.

For Slade, it was nothing. During his days as a frontline Marine in Vietnam, he had been shot, stabbed, and struck with grenade and artillery shell fragments so many times there were hardly two square inches on his body that weren't scar tissue. He had been stitched up so often it looked as though someone held him under a sewing machine. A few rock splinters didn't compare.

"We can't return fire because we can't see them," offered Slade. "They could be anywhere in those bushes."

"Now what?" asked Poet.

"I'm thinking," said Slade.

"Well, think about this, amigo," said Stanley. "We're trapped in a cave by a bunch of deranged, inbred mountain moonshiners who want to kill us. What the hell are our options?"

We had been in trouble before, but always had some kind of an escape plan, no matter how dangerous or bizarre, at our disposal. This time, we were stumped.

Another shot rang out, rock fragments exploded from the wall, and the shell ricocheted into the passageway, striking the heel of Poet's boot.

"Those guys are starting to piss me off," said Slade. Stanley motioned us farther back into the cave.

Breathless, we returned to the large, smelly chamber and took positions on either side of the passageway in case our attackers decided to fire through the opening. I leaned against the rock, taking deep breaths and trying to cope with a feeling of hopelessness. Poet was right. We were trapped, had no apparent way out, and there were men outside who gave little indication they wanted to discuss matters.

I closed my eyes in the belief it would help me think better. It didn't work, so I opened them and stared at the still several feet in front of me, illuminated by the light from my headlamp. I stared at the curious structure with the two-and-a-half-foot-tall copper vat before noticing the fire pit beneath it. It was ringed with rock and filled with the ashes of hundreds of fires. Nearby was a low stack of cordwood, oak and hickory, the fuel used to heat the corn mash. What a chore it must be pushing firewood all the way through that low tunnel to this point, I thought.

Fire! That was it! To corrupt an old saw: where there's fire, there's smoke. Smoke rises and it has to go somewhere. I looked up at the ceiling and saw it was smoke-blackened but saw no evidence of accumulation inside the chamber. If the smoke had no outlet and collected inside, the whiskey makers couldn't remain long enough to manufacture a batch of moonshine. There had to be an exit for the smoke, and it was just possible it might be large enough to afford escape for us.

I rose and walked over to the still, looking up at the smoke-stained ceiling of the chamber, criss-crossing it with my headlamp and flashlight beams. I walked in ever-widening circles around the still, searching.

"What are you doing?" asked Stanley.

Everyone looked at me. Then Slade jumped up and joined me, aiming his light beams at the ceiling too.

"He's looking for the way out," he said, smiling one of his rare smiles.

Slade explained what we were looking for, and seconds later the beams from four headlamps and four flashlights roamed the ceiling. Then, after minutes of searching, Poet called out from thirty feet away on the far side of the still.

"I found it!"

We rushed over and stared up at a rectangular opening in the roof of the cave above us. We could see the traces of several generations of smoke stain on the ceiling up to this point. Beyond the opening, the rock was clean, proof that the smoke escaped through this aperture. The ceiling was nine to ten feet high at this point. We needed something to climb on to get to the exit hole.

Littering the floor of the cavern were several rectangular chunks of limestone that had fallen from the ceiling over the years. Most of them were twelve to eighteen inches thick, corresponding to the limestone deposition from which they broke loose.

Addressing Poet, Slade, and Stanley, I said, "Move some of those blocks under the opening to make a circle about three feet in diameter, the width of that big copper vat. Stack them two-high."

While they scooted and flopped the rocks under the hole, I walked to the still and, picking up a piece of cordwood, began knocking loose all of the copper tubing, the lid covering the vat, and everything else I could see. This done, I pushed the vat off its supports and rolled it toward the circle.

"Well, that will certainly piss them off," Poet said.

I flipped the vat bottom-side up onto the rocks, made some adjustments to the rock circle to ensure good support, then climbed on top of it. It held my weight easily and when I stood to full height, my head and upper torso was inside the hole. Searching around with my light, I found lots of hand- and footholds.

"That's what I like about limestone," I said. "If the rock is not weathered badly, it makes for excellent climbing. I'm going up to see what it looks like. I'll report back as quick as I can."

I climbed up into the opening. The hole went straight up for about six feet, and then leveled out horizontally for a dozen yards. The surface of the rock was flat and I slid along easily. It smelled smoky. Then I found another vertical passageway, this one more difficult than the first but offering no special challenge. I climbed into it and felt fresh air blowing down on me.

The passageway continued in this pattern of vertical, then horizontal, then vertical, and so on, conforming to the eroded-out joints and bedding planes of the highly soluble rock. I was climbing and crawling in a generally westward direction. At times it was narrow and constricting, but mostly it was wide enough to facilitate movement. After thirty minutes of making my way through the snaking cave without pausing to rest, I pushed myself along a horizontal passageway when I saw daylight about ten yards ahead and smelled humid air. I poked my head out of an opening choked with brush and could see the stream below. I recognized enough of the terrain to deduce where the jeep was parked. I enlarged the opening by breaking away some of the brush.

Exhausted, I was now faced with climbing back down to deliver the good news. Whether in a cave or on a mountainside, climbing down is always more difficult than climbing up, and I was not looking forward to it. I slipped and fell twice while negotiating the vertical passages. My pants were ripped, and my elbows and hands were cut and bleeding.

When I finally arrived back at the chamber, Slade said, "Those men are right outside the entrance. I fired a couple of shots in their direction to make them nervous, but they are itching to get at us."

Stanley climbed atop the vat and into the passageway as I made room for him. He was followed by Poet, then Slade. It was slow going this time for I was weak and exhausted. It took more than an hour to reach the end of the passageway and crawl out of the hole and onto the side of the bluff.

"It's only about an hour until sundown," said Stanley between breaths as we rested from the strenuous climb outside the hole.

"There's no trail here," I said, "which leads me to suspect those villagers are unaware of this secondary entrance. If we use the protruding limestone ledges as steps, we ought to able to climb down the side of the bluff with little or no difficulty."

Poet, Slade, and Stanley inspected the side of the bluff.

"I suggest we do it while there is still some daylight," I said.

With nods of assent, we picked our silent way down the steep slope to the valley below.

We made it without incident, arriving at a point about fifty yards upstream from the first cave entrance. From the direction of the ground-level entrance to the cave, we heard voices but could not make out individual words. Apparently a group of men were gathered outside the opening, trying to decide what to do about us. As quietly as possible, we picked our way along the base of the bluff through the brush and briars, calculating the point opposite of where the jeep was parked. Water moccasins slithered away at our approach. We crossed the stream, avoided more moccasins on the opposite bank, picked our way through more undergrowth, and came out about twenty feet in front of the vehicle.

Stanley started the jeep as Poet climbed in beside him. Slade and I piled in the back. At the sound of the engine cranking, we heard a shout from the direction of the cave entrance.

"Take off," I said. "They will be after us in seconds."

Slipping the four-wheel drive into gear, Stanley began inching our slow way up the rutted, twisting, and inclined road. Slade jacked a shell into his Winchester. I reached for mine.

"Those mountain men can run up this road a lot faster than this jeep can make its way over the holes and ruts," Slade said.

We had gone about sixty yards when I spotted the first pursuer: the naked man, carrying a rifle. Barefooted, he ran up the road toward us at a pretty good clip, looking straight at me. When I raised my rifle and pointed it at him, he did not slow his pace.

"Shoot the son of a bitch!" yelled Slade.

I pulled the trigger. The bullet struck the ground in front and to the left of him. Not a bad shot, given the bouncing, lurching movement of the jeep. Without breaking speed, the pursuer dashed into the adjacent brush. Where we had picked and fought our way through the dense, tangled undergrowth, he seemed to slip through it like a snake. I fired two more shots into the brush where I had last seen him in an attempt to convince him to lay low.

We saw no one else during the agonizingly slow climb out of the valley, and thirty minutes later we left the poor road and came onto one slightly better. Breathing sighs of relief, we bounced along at a comfortable twenty miles per hour.

Hours later, we pulled into a parking lot outside a restaurant and spent some time pulling ticks off each other. My hands, elbows, and knees had scabbed over but were still tender. Finished, we entered the building, seated ourselves around a table, and ordered dinner.

"I need some meat," I said. "I think I'll have a large steak, a baked potato with real butter and sour cream, a big bowl of steamed vegetables, coffee, and blackberry cobbler with French vanilla ice cream."

"Double that," said Stanley.

"Triple," said Poet.

Slade held up four fingers. The waitress finished scribbling on her order pad and strolled away.

I could have eaten a second helping of everything but re-frained. What I did need was a stiff drink and a long, hot bath. All the climbing around in that zigzag hole pushed the limits of my endurance and played havoc with my already bad knees. Because my elbows were skinned so badly, I couldn't rest them on the table. Pain pulsed through my body.

"This little trip reminds me of most of our expeditions," said Poet. "Lots of action, nothing goes as planned, we get shot at, and we come back empty-handed."

Stanley chuckled. Slade said, "Not funny."

Poet said, "I'm thinking those strange people found the James cache a long time ago."

"They don't strike me as a community that would care one way or another about gold," said Stanley. "Even if they knew what it was, what in the hell would they spend it on? Certainly not clothes."

"You've got a point," I said. "So we're back to square one. Are we thinking the gold coins from the James robbery are still stashed in that cave somewhere?"

We looked at each other and shrugged.

"Do we want to go back and search the cave?" I posed.

"I vote no," said Poet.

"I vote yes," said Slade.

"I can go either way," said Stanley.

"Goddamnit," said Slade, looking at me. "Another tie, and you get to break it again. And we already know how you're gonna vote."

"I vote we go back," I said without hesitating. "I say we hike in next time. Make it winter when there are no ticks and snakes. Stay away from the road if possible. And we enter the cave through the passageway we came out."

"It's got possibilities," said Stanley.

"Damn right," said Slade.

"Shit," said Poet.

"I vote we try to clean up Poet's language," said Stanley.

With that, we left the restaurant, checked into a motel, and had the best night's sleep we'd had in weeks.

POSTSCRIPT

Two months following the incident at January Cave, I visited an anthropologist I knew at the University of Texas at Austin. I told him about the adventure we'd had in the remote section of the Oklahoma Ozarks. In the course of the telling, I described the strange, self-sufficient people living in the secluded hollow, the absence of electricity, plumbing, roads, and other aspects of civilization most of us take for granted. I also described the physical characteristics of the denizens.

The anthropologist told me this population represented, based on my descriptions, a case of multiple generations of inbreeding, and other researchers had identified the characteristics I described as common to the practice. He said he was aware of similar small inbred populations in Arkansas and West Virginia.

Several weeks later while doing some research, I found out that January was a common surname in that part of the Oklahoma Ozarks, and that many Januarys possessed Cherokee blood.

Poet, Slade, Stanley, and I discussed the possibility of returning to January Cave to continue our search for the gold coins allegedly buried by Jesse James. During the time we were in the cave, we had seen no sign of any treasure, but then, we were pretty busy trying to figure out a way to remain alive and escape people who were trying to kill us, and had no time to explore the two passageways leading from the main chamber.

Playing the devil's advocate, Poet expressed the notion that it seemed ridiculous that Jesse James, or anyone else, would push or pull the heavy loot through forty yards of crawl space, carry it across the chamber, then transport it even further into one of the other passageways.

Stanley agreed, stating that it did seem like a lot of effort beyond what was necessary, but he also pointed out that it was Jesse James's own handwriting that described the caching of the gold in that very cave. Though he may have robbed trains and banks and killed people, Jesse, as Stanley pointed out, was never known to lie, and was regarded by the folk in southwestern Missouri as being more trustworthy than most of the preachers of his day.

"And probably to this day," contributed Slade.

"I believe the treasure is still there," said Stanley. "And I'm betting it's in one of those passageways we didn't get to look into."

The treasure awaits.

11

QUICKSAND!

To live without risk is not really living.

—Max McCoy

Growing up in the desert and mountain environs of West Texas, a region lucky to receive more than eight inches of rainfall per year, I was rarely bothered by thoughts of quicksand.

Quicksand, as I understood it from watching old Jungle Jim and Tarzan movies, was a liquidy mass of super-saturated sand that entrapped unwary explorers, causing them to sink to horrible unknown depths if they were unlucky enough to be unable to reach an overhanging vine or summon help.

I always considered most of the stories about men, animals, and even automobiles disappearing into quicksand as mostly fiction and folklore, a product of storytellers and screenwriters. While involved in an expedition to locate the famous Lost Bill Kelly Mine near the Texas-Mexico border one spring, however, I learned the hard way that quicksand was real and every bit as treacherous and deadly as the movies and lore depicted it.

The Lost Bill Kelly Mine, a mysterious and elusive deposit of rich gold, was named for a Black Seminole who had migrated to West Texas around 1900 from his adopted homeland near Muzquiz in the state of Coahuila, Mexico. Hitching rides and traveling on foot throughout the Big Bend country, Kelly eventually found work on the Reagan Brothers Ranch located near the Rio Grande. Kelly, an adept horseman, impressed the Reagans with his ability to break and train mustangs.

One day while searching for stray horses, Kelly crossed the Rio Grande into Mexico and rode into the Ladrones Mountains. At the top of a ridge, he discovered the remains of an ancient gold mine that had apparently been abandoned centuries earlier. On closer inspection, Kelly found a large amount of wire gold that eventually assayed out at a surprising $80,000 per ton, a formidable amount of money at that time. When the Reagans learned from Kelly of the potential fortune in gold that might lie in the mountains across the river, they attempted to get the hired hand to lead them to the lode. Kelly, who did not trust the brothers, feared they intended to kill him after being shown the gold. One evening he stole a horse and disappeared.

Since that time, a great deal of evidence has surfaced to substantiate the existence of such a mine. The exact location, however, remained a mystery for more than a century. Perceiving the Lost Bill Kelly Mine as an attainable challenge located in a portion of the Mexican state of Coahuila we were familiar and fascinated with, I, along with Poet, Slade, and Stanley, began making plans to search for it. The supposed location lay in one of our favorite environments, and the opportunity to spend time in the Big Bend country and Ladrones Mountains of Mexico was not to be wasted.

During the spring of 1985, the four of us arrived at a Brewster County, Texas, ranch near Maravillas Canyon with the intention of leasing some horses to carry our gear and us across the Rio Grande into Mexico. Arrangements to do so had been made earlier and a price agreed upon, but when we got there we learned from the proprietress of the ranch that the transaction had to be cancelled. Two of her horses had been victims of mountain lion attacks, a third lost or stolen, and three more borrowed by neighboring ranchers to use in a gathering of stray cattle. This left her with only two mounts. They were old and not trail-worthy, more pets than riding stock. Furthermore, she told us, it was risky taking the animals into Mexico. In recent weeks, she explained, riders had been attacked and mounts stolen. We regarded the unavailability of riding stock inconvenient and a disappointment, but ultimately a minor setback. We had conducted numerous expeditions in the past on foot and this would just be another one.

The following morning, we arrived at the point on the Rio Grande where we would cross into Mexico and thence into the Ladrones Mountains. We were pleased to see the river was relatively low, the spring rains still a couple of weeks away. We figured the depth at mid-stream to be about hip-high.

Since it was lunchtime, we prepared a quick meal in the shade of some willows, listened to the ambient desert sounds, prepared our packs, and checked supplies and firearms. We stretched out for a short nap before making the crossing. About a half-hour later, Stanley recalled some petroglyphs under a rock overhang about a mile away that he had encountered the previous summer. Since we were in no hurry, he, Poet, and Slade decided to go investigate the rock art. Since I had seen them before and was enjoying my nap in the desert air, I opted to remain riverside and keep an eye on the equipment.

Swarms of annoying flies buzzing about my head made sleep impossible. With the Rio Grande just a few feet away, I stripped off my clothes to bathe in the cool, muddy water.

Standing at the river's edge, I noticed at my feet an abundance of fine, moist sand, soft and squishy, which gave way easily under my weight. As I walked along the slightly sloping shore at the margin of the water, I left footprints nearly two inches deep in the wet sand, and each time I pulled up my trailing foot it made a loud sucking sound. If I stood in one place for more than a couple of minutes without moving, I sank up to my ankles in the curious stuff.

Naked, I entered the river until the water was up to my thighs. The bottom consisted of the same fine sand and there was an absence of stones and gravels. Had I been more experienced in such things, I would have suspected something. Twelve feet from the shore, I splashed cool liquid onto my face and torso and gave myself a primitive bath. While I slowly sank up to my ankles in the soft bottom of the river, I gave it little thought, believing I would descend no further. When I decided to return to the shore, I realized that I had sunk almost up to my knees and couldn't move.

Suspecting this would only be a small and slightly irritating predicament, I tried to pull one leg from the sand, an action which only served to force the opposite leg an inch or two deeper. With birds chirping in the nearby willow trees, the sun shining bright in the clear sky, and a cool breeze flowing down the canyon, I felt completely out of place stuck in the saturated sands of the river. Trying to remain motionless, I decided to wait until my companions returned from the hike and get them to pull me out. Minutes passed, however, and I found myself a couple of inches deeper into the bottom.

My situation worsened as I sank into the quicksand I always believed to be an element of tall tales and Hollywood movies. Within the hour I could be dead, and there was no one nearby to help me extricate myself from the trap.

The water level crept up to my navel. There existed a growing chance that I might drown and that there was nothing I could do. Oddly, I was overcome with a sensation of calm, a kind of resignation to the strange events transpiring.

So this is what it is like to die, I thought. An interesting feeling, this sinking into quicksand: a combination of helplessness, hopelessness, resignation, and a curious anticipation. The calm feeling lasted for several more minutes before my survival instinct kicked in, an urge to fight for life in whatever time I had remaining. Since struggling in the sands only served to pull me deeper,

I screamed, calling to my companions for help, hoping they were close enough to hear.

After minutes of hollering, I realized the sound was absorbed by the water and carried away by the stiff breeze blowing down the canyon and away from my friends. Most likely I could not be heard more than forty or fifty yards away. Then I remembered that whistling carries farther in the desert air than shouting. Mexicans know this and often communicate with one another over long distances with a series of whistles. I whistled until my mouth and throat were dry and sore and the water was up to my shoulders.

More time passed and my three companions rounded the corner of a huge boulder in the distance and paused to examine the half-dozen *tinajas* in the rock at their feet. Stanley looked up, saw me in the river, and waved. For all he knew, I was taking a swim. I whistled again and waved my arms frantically. Stanley said something to the others, and the three of them raced toward the river.

Poet, Slade, and Stanley formed a human chain connected by wristlock grips. Slade, the strongest and heaviest, positioned himself on the shore and leaned far back. Then came Stanley and Poet, who reached out to me with his free hand. The water lapped chest-high. I grabbed his right wrist with my right hand, and as a unit, the three of them heaved toward the shore. It accomplished nothing more than pulling my head under water. I came up sputtering and spitting gritty river water. Poet told me to take a deep breath, and then they tried again. Another dunking, and I was no closer to being pulled from the sucking sands. If anything, I was an inch deeper. Poet, Slade, and Stanley acted unconcerned about my situation and even made several bad jokes.

The three pulled and tugged, all the while complaining that saving lives was hard work and it might be simpler to let me go under. Once, Poet became dangerously mired in the sands himself and almost shared my predicament. Efforts were redoubled, and

I finally felt myself being pulled from the bottom, a millimeter at a time.

Several more minutes passed, and when it seemed like we had run out of strength and endurance, I was dragged free and hauled to shore. The four of us lay on the sand, exhausted.

"You owe us," Poet said to me.

"I wonder if it was all worth the effort," said Slade, breathing heavily.

Within minutes, we were all asleep on the ground.

The next morning we explored upriver several hundred yards until we found a suitable ford, a hard bottom with stones and gravels that could support our weight. We crossed safely and entered the Ladrones Mountains, where we spent the next seven days.

During our stay in the small range, I had ample time to reflect on my experience with the quicksand and marveled, not for the first time, how easy it is to die in the wilderness, how one small, careless act can cost a life. It occurred to me with sharp dramatic impact how the landscape is often an antagonist, an obstacle, even a foe. During the years my partners and I have undertaken dangerous expeditions into remote areas of the United States and foreign countries, we have encountered bandits, drug smugglers, raiders, and competitors. We have been ambushed, followed, chased, shot at, and occasionally hit. We have encountered bears, wolves, mountain lions, feral hogs, rattlesnakes, poisonous insects, and deadly arachnids. But some of our most dangerous moments had to do with responding to the threats offered by the physical environment—the land and the weather. We have fallen from cliff faces, been trapped in mines and caves, been exposed to deadly gases, nearly drowned in flash floods, fled from rock slides, and more. And now, when least expected, we experienced quicksand.

Nature, while a beautiful and loving mother, can also become an unforgiving mistress. I promised to treat her with more respect.

What about the Lost Bill Kelly Mine? It exists in the Ladrones Mountains. The Spanish word *ladron* means thief, robber, bandit, all appropriate names for this range that has for generations been home to border bandits, drug smugglers, and bootleggers. We spent most of our time trying to remain out of sight of the local residents and were not always successful. We returned with only a pocketful of gold, but enough to ignite a desire to return.

Given our encounters with men who were hostile to our presence in the range, we consider ourselves lucky that we got back alive. There will be a better time to attempt a return to the Lost Bill Kelly Mine.

12

SPANISH SILVER IN A KENTUCKY SINKHOLE

It is by going down into the abyss that we recover the treasures of life.

—Joseph Campbell

One of the best known and most widely related lost treasure tales is that associated with the Jonathan Swift Silver Mines located somewhere near the point where the borders of Kentucky, Tennessee, and Virginia meet in the rugged Appalachian Mountains. Generations old, this lost mine has been searched for by thousands for more than two-and-a-half centuries, each of the seekers hopeful they will be the one to relocate them.

Less well known is that, according to documentation, long before Swift began taking silver from these mines around 1760, they were worked intensively by the Spanish, perhaps as much as a century or more earlier. The Spaniards, after processing the silver ore into ingots and accumulating forty to fifty burro loads of it, would transport it westward through the Appalachian Mountains and across the Midwestern prairies to the Mississippi River. At some location believed to be just north of Memphis, Tennessee, the ingots were transferred onto rafts and floated downriver to where they were loaded onto ships that would carry the wealth across the Atlantic Ocean to Spain. Research also reveals that more than one such pack train of silver never reached its intended destination.

A journal found in a monastery archive in Spain relates the story of one such ill-fated pack train that never arrived at the banks of the Mississippi River. In response to an Indian attack, forty burro loads of silver ingots were hidden at a location in western Kentucky and never retrieved. Because this document was stored in an obscure location and generally unavailable to anyone but serious and credentialed researchers, few knew that it existed. Furthermore, the location of the hidden treasure was not what it seemed, and that fact created a major search and recovery problem.

The old journal had been stored in a musty basement in a Catholic monastery in a location outside of Seville, Spain. It was penned by Padre Antonio Segovia, an unimportant monk whose duty was to serve his superiors. The journal was never placed on display and, as far as could be determined, had never been read until my partner and historian Dr. Trenton Stanley accidentally discovered it in an aged, cracked wooden trunk. Painstakingly, Stanley translated the document over a period of five months, aided by no less than three Castilian language scholars, two in Spain and one at the University of Chicago.

When he was finished, this is what Stanley shared with Poet, Slade, and me:

Sometime during the seventeenth century, a slow-moving pack train consisting of forty or more burros carrying thousands of eighteen-inch-long ingots of almost pure silver was making its way from the rich mines across what is now the western part of the state of Kentucky and heading toward the Mississippi River. The ingots were tightly crammed into heavy leather packs specifically made for that purpose. These, in turn, were lashed to handmade wooden packsaddles that were cinched securely to the burros. The pack train was accompanied by twelve Spaniards, including soldiers, at least two monks, and the herders.

Having enjoyed a rather uneventful journey up to that time, the complacent escort was surprised by a sudden attack from a band of approximately fifty indigenes, on foot, at a location in present-day Logan County, Kentucky. Initially, the commander of the pack train attempted to outrun the attackers, but the heavily laden burros were unsuited for speed. Irritable from an already long day of hauling the heavy burdens, they proved difficult to handle. After entering what was described as a *prado grande*, a large meadow, the Spaniards guided the burros into a circle and prepared to defend themselves against the marauding Indians.

One by one, according to the journal, the Spaniards fell to Indian arrows and lances launched unceasingly into their midst. Captain Juan de la Garza, the officer given responsibility for delivering the silver to the Gulf of Mexico, decided he and the few remaining survivors should attempt an escape. Before doing so, however, he determined to hide the silver so that he, fortified with a larger armed force, could return and retrieve it at a later time.

As de la Garza searched for a suitable place to conceal the ingots, one of his soldiers called his attention to a nearby "well." Believing the silver would be safe until such time as he could mount an expedition to return for it, de la Garza and three of his charges pulled the pack saddles from the animals and tossed them, along with the leather packs and their contents, into the opening.

Minutes later, de la Garza and several others were killed. Only two men managed to escape, a monk and a soldier of low rank. One week later, the soldier died as a result of complications from an arrow wound. The monk managed to reach the Mississippi River and, months later, made his way to New Orleans, where he was taken in by the residents of a small trapping community and restored to health. Three years passed before he was able to make his way back to Spain. It was the journal of that monk, Padre Antonio Segovia, that was discovered by Stanley in the Spanish monastery. After reading and studying the translated document, we determined there was an attractive possibility that the location of this cache could be found and the silver recovered. We decided to try.

Stanley and I spent countless hours with copies of the journal's pages and topographic maps, studying the cryptic notes and trying to interpret and understand descriptions of the terrain across which the pack train traveled. Though the directions and landmarks were vague, they invariably pointed toward a location in western Kentucky. Finally, the four of us traveled to Logan County to see if we could match some of the environment there with the descriptions provided by Padre Segovia. It took three trips over a period of eight months, but we finally found what we were looking for.

Western Kentucky had changed dramatically since the Spanish traveled it over three centuries ago, and retracing a three-hundred-year-old route was difficult. The construction of roads, towns, and subdivisions, along with a variety of agricultural activities, had modified the environment considerably, and descriptions of presettlement landscapes were difficult to reconstruct. We checked into a motel in Munfordville, a town of about 1,500 people just off Interstate 65 in Hart County about forty miles northeast of Bowling Green. From there we would conduct a more thorough search.

From Munfordville, the county seat, we traveled southwest, entering a region underlain by eons-old limestone replete with caves and sinkholes. Indeed, not too many miles away was Mammoth Cave National Park, a popular tourist attraction. After spending three days in the area exploring via paved and dirt back roads, on foot, and using topographic maps, we decided to concentrate on a location that we believed best matched where the attack on the pack train took place as described in the monk's journal. Here we encountered our next obstacle, one that we expected, and one that is the constant bane of professional treasure hunters. It was on privately owned land.

During a visit to the county courthouse, we identified the owner of the land and called to arrange an appointment. We found him to be a pleasant man, interested in local history and fascinated by the story Stanley found in the monk's journal. He gave us permission to continue our search on his property. During the discussion, we agreed on a mutually satisfactory division of any of the silver we might find.

When we asked him about the possible existence of an old well on or near the location we targeted, he said he was unaware of one. In fact, he told us, in his memory no one had ever lived out there and thus there was no reason for a well. This was puzzling.

The following morning after a cafe breakfast of country smoked ham, eggs, homemade biscuits, and hot coffee, Stanley steered his Land Rover toward the large field we previously identified. On arriving, we found it contained endless rows of corn, each young stalk about three feet high. Taking note of the surrounding environment of ridges and valleys, nearly everything matched up with the descriptions from the journal. It was only a matter of time, we calculated, before we discovered the old well.

For two full days we searched the seventeen-acre cornfield, walking up and down the rows. It was hot and humid during that time of the year, but even more so in the cornfield where the air was still and the plants and ground absorbed and reradiated the heat. During dinner at the end of the second day of searching, we talked about giving up, believing that we had somehow misinterpreted the directions, that the quest was fruitless. I reminded everyone that our successes in the past were never associated with giving up, but rather enduring, persisting until every avenue of opportunity was exhausted. There were only a few acres of the field left to cover, so everyone agreed to give it one more day.

The following morning we had been in the cornfield for less than an hour when Poet whistled up our attention. Looking, we spotted him several yards out of the field and standing on an exposed layer of limestone near the northwestern corner of the property. As we approached, we could see he was staring intently at something on the ground. Smiling, he pointed to a circular hole about three feet in diameter. Here, he proclaimed, was the "well" we had been searching for.

As we approached, we could see that it was not a well but the small opening to a sinkhole. We also realized at that moment that three hundred years ago, Captain de la Garza and the monk, probably having no idea what a sinkhole was, simply mistook it for a well. The opening was only three feet across. We dropped to our knees and peered into the depths but could see nothing beyond the few feet illumined by the day's light. We dropped several fist-sized rocks into the hole but never heard them strike bottom.

Convinced this was Padre Segovia's well, we spent the remainder of the day making plans to descend into the hole, hoping we had brought along enough rope. Just before dinner, we abandoned the site and drove over to the farmer's house, explained what we had found, and told him what we planned to do should he grant us permission. I told him it was necessary to drive the Land Rover from the road to the sinkhole, and in doing so we couldn't avoid running over portions of two to three rows of corn. We promised to compensate him for any loss from his crop. He granted permission freely and with enthusiasm. That night, none of us could sleep as we lay awake anticipating the descent into the sinkhole, wondering what we might find, and hoping it would be the Spanish silver.

The next morning found us at the hole a few minutes past dawn. Stanley had parked the vehicle ten feet from the opening. Poet, Slade, and I unloaded ropes, carbide headlamps, flashlights, canteens, and various climbing apparatus. As we worked, we breakfasted on cinnamon rolls, fruit, and coffee purchased at a convenience store.

Lying flat on the limestone outcrop, we leaned into the opening and probed the interior of the dark chamber with powerful flashlights but could see very little. As the hole deepened, it also widened appreciably such that the sides could not be seen beyond the first forty or fifty feet. The chamber was shaped like a giant bell, with us perched at the top of it. Below, there was nothing but darkness—and silence.

It was Slade's turn to remain above ground. Our policy was to always leave one man at the surface in case of an emergency. I won the honor of descending into the hole first, Poet second, and Stanley third.

Stanley tied the end of the yellow rope to the front bumper of the Land Rover. This done, I uncoiled it into the hole and placed a leather pad under it where it made contact with the rock to help avoid fraying against the sharp limestone. Reaching as far into the hole as possible, I swung the rope back and forth, ascertaining it was hanging free and not touching bottom. Our ropes came in 150-foot lengths. I would have to carry an extra rope down with me as I rappelled into the hole and connect it to this one. It was inconceivable to me, but entirely possible, that this sinkhole could be deeper than 300 feet. If it were, we would require at least three lengths of rope. Carrying one extra rope into the sinkhole was enough trouble. The prospect of carrying two was not appealing. Two coils of rope were heavy, and descending on one rope while carrying the extra weight restricted maneuverability and control. If I needed a third rope, one would have to be lowered.

After fitting the yellow rope through a series of locking and nonlocking carabiners attached to my seat rigging, I placed a coil of blue rope over my shoulder and dropped through the opening. After six feet, my boots were no longer touching the sides and I swung freely. Slowly, I lowered myself via a controlled releasing of the rope through the carabiners. As I descended, I began rotating on the rope, common to a free-drop. I looked up to see the silhouettes of my three partners peering down at me from the opening, but they were indistinguishable. Each of us was an accomplished mountain climber and caver with hundreds of hours of experience, but none was prepared for what was to follow.

The eerie silence of the sinkhole was broken only by the occasional chirp of a disturbed bat. From somewhere far below, I could hear the faint sound of dripping water. At fifty feet down, the walls of the chamber had widened such that they could not be seen, the light of my carbide headlamp falling far short. My breathing echoed in the darkening chamber.

Deeper and deeper into the abyss I lowered myself, dangling freely while rotating on the twisting rope. Every thirty seconds or so I blew a short burst on a whistle that hung from a lanyard around my neck, our signal that the descent was going as planned. At about 120 feet, I could still see nothing below and resigned myself to having to connect the second rope. Moments later, I saw the end of my rope dangling several feet below.

Now came the dangerous part. I stabilized my position by taking several wraps of the remaining yellow rope around my thigh and placed the end between my teeth. I freed a coil from the blue rope over my shoulder and, with deliberate care and control, tied the two ends together. I examined the knot several times to make certain I had eliminated any chance of slippage or parting. Satisfied, I pulled the spare rope from my shoulder and uncoiled it into the darkness below. I thought I heard the end of the rope slap against moist ground somewhere below but could not be certain.

Taking a deep breath, I steeled myself for the tricky maneuver to follow. It was necessary to unhook myself from the lead rope and reattach to the second one below the knot. If mishandled, I would send myself to serious injury or death. I removed a homemade prusik loop from my belt and attached it to the yellow rope at head level, pulled the knot tight, then clipped the other end, looped, into a carabiner attached to my harness. For good measure, I added a second prusik loop.

I lowered myself a few inches, allowing the two loops to support my entire weight. When I was certain they would hold, I unhooked the carabiners holding me to the yellow rope and reattached them to the blue rope below the knot. Using my feet to manipulate a crude stirrup with the remaining length of yellow rope, I lifted myself such that I could loosen the prusik knots. This done, I unclipped them from the carabiners and replaced them in my belt. Slowly, I lowered myself a few inches at a time, keeping an eye on the knot. The new rope squeaked as the knot tightened under my weight, but it held.

I blew a blast on the whistle and lowered myself another twenty feet. At this point, I could make out the sound of a small, trickling stream below. Another fifty feet down, my headlamp illuminated a portion of the sinkhole floor below me. Scattered about were hundreds of rocks ranging in size from medicine balls to tractor-trailers, remnants of long-ago collapses of the ceiling. Among this jumble flowed a clear, shallow, narrow stream, almost directly below the opening. Though the stream was only two feet wide, the channel through which it flowed ranged from four to twenty feet wide in places, suggesting much greater flow in times past.

I swung myself on the rope several times and, when I had cleared the stream, landed atop a low boulder. After two sharp blasts on the whistle to indicate I was safely on solid ground, I began unhitching from the blue rope. As I stashed my gear near the edge of the rock, I saw the rope twitching, indicating Poet had hooked on and was descending. I decided to await the arrival of him and Stanley by exploring the bottom of the hole.

Large rocks, illuminated by my light, cluttered the floor of the chamber, and over the millennia, the stream had carved a path through and around the maze of boulders. I stepped into the silty bed to test its consistency. Applying only the slightest bit of weight to my right leg, I sank several inches into the soft, yielding muck. Alarmed, I scrambled back to solid ground and let my heart rate return to normal. Previous experiences with quicksand had rendered me cautious.

By the time Poet joined me, I had explored several hundred square feet of the bottom of the sinkhole. Several minutes later Stanley completed his descent, and the three of us systematically examined the area in order to get a feel for the layout and to try to find some evidence of the silver we were convinced had been thrown into this huge geological pit.

About forty-five minutes later, Poet whistled for us to join him. When we arrived back at a point almost directly beneath the opening, he pointed to what appeared to be a piece of wood sticking out of the moist silt about two feet from the streambed. He reached down and pulled it out. At first there was resistance, but a moment later it was yanked free of the mud accompanied by a sucking sound. Avoiding the soft bottom, he knelt close to the water of the stream and cleaned the muck off the object. Immediately, we could see it had once been a part of a packsaddle.

Encouraged, we diligently searched the immediate area with greater care. After an hour, we were rewarded with the discovery of two more pieces of hand-hewn packsaddle. Another hour passed, and Stanley, with a cry of delight, held up yet another piece of wood.

"I have no doubt now," exclaimed Stanley, "that we have found Captain de la Garza's well!"

We spent a few more hours exploring around the sinkhole searching for the silver before coming to the conclusion that when the heavy ingots of silver hit the streambed, it was only a matter of a few seconds before they sank out of sight.

We discovered the sinkhole was part of an extensive cavern system. I followed the channel upstream and found it entered the chamber at a point near the northeast, flowing through a well-developed passageway. About fifty yards into this part of the cave, however, the route was blocked by fallen rock, under and through which wound the little stream.

I retraced my steps and walked along the watercourse out of the sinkhole chamber and into another section of the cave that trended southwest. At about one hundred yards into this portion, my progress was halted again by a massive roof collapse. On the way back to the main part of the sinkhole, I spotted a trickle of water dripping from the small opening of a narrow feeder cave.

The entrance to this little tunnel was about waist high, and the water flowing out of it formed a miniature waterfall at my feet. I touched a finger to the water, brought it to my lips, and tasted it. It had flowed in from the surface. I don't know how to explain how I knew, but through years of experience, I've learned the subtle difference in the taste of water that comes from the surface from that which flows underground.

I probed the narrow cave with my flashlight and saw that it angled upward at about thirty to thirty-five degrees. Along the bottom were tiny gravels that had been washed in from above. Poking my head into the opening, I sensed a barely discernible flow of air. This, I knew, was a passageway to the surface.

This was good news for two reasons. First, in the event of a disaster such as a broken rope, this passageway might serve as an alternative route to the surface. Second, I suspected it had never been investigated, and nothing tempts an explorer more than someplace that has never been visited before.

I returned to the middle of the chamber where I found the others waiting for me. While I was gone, Stanley had suffered a severely sprained ankle while clambering across a slippery boulder. The ankle had swollen dramatically and he was having difficulty walking. As Poet and I rigged a climbing harness for him that would not necessitate the use of his ankle, I described the small passageway in the cave I was convinced led to the top. I told them that while the two of them prusiked back up the rope, I was going to try to make my way back via this route, that I was curious to see if it went all the way to the top and if it remained large enough to accommodate a man.

As I spoke, Poet, using one of the pieces of wood we found, probed into the soft bottom of the stream channel. I noted the ease with which it entered. Poet thrust it in clear up to his elbow before pulling it out. He then picked up a stone about the size of a fist and plopped it into the muck. Within seconds, it sank into the ooze. After waiting five minutes, Poet probed the place where the rock went in with the piece of packsaddle wood but could not find it.

Straightening up and pointing down at the streambed, Poet said, "That's where the silver is. The weight, the specific gravity of metal such as silver, gold, or lead is such that it would be carried down through soft, unconsolidated sediments like this quicksand until reaching bedrock. How far down bedrock might be is any-body's guess."

Using the palm of his hand, Poet shoveled several hands full of silt from the channel onto the bank. Though he removed a lot of the soft mud, the shallow openings he created filled within seconds.

"If we hope to retrieve the silver ingots from this quicksand," he said, "we would have to have some kind of equipment that could probe the depths of this deposit, grasp the bars, and then pull them up."

Peering down at the stream, he continued, "We could make something, I suppose, but the first order of business would be to ascertain how deep this mother is."

We all agreed. There was nothing more we could do at that point, and it was time to get back to the surface. A check of my watch showed it was just past noon. After hitching Stanley to the blue rope and watching him inch his way upward, I chatted a few more minutes with Poet. He would wait until Stanley reached the top and blow his whistle, then begin his own ascent. I refilled and relit my carbide lamp, reattached it to my helmet, waited another ten minutes, then made my way back to the small cave I wanted to explore.

Would it lead to the surface? I was certain it would. However, if it narrowed somewhere along the way preventing me from pro-ceeding, I would be confronted with backing down the narrow passageway, a difficult and tiring exercise. If I became trapped and did not return to the surface in a reasonable time, Poet would have to rappel back down and go in search of me. When I reached the tiny opening, no more than two-and-a-half feet across, I took a deep breath, hoped for the best, and crawled in.

It was rough going from the start. I could only inch my way along and upward by pulling myself forward with my elbows, my headlamp illuminating the way. Ten minutes later my neck, unused to holding my head at that angle, was tired and sore. Here and there where the passageway narrowed, progress was made more difficult as I scraped joints and limbs and helmeted head against the rough sides and bottom.

After several yards of crawling, the small, sharp gravels that had been washed in from the surface began cutting into the thin flesh of my elbows and forearms. By the time I had gone fifty feet, my shirtsleeves were bloody.

The passageway twisted and turned as it continued surface-ward. Sometimes the bends were so sharp I could barely negotiate them. I was now hoping fervently that this cave opened to the surface, for returning along the same route backward would be next to impossible. I began to feel trapped.

That kind of locomotion, propelling oneself along and up-ward using solely shoulder, arm, and pectoral muscles, was dif-ficult and exhausting. I was beginning to cramp severely and had to pause often to rest and massage my arm and chest muscles. I had no idea how much farther I needed to travel before reaching the end of the tunnel. I tended not to worry about such things, but I was growing concerned that I might run out of strength and energy before I conquered the passageway.

After another thirty yards of snaking along, I was forced to stop once again to rest my muscles, now screaming with pain. With difficulty, I rolled over onto my back, closed my eyes, and tried to nap for a few minutes. Exhausted, within seconds I was dozing.

I awoke when something brushed my cheek. Eyes still closed, I swiped a gloved hand across my face. A few seconds later came a similar sensation, then another. Then I felt something crawling down my neck and into my shirt. I pulled off a glove, slapped at it, and held the object up close to my eyes. It consisted of a tiny smashed body and an array of thin limbs each about three inches long.

"What the hell . . . " I mumbled, then looked up at the roof of the passageway, mere inches from my face.

In the light of my headlamp, I could see the ceiling undulating in a series of waves, the movement making a barely audible hissing sound. At first I was convinced I was hallucinating as a result of fatigue. I blinked several times and tried to focus. Then I saw them.

The ceiling was carpeted with thousands of albino granddaddy longlegs cave spiders, the population growing disturbed at my presence and, no doubt, from the heat and glare of the headlamp. I quickly shut off the light and lay very still. But the damage had been done.

One by one, spiders dropped from the low ceiling onto my face and body. In a matter of seconds I was covered, could feel the tips of their legs moving lightly across my face, my neck, felt them crawling into my shirt, across my hands.

I had to move on. By now my aching muscles were stiff, and with great difficulty and pain, I turned over onto my stomach, relit the carbide headlamp, and began inching forward once again. As I moved, the spiders fell onto my neck and back, onto the floor of the tunnel in front of me, growing thicker and thicker. Soon the gravelly floor in front of me swarmed with the milling, spindle-legged arachnids.

Though my chest and shoulder muscles screamed with pain and resisted, I forced myself forward, redoubling my efforts to get through the cave. Panting for breath and in severe pain, I was finally clear of the spiders. I turned over again and, despite the recent adrenaline rush, fell immediately asleep.

Cramping muscles woke me an hour later. Gritting my teeth, I rolled back over and continued on. I moved slowly, only a few inches at a time before pausing often to rest. Though I was in agony, I forced myself into a momentum that resulted in a slow but steady movement upward and through the passageway. One-two-three, forward. One-two-three, forward. I advanced six to eight excruciating inches at a time.

Hours passed. I ran out of carbide and my lamp died. I also used up a set of batteries in my flashlight and replaced them with spares, but now these had grown weak and dim. If the flashlight faded before I reached the surface, I would be forced to grope along the narrow tunnel, feeling my way in total darkness.

After negotiating a slight curve in the tunnel, I thought I saw light ahead, though very dim and distant. I switched off the flashlight, let my eyes adjust to the darkness, and then peered ahead again, hopeful. Yes! There it was, faint and far away, but it was light, the glow of an evening transitioning into night. I forgot about my pain and crawled forward, inch by inch.

Another hour passed before I approached the opening. I could feel the fresh air from the outside passing into the cave, blowing across my face. It smelled like humidity and corn stalks, but I never smelled anything so sweet. No more than six feet from the surface, I was on the verge of shedding tears of gratitude when I came face to face with another obstacle.

My reverie of relief was shattered by a cacophony of deep, continuous buzzing only three feet in front of me, the sound growing louder, more intense. I directed the beam from my failing flashlight toward the source of the noise and saw a cluster of four large eastern diamondback rattlesnakes, the longest about five feet.

I tried to call out. I had no idea how far this opening was from where the Land Rover was parked, but I was hopeful that my companions were close enough to hear me, to come to my rescue by removing the serpents blocking my path and pulling me out into the cool night air. I tried, but so dry was my throat that no sound came forth. I remembered my whistle and groped for it.

It was gone, lost somewhere back in the passageway. I could only mumble a single word.

"Shit."

I was at a loss. If I were on the outside, it would have been a simple matter of removing the serpents with my snake stick. Here I was—unarmed, defenseless, helpless—with four poisonous cave residents between freedom and me. I lowered my head onto my forearms to ease the pain in my neck, considered my options, and decided I had none.

In a fit of annoyance, I picked up a piece of gravel from the floor in front of me and flipped it at the nearest snake, then another, and another, until after being pelted enough, the snake broke out of its coil and slithered a few inches to my left and disappeared into what must have been a crevice in the limestone. Shining the light of my headlamp at the place where the snake vanished, I could see several narrow fissures, common to the highly jointed, thinly bedded limestone rock.

I picked up more gravel and selected another crotalian target. After a dozen direct hits, this one, too, slithered away into a crack. Two down, two to go.

After another half-hour to forty-five minutes, I managed to disturb the remaining rattlers enough to send them seeking the shelter of the numerous crevices that laced the floor of the cave entrances. I pulled myself forward a few inches, then a couple more.

My neck hurt so badly I could no longer raise my head and merely slid my face along the floor of the passageway. I tried to look into the crevices to see how deep they were, but from my position could see nothing. A few more inches. I put pain and fatigue out of my mind as I considered that I was less than five feet from safety. A few more inches. A few more.

Close to one of the crevices, I focused my light and peered in. A thick-bodied rattler was wedged into it only two inches below the level of the floor. Worse yet, I would have to crawl over it on my way out of the cave. I moved forward another few inches and found another crevice. There, stretched out along a length of the crack was another rattler, its backbone even with the rock surface. I would have to negotiate across this one too, and in the course of my passing would likely touch the serpent. I found another snuggled into a crevice within an inch or two of the surface. I never did locate the fourth rattlesnake. By then I didn't care; I just knew I could not remain where I was a minute longer.

I was certain of one thing. Stretched out, they were not likely to strike. Except in rare circumstances, a rattlesnake only strikes from a coiled position. I was less certain, but hopeful, of one more thing. I was praying that the slight coolness of the late evening would render the cold-blooded snakes a bit torpid, less energetic than they would be during the warmer portion of a sunlit day.

Slowly, I crept forward another two to three inches, then again. Soon, I was directly atop one of the crevices, looking down at a snake. I held my breath, daring not to move. I needed to crawl across approximately four more feet of cavern floor before I was safely out.

I girded myself; allowed a long, slow, deep breath; then, ignoring the extreme pain in my arms, shoulders, neck, and chest, low-crawled out of the cave with a sudden burst of speed generated by an adrenaline-fueled concern about getting bitten.

Once out, I rolled several feet down a shallow bank to the bottom of a dry creek bed, gasping for breath, and feeling nothing more than relief along with intense pain in every muscle and bone of my body. I lay unmoving, staring up at the starlit sky. I was curious to know what time it was, but I could not muster the strength to raise my arm to look at my watch. I fell asleep and dreamed of dark, tight spaces and rattlesnakes.

Slade found me about an hour past dawn and shook me awake. I was lying in the same position I assumed when I had fallen asleep. He was holding a live rattlesnake behind the head and told me it had been coiled up next to my body. He flung it into the brush.

Though I tried to rise, I could not make my muscles obey. Finally, Slade grabbed me under the arms and helped me to stand. Poet and Stanley appeared and together, the three of them helped me back to the Land Rover.

Two hours later we were in the emergency ward of a clinic in Elizabethtown, Kentucky, where I was treated for severe muscle tears in my chest and shoulders, bone-deep cuts on my elbows, and cuts along my forearms and thighs where I scraped along the sharp gravel. My pants and shirt had been torn to shreds and were little more than rags. The toes of my boots had been worn completely through.

The injuries were a small price to pay for the fact that we had found the lost silver of the de la Garza expedition. Now all we had to do was retrieve it.

Returning to the silver turned out to be more difficult than we calculated. Before leaving Kentucky, we met with the farmer on whose land the sinkhole was found. We explained what we had discovered, how we expected to recover the ingots, and that we planned to come back to Kentucky in approximately two to three months to undertake the salvage operation. We shook hands all around, and he said he looked forward to seeing us again.

During the first week of September, we called the farmer to make arrangements to renew our attempt at recovering the silver. A woman answered the phone, identified herself as his daughter, and informed us her father had passed away, having succumbed to a heart attack two weeks earlier. I commiserated with her on her loss and explained that he and I had an ongoing business arrangement and that I would call her back in a few days to explain.

One week later, I placed a second call to the daughter, reminded her of who I was and the arrangement we made with her father. I left out details as to the exact location of the sinkhole and what was in it. She said she was not interested and informed me that the land, as well as other properties owned by her father, had been put up for sale, the income from which was to be divided among her and her siblings. As politely as possible, I pursued my desire to return to the cornfield, but she hung up on me. We could do little but wait to see what happened to the property.

I placed a weekly call to the real estate agent handling the sale of the property to ascertain its status. Sometime in November, the property was sold. When I asked who the buyer was, the agent declined to provide the information.

During Christmas break, Stanley and I traveled back to the county courthouse and looked up the name of the buyer. It was a development company based in Florida. Several names were attached to the paperwork. I selected one to call and after more than a dozen attempts finally made contact. When I inquired about the land, I was told the company had no definite plans for its use at the moment. I asked about the possibility of gaining access to the land but was refused and informed that it was under the care of a property maintenance company from Bowling Green. It was posted, I was told, a lock was placed on the gate, and admittance was forbidden.

The property has changed hands twice since then, with each new owner forbidding access. If we were able to gain access, the first order of business would be to determine the depth of the quicksand to bedrock. If within twenty feet, claims Stanley, the silver is retrievable. He and Poet designed a piece of equipment they believe can penetrate the sand and retrieve any loose ingots, a kind of sophisticated grappling scoop. It is lightweight, fits together like a fishing pole, disassembles into a package only five feet long, and can be easily lowered or carried into the sinkhole.

No doubt the silver still lies at the bottom of the quicksand. A rough estimate of the value of the ingots tossed into the so-called well by de la Garza and his men is around two million dollars. We believe we have everything we need to recover the silver except access to the site as well as a formal agreement with the current owners pertinent to the salvage project. We continued negotiations over several months but had no success.

Without legal permission to retrieve the treasure, Poet, Slade, Stanley, and I had discussed a renegade action—sneaking onto the property in the dark of night and entering the sinkhole. Ultimately, we determined the likelihood of being observed was too great and the logistics of entry and removal too complex and far too labor intensive.

The silver is still there, and nobody knows the location but us.

13

SPANISH GOLD
GUARDED BY RATTLESNAKES

When sitting around a campfire during a Mexican expedition with Jameson, I often wondered if my health and life insurance were paid up.

—James Poet

For several generations, many beguiling and curious tales of lost mines and hidden treasure have emanated from the foothills region of the Sierra Madres along the Chihuahua-Sonora border. One, a story that has achieved the status of legend in the area, involves a very rich and productive gold mine located near a long-abandoned Spanish mission in a remote section of the mountain range. A rich outcrop of gold, as near as can be determined from the translations of centuries-old documents, was discovered by Spanish explorers during the late seventeenth century, probably around 1680. Local Yaqui Indians, as well as members of other tribes, were enslaved to work in the mines. A short time later, a mission was constructed and staffed with a dozen monks, a cook, some workers, and a handful of soldiers. The job of the monks was to convert the local Indians to Christianity, by force if necessary. Though the Catholic Church is loath to admit it, those potential converts who resisted the yoke of the papacy or refused to work in the mine were put to the sword. That was the job of the soldiers.

The mine was operated under the watchful eyes of the padres for decades. During that time it yielded tons of rich gold that was separated from the rock in an *arrastre*, refined, and cast into ingots. The Indian workers, chained together at the neck, dug the ore using crude tools, gradually extending the shaft deep into the side of the mountain. They began work around dawn following a poor meal of watered-down gruel and were not allowed to quit until sundown. Herded back into meager and squalid living quarters, they were given stale bread for dinner. It has been written that many of them died in their chains while working.

Every two or three months, the padres had the gold ingots loaded onto burros and transported to church headquarters near Mexico City. The route from the mission wove sinuously through the mountain range before reaching the plains. The trip took several weeks.

One morning during the summer of 1722, a shipment of six hundred gold bars was being readied for the long journey to the church treasury. As one of the holy men barked orders, the slaves carried the accumulated ingots to the nearby burros and packed them into the stout leather bags fastened to the wooden frames.

A half-dozen burros had been loaded when a band of fifty Yaquis, armed with bows, arrows, lances, knives, and clubs appeared in a line across a low ridge opposite the mine.

The monks, mistakenly believing the Indians were after the gold, ordered the ingots to be carried deep into the adjacent mine shaft where the treasure could be more easily defended. Lashing viciously at the slaves with long leather whips, they cursed and kicked the workers into action. Dozens of yards inside the mine, the ingots were stacked against one wall two to three feet high and extended for several yards. This done, the monks exited the mine shaft in time to observe the Indians swarming down the hillside and into the small settlement, clearly intent on killing all of the churchmen and freeing the prisoners, their countrymen.

During the ensuing melee, the soldiers and monks put up a futile effort at defending themselves. Most were slaughtered within minutes, their bodies mutilated, their ears cut from their heads. Three were taken prisoner.

While the attention of the angry Yaquis was on the robed clerics, two of the mission residents hid behind a jumble of boulders near the base of the cliff. One was a mere boy who was studying for the priesthood, the other a soldier. They watched in horror as the Indians hacked the dead Spaniards to pieces and pulled the remaining residents of the settlement from their dwellings and killed them.

As the frightened pair watched from hiding, the three captured monks were ordered to unchain the Indians. This done, they, in turn, were shackled with the same cruel irons they had placed on their slaves and pushed roughly toward the church.

After cursing and whipping the monks for the treatment of their fellow tribesmen, the Yaquis subjected them to unspeakable tortures while keeping them alive for several days. Initially, they were tied to fence posts and whipped until their flesh hung in strips on their backs, not unlike the way the papists treated the mineworkers. They were then spread-eagled on the ground and small fires built atop their stomachs, burning slowly into their intestines. Following this, the monks were hung by their wrists from low branches, their tongues cut out, and burning sticks plunged into their eyes. The genitals were excised and stuffed into their mouths. This done, the Yaquis, gathering up any usable items from the mission settlement, vanished into the mountains from whence they came, leaving the suffering monks to the mercies of the wolves and vultures. It took them two more days to die.

When the last of the Indians disappeared over a nearby ridge, the boy and the soldier crept from their hiding place. Having not eaten during the entire time they were witness to the horrible tortures, they were weak, dazed, and uncertain of what to do. They remained in the area of the mission for a time, scavenging a few food items missed by the Indians. They moved about fearfully lest the Yaquis return.

Deciding that trying to find their way to Mexico City was better than lingering at the death site, the two stole down the trail that led from the settlement and wound across ridges and through canyons. Months later, they arrived at the monastery. After being allowed only two days to rest and recover, they were brought before Catholic authorities to relate their experiences. A church scribe wrote down their story.

Because of the growing Indian menace throughout the Sierra Madres, coupled with the shortage of manpower and soldiers, the church leaders decided it would not be in their best interests to organize an expedition to the remote mission to retrieve the gold. The transcripts of the survivors' testimony were filed away in the archives and remained untouched until they were found over two centuries later.

As time passed, the mission in this remote section of the Sierra Madres gradually succumbed to the elements, collapsing into a rectangle of low walls. Dwellings and rock fences likewise retreated under the onslaught of rain, wind, and time. A small rockslide, likely generated by one of the rare earthquakes known to strike that region, covered the entrance to the mine shaft. For well over two hundred years, this area was not visited save for an occasional prospector or trapper.

The gold ingots, stacked deep inside the old mine and representing a fortune of several million dollars, lay untouched.

Dr. Trenton Stanley taught history at a midwestern university until he grew weary of the childish politics, jealousy, and sniping common to such institutions. Unlike his obsessive-compulsive and anal-retentive colleagues, Stanley believed a grand adventure-filled and satisfying life existed beyond the stifling walls of academe.

A successful collector and dealer in antiquities and a professional treasure hunter, Stanley continued to pursue his love of history as well as satisfy his craving for experience and escapade. For years, he journeyed to Mexico City and environs where he studied Indian statuary and old Spanish documents associated with early efforts at colonization and mining.

During one of his visits in 1985, Stanley discovered a number of Catholic documents stored in an old metal case in the basement of a museum on the outskirts of the capital city. Among the materials were sheets of parchment containing an account of the escape of the soldier and boy from the small Spanish mission in the Sierra Madres following the Indian attack. The account detailed the enslavement of the local Indians to work in the gold mine and the massacre of the Spaniards in the tiny settlement. Of particular interest to Stanley was a portion of the account that detailed the caching of more than six hundred gold ingots in the mine shaft. Accompanying the sheets of parchment was a crudely sketched map purporting to show the location of the mission, some landmarks, and the mine.

A few weeks following his return from Mexico City, Stanley contacted me at my home. At the time I was living several hundred miles from El Paso and, like Stanley, teaching at a small university. I invited him to travel to my home, but he was unable to leave his business at the time. With the profits realized from several successful treasure-hunting ventures, Stanley had been able to set himself up in a lucrative El Paso–based antiquities operation—buying, selling, and consulting. In turn, he asked me to meet him in a quiet tavern near the campus of the University of Texas at El Paso.

As the cool interior of the tavern provided relief from the 100-degree temperature outside, Stanley related aspects of his recent visit to Mexico and showed me his handwritten translation of the old mission document as well as a copy of the map. The account fascinated me, and I found myself wondering what thoughts occupied the soldier and the young boy as they watched from hiding as the Yaquis tortured and slaughtered the occupants of the small village. I likewise marveled at the fortitude it must have taken to make the long journey on foot from that isolated part of the Sierra Madres to Mexico City far to the southeast. They were forced to find water and food along the way, and that they survived at all is remarkable.

According to the map, the mission and mine were located more than two hundred miles south of the border between Mexico and New Mexico as the crow flies. It lay right inside the state of Sonora in a rugged, mostly trailless portion of the Sierra Madres. In years past I had hunted deer, dove, quail, and lost treasure in that region and had camped in the adjacent foothills, and I was somewhat familiar with the environment. Here, one could find mule deer, black bear, a Mexican species of grizzly bear, wolves, mountain lion, jaguar, and ocelot. Day-to-day hazards included rattlesnakes, scorpions, tarantulas, and poisonous centipedes, along with dangerous narrow mountainside trails and occasional rockslides.

Unknown to many outside of the region was the fact that several tribes of Indians, notably Yaqui, Tarahumara, and even Apache, still lived there in a more or less wild and primitive state. Most of them resented intrusion. Occasional visitors into this remote area of deep, twisting, forested canyons, high peaks and ridges, and steep cliffs were seldom seen again. During the 1960s, an anthropological team entered the area and learned the Tarahumara still practiced cannibalism.

Following two days of discussion relative to the potential of finding and retrieving the Spanish gold as well as some important mission artifacts, Stanley and I began making arrangements to travel to the Sierra Madres. Our first act was to enlist the participation of fellow expeditionists James Poet and Mungo Slade.

Several weeks later when we were all able to allocate the time, we invested nearly a week into preparation, acquisition of supplies, and processing the necessary paperwork. This done, Stanley, Poet, Slade, and I crossed the Mexican border from

El Paso, Texas, to Ciudad Juarez, got our paperwork filled out and visas stamped, and took a leisurely drive south on Mexican Highway 45 to Ciudad Chihuahua, a city of approximately three hundred thousand people at the time and the capital of the state of Chihuahua.

On arriving we checked into the Hotel Victoria, where we dined on broiled Boquillas black bass, grilled asparagus and zucchini, and cool, crisp Herradura margaritas made with hand-squeezed lime juice. For the next two days we invested more study into the documents and maps, rechecked gear, arranged our backpacks, and cleaned firearms. From time to time we took a break and cooled off in the large hotel swimming pool, walked around town, and chatted with locals. During the evenings we enjoyed exquisite meals of bass or aged steaks in the hotel dining room, amazingly inexpensive and worthy of any five-star restaurant in the world.

On the morning of the third day, we departed Ciudad Chihuahua and drove west through the towns of Cuautemoc and La Junta. The roads were two-lane all the way and poorly maintained but passable. Here and there, portions of the road had been washed away as a result of flash flooding. Now and then we were forced to negotiate perilous stream crossings. Stanley's International Harvester truck performed nobly.

We spent a night in La Junta. Green chile and chicken *enchiladas*, *frijoles*, music, tequila, Dos Equis, Tecate, and friendly citizens were available in the hotel restaurant. In the morning, we took the main road out of the town for several miles, then turned onto a poor dirt road, one never graded or maintained. Because of its condition, travel was slow.

While we occasionally saw livestock grazing on the native grasses of unfenced fields, we traveled for miles without seeing another human being. It was only on entering the small community of Tomochic after six hours of difficult and slow going that we encountered people, and the reception was unlike what we had previously experienced. The townsfolk of Tomochic remained distant, suspicious, almost elusive, and provided no answers to questions regarding certain landmarks farther up in the nearby mountains.

Getting nowhere, we decided to drive on in the general direction of our destination until we ran out of road, which occurred about seven miles out of town. Here, we set up camp and made preparations to pack into the mountains the following morning.

The foothills in that part of the Sierra Madres were rugged, sparsely populated, and fringed with a mix of pine trees and desert vegetation. It was a cool morning as we shouldered our backpacks, left the campsite, and began the long climb to the location high in the range previously determined by Stanley. We made our way along narrow game trails that crisscrossed the slopes, gradually gaining in altitude. As we ascended into the higher reaches, the desert scrub and cacti gave way to a thicker cloak of pines, accompanied by stands of spruce. Small streams trickled down the slopes, evidence of springs higher up.

We followed a copy of the map carried by Stanley. After hours of hiking, we noted that we were on a dim trail that had seen rare use over the past decades. It was wide enough to have accommodated carts at one time, and we suspected it might have been the same trail used by the monks when they led the pack train from the mine to church headquarters in Mexico City.

After arriving at dead ends twice, we found the remnants of a trail that led higher and higher into the range. Two days later, we arrived at an area of level ground several acres in extent, and at the far end we spotted what appeared to be the remains of a structure. On closer inspection, it turned out to be the crumbling, weatherworn rock and adobe walls of what must have been the mission church. It was much smaller than we expected, but congregations were apt to be tiny in an area this remote. Not far away we saw the crumbled foundations of other rock structures, smaller ones we assumed were habitations. Nearby, a tiny spring trickled from the wall of a cliff, filling a pool five feet wide with clear, cool water.

After exploring the region for hours, we discovered several artifacts that were clearly Spanish in origin, including tools, nails, and hinges, along with bridle and saddle fittings. These convinced us that we were in the right place. That night, after removing the rattlesnakes that had taken refuge there, we set up camp within what remained of the old mission walls and made preparations to search for the mine on the morrow.

During the night, the vipers found their way back into the enclosure. We awoke within inches of six or seven of them. They were lethargic in the cool morning air on the mountain, and it was a simple matter of picking them up and flinging them back over the wall.

We finished a breakfast of *tortillas de maize*, goat cheese, and coffee just as the sun topped the eastern ridge. With the new light, we consulted the map once again, and then set out to look for the mine. We followed a trail overgrown with vegetation from the mission into a nearby wide, shallow canyon. At a location near a steep rock wall less than a quarter of a mile from the mission was a dense tangle of low-growing vegetation. We decided to take a closer look to see if there might be another spring located there. No spring, but Stanley retrieved a rusted mattock head lying on the ground and, after a close inspection, declared that it had been forged by Spanish craftsmen centuries earlier and likely used during the excavation of the mine shaft.

As we searched the bushes for more artifacts, Poet called our attention to the canyon wall opposite from where we stood. There in the early morning shadows was the vague hint of a mine entrance partially covered by a small landslide. We hurried to the feature and could see that beneath the layer of rock and debris was the opening to a man-made tunnel.

Unfortunately, several tons of material from the slide prevented immediate entrance. While Poet, Slade, and I pondered the task of removing the obstructing earth and rock, Stanley unfolded the map and consulted it.

"By God, this is it!" he declared. "This is the spot marked on the map. If the record is correct, there should be six hundred gold ingots stacked against one wall several dozen yards down in the shaft."

For the next two days, the four of us pulled, pushed, rolled, and levered rocks and boulders from the mine entrance, stopping only to rest, sip water, and have a quick meal of dried fruit and jerky. By the time the sun was descending behind the west ridge on the second day, we had opened barely enough space to allow entrance into the mine. It was all we needed. Exhausted, we retreated to the campsite, removed the rattlers that had once again returned to reclaim their space, and fell asleep, each of us anxious to enter the shaft in the morning. Poet, Slade, and Stanley said they dreamed about the gold in the mine shaft. For some reason, I dreamed of rattlesnakes.

Following a quick meal of grits and strong black coffee, we gathered up flashlights and helmet-mounted carbide lamps and headed for the mine entrance. Once there, we decided it was Poet's turn to remain outside. Though he was unhappy about not getting to explore the shaft, he agreed to the role and found a comfortable perch on which to rest. One by one, the rest of us wormed our way into the tunnel through the opening created by moving aside the boulders and rocks.

It was also agreed that it was my turn to be the first to proceed. Contrary to what a lot of people might believe, this is neither honor nor privilege. The first man into an abandoned mine shaft or cave must deal with the creatures that normally live in such environments, mostly snakes, spiders, and in that part of Mexico a particularly poisonous centipede. In addition to the unwanted wildlife, one must occasionally cope with deep pits, loose cave-in-prone rock, toxic gas, and sagging timbers.

I encountered a number of spiders (all harmless), no snakes, and one centipede. The centipede was thick-bodied and nine inches long, the exoskeleton shining neon green in my flashlight beam. I dispatched it with a rock, continued on, and called for Stanley and Slade to follow.

The walls and ceiling of the shaft evidenced crude excavation technique, and support timbers, aged and rotted, were spaced dangerously far apart. The ceiling was low, forcing us to stoop as we walked. In some places we had to crawl on our hands and knees. I marveled at the terrors that must have faced the enslaved Yaquis who worked in the cramped, torch-lit space every day. The closeness of the walls in the dank passageway would have been deathly claustrophobic.

Thirty yards into the tunnel, Stanley called for a halt. Slade and I turned and watched him extract what looked like a crowbar from under a rock. He passed it around and explained it was a digging tool. As we examined the piece of metal, Stanley interrupted us again with a loud exclamation and held up a gold ingot.

Under the glare of our headlamps, he brushed the dust from the bar. It was twelve inches long, three-and-a-half inches wide, and an inch-and-a-half thick. Crudely stamped upon the top was a Christian cross topped with a caret, similar to ingots associated with the Spanish and the church we had found in the past. Stanley ventured the opinion that one of the Indians or monks dropped the ingot in their haste to hide the treasure from the attacking Yaquis. Twenty more feet of crawling into the shaft yielded three more gold bars.

As we examined the ingots, a buzzing sound ebbed and flowed, echoing through the tunnel. We sat motionless, silent, probing the dark recesses with our lights to try to ascertain the source of the sound. Within seconds, the noise intensified, reverberating up and down the shaft. Baffled by the sound and unable to comprehend the source, we stared at one another, unspoken questions of what we should do filling our countenances.

After listening closely, we discerned the sound was coming from about twenty yards deeper in the tunnel. Without speaking, I inched forward, Stanley and Slade following, making our way deeper into the shaft, lights exploring the darkness ahead. I finally determined the origin of the sound but kept the information to myself.

We came to a portion of the shaft that had widened out to twelve feet and stared at what appeared in the beams of our flashlights. Lying before us on the floor of the tunnel was a thick, writhing mass of rattlesnakes. The very floor moved as a series of waves with their movement as they slithered, coiled, and entwined with one another. The buzzing from the hundreds of rattles filled the chamber.

We ventured to within five feet of the dense cluster of reptiles that extended deep into the shaft, far beyond the penetration of our lights. Because further exploration was impossible, we observed the rattlesnakes a long while before making the laborious return to the exit.

I had long heard about such gatherings of rattlesnakes but always regarded them as wild and exaggerated tales. Years earlier while on a treasure-hunting expedition in a remote location in the Mexican state of Coahuila, we encountered such a cluster, but nothing like the one we just witnessed. There was a tangy reptilian scent in the air, one common to rattlesnakes. This scent recognition would serve me well in the future.

Once outside, we seated ourselves next to Poet on a jumble of rocks we had moved the previous day and inhaled the fresh air of the canyon while we debated our next move. Poet listened intently at our description of the mass of snakes we encountered in the shaft.

"How about smoking or burning them out?" he suggested.

"Think that will get rid of them?" asked Stanley.

"I've cleaned out nests of rattlers in small caves by stuffing brush on top of them, dowsing with kerosene, and lighting it," said Slade. "They don't like it much and come out pretty fast."

"I've seen it work, too," I offered.

"We've packed a small amount of fuel for the camp stoves," said Poet. "We could make a pile of brush and limbs in the chamber, douse it and light it up, and see if it works."

"Anybody got a better idea?" asked Stanley.

We didn't, so we agreed to give it a try.

For the next few hours we cut dry and green wood and brush, dragged it into the shaft, and tossed it on top of the writhing snakes, with the buzzing of the rattles providing a background din such that we had to shout to be heard. After splashing the pyre with our cooking fuel, Slade flipped a match onto it and we watched it grow into flames. Dense smoked filled the chamber immediately, forcing us to scurry back out of the shaft.

We waited for three hours before reentering the tunnel. As we crawled along, smoke hung thickly along the ceiling and in corners, making breathing difficult. On arriving at the site of the fire, we found a pile of ashes and a few smoldering limbs, but most of the snakes were gone. Stanley pointed to several large clefts in the wall of the shaft around which a number of the rattlers were coiled. The openings, he suggested, led to the outside and allowed ingress and egress for the reptiles.

Though the population of rattlesnakes in the tunnel was significantly reduced, many still lurked in the darkness. We passed over the still hot ash and dozens of charred snakes, making our way through the wide chamber and toward the narrowing shaft beyond. We proceeded cautiously, for we heard the buzzing of rattlers ahead of and alongside us. In this part of the mine, the ceiling was high enough that we could walk upright. Where possible, we eased past the snakes without incident. At other times we were forced to move some out of the way.

As we made our way deeper into the shaft, we found two more gold ingots. The realization washed over us that we were only a few yards from the huge cache of gold. Though no one spoke a word, the excitement of being moments away from the hoard was contagious.

As we inched forward, step by calculated step because of the snakes, our flashlight beams showed that the tunnel made a sharp turn to the right. After negotiating the angle, we were confronted by another cave-in. One by one, we crawled over the obstruction to the other side, barely squeezing through the small passage between rubble and ceiling. Stanley went first, and we heard him emit a cry of surprise as he was making his way down the opposite side out of our sight. I squirmed though the opening as fast as possible only to be calmed by his voice, stating he had been struck by a small rattlesnake. The serpent's fangs struck his boot but bounced off without penetrating. A tiny squirt of venom remained where the reptile had hit the leather.

Once we completed the crawl through the narrow passageway, we proceeded forward a few steps only to be confronted with another obstacle. An even larger collapse sealed off the tunnel ahead of us. On first inspection, it appeared as though tons of rock had caved in, and it was evident that the debris extended several yards through the shaft. According to the specifics carried by Stanley, the cache of Spanish gold ingots lay just beyond this huge cave-in.

We spent nearly an hour assessing the extent of the collapse. The best way to remove the heavy boulders, we considered, was with jackhammers, which would be difficult to transport up the mountain to the site and then this far into the mine. Using the appropriate tools, it would be possible for the four of us to break up the rock and move it to different areas in the shaft, but it would take weeks. Slade suggested using small charges of dynamite to break up the large rocks, but we decided it was out of the question due to the weak and crumbly nature of the granite through which the shaft had been cut. There was a good possibility that a blast would generate another cave-in.

We had no choice but to turn back. As we made our laborious return through the tunnel, we encountered more rattlesnakes. When we reached the wide chamber, Stanley pointed out snakes slithering back in through the clefts, resuming their massing. Had we waited much longer, the chamber would have been once again filled with the serpents, making passage impossible. As it was, we had to negotiate our way through the passageway delicately, passing within inches of some of the vipers. I led the way out of the chamber and into the narrow shaft on the opposite side, followed by Poet and Slade with Stanley bringing up the rear. When I looked back to make certain everyone had made the passage safely, I spotted Stanley slapping wildly at his left calf. Eight inches away, a large rattlesnake was recoiling, having just struck.

"I'm hit," yelled Stanley, panic rising in his voice. It was his first snakebite.

We needed to get away from the chamber and the growing number of snakes, but we needed to keep Stanley calm, quiet, and still. An elevated heart rate would carry the poison through the bloodstream too fast to be assimilated and could result in death.

After ripping open his pants leg, I squeezed the area around the two puncture marks. A tiny bit of milky venom bubbled out, but some of it surely had gotten into the bloodstream. I cut a strip from the bottom of my shirt and fashioned a tourniquet that I applied on the upper thigh just tight enough to slow the blood flow. I pulled Stanley several feet into the shaft and stationed Slade between us and the chamber to keep the rattlers at bay. As I used water from my canteen to wash the bite, I knew Stanley was in for a rough time.

Speaking in slow, deliberate tones, I addressed Stanley. "I'm going to drag you out of the tunnel. I want you to try to relax and not move. Let me do all the work."

I could tell by the look on Stanley's face that he wondered whether he would live or die. "You'll be fine," I said. "Most people bitten by poisonous snakes don't die, but it's going to swell up and pain you for a while. Let's get your boot off before the limb swells."

"Get moving," called Slade. "The snakes are coming in fast."

I positioned myself in a seated position behind Stanley with my back toward the exit. I grabbed him under the armpits and pulled him a few inches. I sought and found a new position and repeated the maneuver. In this manner, I dragged my friend's

165 pounds out of the tunnel and into the fresh open air. Slade followed, dragging along three gold ingots we had found on this second trip.

We carried Stanley to the campsite and checked his bite. I cleaned it again with water from my canteen, applied alcohol and antiseptic I found in our tiny first-aid kit, and rewrapped it. This done, I collapsed back on the grass and fell into a deep sleep brought on by exhaustion.

I awoke sometime during the night. For a moment, I didn't know where I was and lay still for several minutes reconstructing the events of the previous day. A nearly full moon illuminated the camp inside the remains of the old mission walls. Stanley lay next to me, his leg propped up on a rock about twelve inches off the ground. He slept fitfully. His calf had swollen to nearly twice its normal size and he was moaning.

Slade appeared at my other side, silent as a ghost. He squatted down and offered me his canteen. I drank half of the water before handing it back. I asked about Stanley.

"He's had fits of vomiting," said Slade. "He tries to sleep but wakes up from the pain, crying out. I've been sitting up with him."

I started to rise, saying, "Get some rest. I'll look after him for a while."

Slade pressed me back down on my bedroll and said, "Go back to sleep. You've got to be worn out from dragging Stanley all the way out of that shaft. Besides, I can't sleep anyway."

In the morning I examined Stanley's leg. It was a ghastly color, a sickening mix of green and purple, but the swelling had gone down a bit. While it was still painful to the touch, he managed a smile and thanked me for pulling him out of the shaft. That night we dined on a concoction prepared by Slade that included some of the provisions we carried, some wild onions found nearby, and some kind of meat I couldn't identify. When I asked him what it was, he replied, "Rattlesnake." Stanley looked up in surprise, put his plate down, and didn't eat another bite.

Three days passed before Stanley could walk on the leg without pain. The swelling had gone down and while still discolored, it looked markedly better than before. Though it pained him, he was able to take a few steps at a time. He declared himself ready to travel and expressed a desire to leave the mountains and return home.

On the fourth day following our adventure in the mine, we set out for home. We divided the contents from Stanley's backpack and placed them into our own. I tied his empty pack to mine. We had retrieved a total of eight gold ingots from the mine. Slade, Poet, and I each carried only one since they weighed over twenty pounds apiece. We buried the remaining five in a location marked with a rock shaped like a frog.

It took four long days to return to the place where we had left the International Harvester. When Stanley grew fatigued, the rest of us took turns carrying him piggyback while someone doubled up on backpacks.

None of us returned to the site of the old mission and mine containing the six hundred gold ingots. For the rest of his life, Stanley suffered from slightly limited movement in his lower leg as a result of the snakebite and walked with a barely noticeable limp. He refused to be part of a return expedition.

Slade, Poet, and I discussed going back to the remote shaft but remain baffled about how to remove the obstacle of the cave-in. We visited with an engineer to discuss potential solutions and received some encouragement, but in the meantime other searches, other expeditions seized our interest and attention.

The gold, estimated by Stanley to be to be worth close to ten million dollars, still lies deep within the old Spanish shaft in the Sierra Madres. Only a handful of people know about it, and the site is difficult to reach. Then there is the problem of the incredible amount of work it would take to remove the tons of rock separating the fortune from the seeker.

But first, you have to get past the rattlesnakes.

14

THE LOST HAP
SWEENEY GOLD CACHE

To be lucky, you must know what you are doing

—Roald Amundson

The Guadalupe Mountains of West Texas is the setting for
more lost mines and buried treasures per square mile than any
other location on the planet. I have heard similar claims regarding
other areas, but decades of experience and research have proven
they take a backseat to this special mountain range. In the case of
the Guadalupes, the claim is backed up by documentation relative
to some impressive recoveries. In addition, there are many more
legitimate treasures in and near the range that continue to lure
treasure hunters, professional and amateur, to this day.

One particular treasure cache that has intrigued and tempted
me for years involves forty gold ingots, a fortune worth millions.
My own search for this cache began with coming into possession
of a map and some scribblings in a journal, both made in 1910
by a man named Hap Sweeney. As it turned out, there were two
principal obstacles associated with the process of recovering this
cache: first, the map, along with the writing in the journal, were
unintelligible and all but undecipherable; second, the purported

---

Because permission was neither asked for nor given, the names of a number of principals in the
following account have been changed.

gold cache lies within the boundaries of the Guadalupe Mountains National Park. Treasure hunting and recovery are illegal in national parks, punishable by huge fines and jail terms. I preferred to look upon these two as not so much obstacles but as challenges. I have employed old maps in the past with numerous failures but some successes. Furthermore, I have never let absurd restrictions such as are sometimes applied by the National Park Service deter me from what promised to be a great adventure.

The extreme difficulty in determining the location of the cache based on Sweeney's crude map was compounded by the fact that park service employees, suspicious of my activities, followed me into the range. Interpreting the map turned out to be a challenge. Eluding the park service tracker was much easier.

Hap Sweeney was a sometime cowhand who worked on ranches throughout West Texas and southeastern New Mexico. A Sweeney family descendant once told me Hap was born and raised in Kansas and came to Texas during the 1880s when he was sixteen years old. No one knows why, and much of Sweeney's life has gone unrecorded. When Sweeney was in his late thirties and early forties, however, it was known that he lived in a crude shack in the Guadalupe Mountains in a topographic feature called The Bowl, a concave setting ringed by low ridges. Game was plentiful here and freshwater springs were nearby.

Some claim Sweeney lived in this shack while tending cattle that grazed here, but there is precious little documentation of cattle ranching at this altitude during that time period. Others suggest he lived in the shack while he prospected for minerals in the surrounding rock. All of this was conjecture; there exists no evidence for either. The family descendant stated that Sweeney had a dark side and suggested that he lived in this remote area because he was hiding out as a result of an earlier brush with the law, though no one knew for certain from what. Again, conjecture, no evidence.

In 1913 Sweeney rode out of the Guadalupe Mountains and up to a ranch house located not far from the present-day location of Pine Springs. He was gaunt and pale and appeared near death's door. The rancher loaded Sweeney into a horse-drawn wagon and instructed a hired hand to drive him to Van Horn, the nearest settlement where a physician could be found, located some sixty miles to the south. During the trip, according to the hand, Sweeney was delirious and prattled on about "my gold" and "what would become of my gold" if something should happen to him.

After dropping Sweeney off at the small hospital, the hired hand returned to the ranch and told his employer about the recluse's ravings and the constant mention of his gold. No one knew what any of it meant, but the account was repeated often throughout the area. It was later learned that Sweeney passed away two days after being delivered to the hospital. Curiosity about Sweeney's gold percolated for a while, then ebbed. With the passage of a few years, the tale was all but forgotten. Twenty years later, however, an event occurred that revived the story of the gold cache.

During the 1930s, devastating fires raged from the foothills and slopes to the forested high country of the Guadalupe Mountains. The fires destroyed hundreds of acres of trees, brush, and meadow. The tiny clearing where Hap Sweeney's cabin was located was not spared. A few weeks following the fires, a deer hunter who visited this area every autumn chanced onto the old home site. Only a few charred poles were left of the corral where Hap penned his horse. All that remained of the cabin was the twisted metal roof, bedsprings, a pot-bellied stove, and scattered nails and hinges. As the hunter examined the burned-out landscape, he was distracted by the jerky movement of a squirrel exiting an oversize knothole in a nearby oak tree. He rode over to investigate.

The thick trunk of the tree had survived the conflagration, but most of the smaller limbs had been burned away. The knothole was shoulder height to a tall man and as large as a human head. Curious, the hunter dismounted and peered into the opening.

What he saw surprised him. Stuffed into a thirty-inch-deep cavity was a pair of leather saddlebags. Concerned about spiders and other unfavorable denizens of the small space, the hunter picked up a broken branch and poked it around in the hole in an attempt to generate the dispersal of any creatures that might be lurking within. Satisfied the hole was unoccupied, the hunter reached in, seized the saddlebags, and, with difficulty, withdrew them. He thought them uncommonly heavy.

The leather was old, brittle, and weathered from its residence in the tree trunk. Dropping to one knee, the hunter unbuckled the straps and emptied the contents. From one side, the inventory included a dog-eared Bible, a copy of *Silas Marner*, a pair of leather work gloves, and a journal. From the other bag the hunter withdrew a gold ingot.

The journal entries had been made in pencil, had faded over the years, and were difficult to read, but the hunter encountered a brief description of the discovery of a cache of gold ingots in a cave apparently located in this same mountain range. Tucked inside the journal was a folded piece of brown paper on which was sketched a crude map, also in pencil, also badly faded. The map consisted of images that appeared to be trails and landforms such as ridges and canyons. Here and there the hunter saw the word "spring" and "water." Near the left-center of the map one word caught his attention: "gold."

The hunter had years of experience packing into and hunting for deer, elk, bear, and mountain lion in the Guadalupe Mountains. He concluded that the map only vaguely represented portions of the range and that Sweeney's perception of direction and distance was terribly skewed.

Months later, the saddlebags and their contents were turned over by the hunter to a woman in Pecos, Texas, who was identified as Hap Sweeney's niece. Her name and address were found in the journal and the hunter delivered the items one afternoon as he was passing through that town. He explained he tried to follow the map to the location marked "gold" but could make no sense of it.

The niece, who was twenty-eight years old when she came into possession of Hap Sweeney's belongings, looked them over and placed them in the bottom drawer of a dresser, where they remained for the next forty-five years.

The tale of Hap Sweeney's lost gold cache had been passed down among area ranchers and residents since the time he died in the Van Horn hospital raving about the treasure. Over time, the story, as with most such stories, was embellished with each telling. I found it interesting, even compelling. I was inclined to consign it to that category of elusive and perhaps exaggerated lore associated with the range but for one thing: the existence of the gold ingot.

One day in March in 1981, I found myself in the mountain range visiting with another treasure hunter, a man named Eugene Anderson. The subject of Hap Sweeney's lost gold cache came up, and Anderson, as usual, claimed to know more about it than I did. Anderson liked to talk, mostly about himself, and he rambled on for several minutes about his theories of where the gold came from, how it happened to be hidden in the Guadalupe Mountains, and where it might have been cached.

I knew Anderson well enough to know his credibility was suspect, so I rarely paid much heed to anything he said. At one point in his ramblings, however, he said something that caught my attention: he said that Hap Sweeney's niece, the one who was in possession of his map and journal, was still alive and living in Pecos. I asked Anderson if he had ever spoken with her about the items. He said he had made several attempts to do so, but she refused to have anything to do with him. Anderson had that effect on people. I asked him what her name was, and he told me. I decided I would try to contact her.

On my return trip to Arkansas, where I was living at the time, I stopped in Pecos long enough to look up the niece's name and address in a telephone book. I copied the information and during the rest of my trip mentally composed the letter I would write to her explaining my interest in Hap Sweeney's lost gold cache.

I wrote and mailed the letter two days after my return. In it, I informed the niece of my interest in what I referred to as the Lost Hap Sweeney Gold Cache as a collector of folklore and collector of tales related to the Guadalupe Mountains as well as my interest in it as a professional treasure hunter. I requested permission to examine the journal and the map. I told her I wanted to under-take a search for the cache and, if located, would divide it with her. To my surprise, I received a response within two weeks. The niece was amenable to my request to examine the documents and invited me to do so at the earliest opportunity.

Weeks later I traveled to Pecos, located the home of the niece, and knocked on her door. A pleasant elderly woman an-swered; I introduced myself, and she invited me inside. I was seated at the kitchen table and presently served a generous piece of spice cake and a hot cup of coffee. When the niece was satisfied I was properly accommodated, she went into an adjoining room and returned with Hap Sweeney's journal, which she placed in front of me. She retreated from the kitchen a second time and returned with a gold ingot, which she set beside me. I examined it and determined it was authentic and probably refined during the mid-1800s. The niece and I talked for several minutes, and then she excused herself and invited me to spend as much time with the journal as I wished.

Reading Hap Sweeney's journal was not easy: Sweeney's light touch with the pencil, coupled with the age of the docu-ment, made it very difficult. Though laborious, I eventually tran-scribed most of the sixteen pages of the journal and made a copy of the map.

According to Sweeney's journal, he spent much of his time in the Guadalupe Mountains exploring on foot and on horseback. He never explained why. During one of his forays a short distance west of The Bowl, he came upon the opening to a cave. The opening was vertical and was difficult to see if one was standing more than ten feet away.

Dismounting and hitching his horse to a nearby branch, he walked over to the cave and peered in. It went straight down for ten feet then made a ninety-degree turn to the east. Sweeney noted that the rough limestone wall of the opening offered numerous hand- and footholds, so, curiosity getting the better of him, he climbed down. On reaching the bottom of the vertical opening, he was forced to crawl on his hands and knees into the horizontal passageway. There was sufficient light that he could see several feet into the tunnel. What he saw caused his heart to beat rapidly. Moving closer, Sweeney placed his hands on a pile of gold ingots, forty in all. He retrieved one and climbed back out.

On returning to the surface, Sweeney realized he was a wealthy man. What was not explained in the journal was why he chose to remain living in the tiny cabin in the Guadalupe Mountains for the next few years. Time and again, according to the journal, Sweeney revisited his cache of gold, counting and restacking the ingots in different ways. There is nothing in the journal to suggest that Sweeney removed any more of them. It would therefore be logical to conclude that thirty-nine of them remained stacked in the cave when Sweeney left the mountain and was carried to the hospital in Van Horn in 1913.

I explained to the niece that I intended to search for her late uncle's mysterious cave. If I found it, and if the gold ingots were still cached within, I intended to retrieve them. I informed her that since the cave was located inside the boundaries of a national park, such a recovery would be illegal, and to be caught doing so could yield a prison term. I further explained that I visited the Guadalupe Mountains several times each year, sometimes searching for treasure and other times to backpack into the high country for the pleasure of it. Because of my continuous presence in the park, I was well known to most of the rangers and other employees.

My comings and goings should, I claimed, arouse little to no interest. I was soon to be proven wrong.

As a result of family responsibilities and administering an academic department at a small university, I was unable to return to the Guadalupe Mountains until the spring of 1984. Alone. I packed enough provisions for two separate four-day explorations and searches for the cave. I intended to start from the location of Sweeney's cabin in The Bowl. Should I experience no success during the first four-day search, I would return to my base camp at the foot of the mountains, rest and repack, and head back up for another one.

On the afternoon prior to my trek up into the range, I decided to drive over to the park's visitor center and look over the book selections and any new displays that may have been constructed since my last visit. On arriving, I found the usual contingent of park employees gone and the center left in the hands of a young intern named John Lucero. He informed me that they all had taken off to render assistance relative to a truck accident several miles to the east on Highway 62-180. I had met Lucero during an earlier visit, liked him a lot, and had had several good conversations with him.

Lucero appeared nervous during our conversation, and I assumed it had to do with his responsibility of running the visitor center alone until his superiors returned. After checking the gravel parking lot to make certain no one else was around, he motioned for me to come back into the tiny suite of offices behind the center. He guided me over to a bulletin board and pointed to what amounted to a wanted poster. It contained my name and likeness and stated that I was sought on suspicion of destroying government property.

Lucero asked me not to tell anyone that he had shown me the poster. He also told me that I was being watched and that when I left to pack into the high country, I would be followed by a part-time ranger named Loomis. Loomis would carry a two-way radio and was to observe my activities in the mountains and report any illegal activity to the superintendent. I thanked Lucero for the information and left.

Early the next morning, I was two miles along the steep climb up Tejas Trail, which led to the interior of the range, when I paused to sip water from my canteen. I scanned the switch-backing trail below me and spotted Loomis about one mile behind. Even from this distance, I could see that he was carrying only a daypack and a single canteen. He had neither enough water nor provisions to stay with me for the four days I intended to be in the mountains.

I had encountered Loomis on previous trips to the park. He was a young, good-natured, redheaded, athletic-looking man who worked as a part-time ranger relegated to trail maintenance and chores none of the full-timers wanted to undertake. When he wasn't rangering in the Guadalupes, Loomis was a firefighter in Idaho and Montana. He was easy to get along with, and we had enjoyed a few pleasant conversations over the past months.

I thought little more about my pursuer. Once I reached the top, I intended to leave the trail and strike out on my own, making my way through the forest and canyons. I also intended to elude Loomis. I rarely followed the established trails anyway. The National Park Service has rules relative to remaining on the trails and not wandering off of them. I had been backpacking into this range many years before it was ever designated a national park and had no intention of adhering to their guidelines.

Two hours later I crested the ridge separating the slope from the interior of the range. At this point was a trailhead. In addition to the Tejas Trail, others headed off to the north, east, and west. At this juncture the park had erected an ugly street sign such as one might find in a subdivision. The sign had the names of the trails painted on green metal with arrows pointing in the appropriate directions. The man-made sign was as out of place in this natural environment as a turd in a punchbowl. Having a more heightened respect for these mountains than did the park service, I pushed and pulled on the sign until it was loosened from the ground in which it was planted. When I had freed it, I carried it over to the edge of the ridge and tossed it into a canyon below. Following this, I stepped off the trail and made my way toward The Bowl.

Two hours later I arrived at the location of Sweeney's old cabin. After withdrawing the copy of the map, I studied it. Sweeney's perception of the surrounding area—indeed, the landscape of the entire range—left a lot to be desired. Here and there on the map I could recognize prominent ridges, canyons, and peaks, but Sweeney's perception of how they related to one another geographically was way off. The maze of trails he drew made no sense at all; despite my three decades of exploring these mountains, they resembled nothing I was familiar with. There was little to do but try to make sense of what Sweeney had drawn, so I hung my backpack on a nearby tree and started out.

For the remainder of the day along with most of the next, I followed trails: game trails, forest service trails, park service trails, and old Indian trails. None of them matched anything on Sweeney's map. Several times I left the trail I was following and worked my way through the forested uplands along routes that might have been implied on the map, but none of these forays made any logical sense. I never encountered any trail indicated by Sweeney, and most of these searches were in areas where neither man nor animal would travel if given a choice. I did encounter four cave openings, however, all with vertical entrances, and all located between The Bowl and the western escarpment and in the general area where Sweeney had marked his cache on the map. I entered and explored each one but found nothing and no indication that anything was ever cached in them. I was beginning to despair of ever finding the Lost Hap Sweeney Gold Cache.

Midafternoon of the second day I chanced upon a single shed elk antler. It was a magnificent multipointed specimen. I searched for the mate to it but had no luck. The antler would yield several excellent knife handles, so I determined to bring it back with me and deliver it to my friend Ken West, a professional knife-maker of some repute. Discouraged by my search for Hap Sweeney's cave thus far and having nothing better to do, I decided to leave my backpack where I had hung it in The Bowl and carry the antler down the mountain and deposit it in my pickup. That night I slept on the front seat of my truck.

The next morning, following a hobo bath in the park restroom and a light breakfast from my glove compartment stash of granola bars, I decided to drive over to the visitor center for no other reason than to annoy those who believed I was in the range committing crimes against the park service.

When I walked through the front door, a sudden hush descended over the gathering of park personnel clustered behind the counter: Lucero, a ranger named Ben Warner, another named Rebecca Castillo, and the superintendent whose name I have forgotten.

"Howdy," I said as I walked over, leaned my elbows on the counter, and smiled. Lucero appeared nervous. I winked at him.

Warner remained where he was behind the counter and glared at me. During my previous visits to the park, Warner took every opportunity possible to try to intimidate and harass me. His demeanor was always hateful, his look reptilian, and I knew that none of the other rangers could stand him. I found him amusing.

"What are you doing here?" he asked

"Isn't this the visitor center?" I said. Warner nodded.

"Well, I'm visiting," I said.

The superintendent who had been glaring at me spoke up and said, "Where's Loomis?"

I told him I had spotted Loomis on the trail behind me when I hiked to the top the previous morning but had not seen him since. The superintendent got a concerned look on his face and mumbled something about Loomis not making radio contact

since he left. Loomis carried a government-issued communica-
tions gadget the park service referred to as a "radio," but in truth
it was little more than a child's cheap communication toy. It was
ineffective a half-mile from the visitors' center.

I asked him what Loomis's assignment was. Lucero, who by
now had moved to the rear of the cluster of rangers, appeared
ready to bolt. The superintendent admitted Loomis had been
given instructions to follow me and see if he could catch me in
the act of destroying park property. I explained that I was clearly
packed to spend several days in the high country but that Loomis carried only one canteen and precious little of anything else
in the tiny daypack he transported. The opportunity to gig the
superintendent was too good to pass up, so I said, "Anyone who
would assign Loomis to follow me with such poor preparation is
an idiot."

The superintendent turned red in anger. I was convinced
he was ready to explode when Lucero stepped forward and said,
"Shouldn't we go search for Loomis?"

After glaring at me for another moment, the superintendent
agreed that a search party needed to be organized. He told Warner
to lead it. Warner responded by saying he was not familiar enough
with the high country and did not know the trails. When Castillo
was asked, her answer was the same. The superintendent got on
the phone and called other rangers but all had the same response:
none of them had enough intimacy with the high back country
to lead a search. They were just as likely to become lost while
looking for someone who was already lost.

"Who knows the goddamn trails?" yelled the superintendent.

"There are two park employees who know them better than
anybody," said Lucero. "James Kirkwood and Anthony Arellano." Kirkwood and Arellano had the responsibility of maintaining the park service trails and had spent hundreds of hours in the
range. Kirkwood had, in fact, been born and raised in these very
mountains.

"Those guys are maintenance men, for god's sake!" yelled the superintendent. "We can't place maintenance men in charge of a search party. It looks bad. It says our cadre of park rangers don't even know the park!"

Lucero spoke up. "There is one man who knows the high country better than anyone. I would guess he'd have the best chance of finding Loomis."

"Who the hell would that be?" said the superintendent.

Lucero pointed at me and said, "Jameson."

I smiled. An embarrassing silence reigned for a full minute. Hate emanated from Warner and the superintendent, confusion from Castillo. The superintendent finally broke the silence and said to me, "Would you consider leading a search party to the top to find Loomis?" He asked the question in a manner that suggested he was hoping I would say no.

"Of course," I said.

"Pick a team, then, and get on it as soon as possible. He's been up there for two days with no food and little water."

Warner and Castillo squared their shoulders and rose to full height in an attempt to appear taller than anyone else. Clearly, they wanted to be selected, though I was not sure why. Perhaps they thought they might be regarded as heroes if they were part of a rescue.

"I pick James Kirkwood and Anthony Arellano," I said.

"You can't pick them," said the superintendent. "They are not rangers. They're just maintenance men."

"Your rangers have no experience," I said. "Besides, most of them are incompetent and not to be entrusted with this kind of responsibility. Kirkwood and Arellano know more about the Guadalupe Mountains than all of your rangers, including you, put together. Call over to the maintenance shed and tell them to gather provisions and saddle a couple of horses to ride to the top. I'll go on foot. Tell them I'll meet them at the trail junction at the top of the ridge."

With that, I walked out the door.

By 1:30 that afternoon, Kirkwood, Arellano, and I were taking a break. We had arrived at the crest and proceeded down the trail I assumed Loomis would have followed. We were seated and leaning against a log a few feet off the trail, sipping from our canteens and allowing the horses a bit of rest. We were discussing separating, each of us following a major trail in search of Loomis, and rendezvousing at a specified location. Just as we stood in preparation to leave, we heard someone whistling a tune as they approached our location from the middle trail. The individual was out of sight behind a curve in the trail.

Curious, we waited, and one minute later we were rewarded by the sight of Loomis hiking toward us, a big smile on his face. Spotting me, he said, "I've been looking for you!"

As I shook my head in disbelief, Kirkwood and Arellano explained all that had transpired during the past two days. Loomis was surprised to learn that he was considered lost and the object of a search. He had survived on some candy bars he stuffed in his pack just before departing. He found sufficient water to slake his thirst in small rock basins that had filled from a rain a week earlier.

After the three park employees started back down the trail toward headquarters, I resumed my search for the Lost Hap Sweeney Gold Cache. I put in a total of seven days on the quest, crisscrossing this part of the range several times from several directions. Due to the gross inaccuracies on the map and an absence of any kind of luck, I had no success whatsoever.

Years have passed. Loomis, who earned the nickname "Lost Loomis" for his misadventure, left at the end of the season to fight fires full time in Idaho. Kirkwood and Arellano are retired from the National Park Service and continue to live in the area. Castillo moved on. Warner resigned from the park service and began a new career teaching in public school. John Lucero went on to work at other national parks and during the mid-1990s, as a result of his dedication, rose into the higher rank of National

Park Service administration. I stayed in touch with Hap Sweeney's niece, keeping her apprised of my search for the lost gold
cache. She passed away in 1990 in Pecos, Texas. She left no heirs.

I made three additional extended and extensive searches for
the Lost Hap Sweeney Gold Cache, none successful. I turned to
the lures and challenges of other treasures. Since they were, for
the most part, useless, I passed all my Sweeney documents, including the map, along to a fellow treasure hunter, but he had no
more success than I.

In spite of the failed searches, I remain convinced the Lost
Hap Sweeney Cache lies somewhere on the Guadalupe Mountain
range in a small cave. Though Sweeney's map and notes were of
little to no help, the evidence points to the notion that his claims
were authentic: his near-death ravings about his gold cache and
the single gold ingot retrieved by the hunter who found the
saddlebags.

There is one more thing. Treasure hunters often talk about
their gut feelings relative to certain caches and mines. In the case
of the Lost Hap Sweeney Gold Cache, my gut feeling is that it
does exist and that someday it will be found.

15

TRAPPED

Asleep or awake, we dream of treasure.

—Evan S. Connell

One of the most unnerving experiences I have ever endured at the hands of other men involved no gunfire whatsoever, but was an ordeal I don't care to ever repeat. During one of our expeditions into the Sierra Madres of Mexico, we entered a remote north-south-oriented canyon in which we were convinced, based on an interpretation of some two-hundred-year-old archival material, lay a cache of silver ingots. We had visited this canyon during a previous expedition and found it to be untouched since the time of the Spanish explorers and miners two-and-a-half centuries earlier. This canyon had a broad, flat floor through which wound a narrow stream.

On this visit, however, we spotted a dramatic change. On the east side of the canyon, someone had constructed a landing pad, one suitable for a helicopter. Forty yards from the landing pad was a sixteen-by-sixteen-foot wooden frame building, a house, with windows on each side and a door opening toward the pad. At the far end of the canyon, the one opposite where we entered, we could see a recently bladed road that snaked from the pass toward the building. We could not imagine what would warrant traffic into an area more than seventy-five miles from the nearest native village. Initially, we suspected it all had something to do with a mining venture since the mineralization in this canyon had attracted prospectors and miners often in the past.

Our arrival in the canyon had gone unnoticed by anyone as far as we could tell. We watched the house for several hours and saw no one enter or leave. We took care to remain out of sight just in case, simply because we did not want to arouse any curiosity pertinent to our mission. After three days of exploring the canyon and searching for clues relative to the location of the cache, I grew curious and suggested we go take a closer look at the building, perhaps see if we could see anything through the windows, which did not appear to be curtained or shaded. My partners discouraged the notion, warning against a sudden return of the owners or occupants during our inspection. Not to be deterred, I decided to investigate one morning after breakfast.

Around mid-morning I bade good-bye to my partners and, using rocks and trees for cover, made my way to a point on the opposite side of the canyon from where we were camped and fifty yards from the building. I was facing the rear of the structure. It rested on a foundation of cinderblocks stacked two-high at the corners and every four feet along the sides. I could see a back door. Just outside this door was a barbeque grill.

All was silence. I rose from my hiding place and strode toward the building. When I arrived within twenty feet from the building, I saw several rattlesnakes taking shade beneath it.

I tried the back door and it was locked. Same for the front. Peering in one of the back windows, I spotted four cots and bedding, a table with a propane cook stove, and a second table stacked with a variety of canned goods. I was beginning to suspect this might be a hunter's cabin when I saw something else that changed my mind. At the far end opposite the cots were stacked dozens of rectangular bundles wrapped in plastic. Each one was about one foot long, eight inches wide, and three inches thick. It took me a moment to deduce this was cocaine. Against another wall I could see more stacks that were clearly bales of marijuana. Against these bales leaned four automatic weapons. The building was clearly a drop and pick-up point for drug runners.

It was imperative that we get out of this canyon before the occupants of the building returned. I was about to make my way back to our camp to warn my partners when I heard the whine of a vehicle straining through second gear, the sound coming from the direction of the far end of the canyon. I peered around the corner of the building and saw a white Jeep Wrangler carrying two men come over the pass and make its way along the winding route toward the building. If I attempted to run back to the point where I came out of the trees, I would be spotted.

This was probably not the most dangerous situation I had ever found myself in, but clearly one of the most uncomfortable because my exit options were limited to nonexistent. Each threatening circumstance dictates a certain response, and the manner in which one responds is a function of experience and preparation. In this case, I knew what my response to discovery would be from the moment I stepped from cover and walked over to the structure.

As the Jeep approached the building, I examined the nearest opening to the crawl space beneath. Assured it was clear of rattlesnakes, I eased myself through it and wiggled my way to a position under the wooden floor roughly in the center. As I awaited the arrival of the Jeep, I counted seven rattlesnakes taking shade near the edges of the building. I could see light through the spaces between the floorboards.

A few minutes later the Jeep arrived. The two men were involved in conversation in Spanish as they turned off the engine, retrieved some items from the rear of the vehicle, and approached the front door. I could tell one of the items was an ice chest from the characteristic sound of watery ice sloshing around. One of them paused and, apparently noticing the slumbering rattlers, said something to the other about the nuisance reptiles. The sound of a key being pushed into the lock was clear, as was the turning of the mechanism and the squeak of hinges as the door was opened.

For the next two hours, I listened to the barely audible conversations from the two men. They talked of women, weapons, and money. I heard the squeaking of the metal springs of a cot as one of them lay down. I heard the slamming of a clip into an automatic weapon and the ratcheting sound it made when cocked. A moment later the front door was opened and the two men stepped outside. An eruption of excited conversation was followed by the staccato burst of the firing of the automatic weapon. They had obliterated one of the rattlesnakes that had slithered out from under the building. I immediately feared the men would decide to look beneath the house for more and find me lying there.

Laughing, the two men fired more automatic weapons bursts at some target in the distance. As I practiced some controlled breathing to accommodate this most recent adrenaline rush, I could see the recently shredded snake some distance away still writhing, its primitive nervous system exhausting its final energies in its death throes. I found myself hoping the two men had satisfied their urges to shoot rattlesnakes for a while.

Another hour passed, and one of the men stepped out of the back door and walked several yards away to urinate. The sequence of noises that followed indicated he was stacking wood into the grill and preparing to cook something. Forty-five minutes later, the aroma of roasting meat wafted under the building, reminding me that I had not eaten since breakfast, six hours earlier. When the meat had been cooked, the two men filled their plates and reentered the building. More conversation followed as they dined, then silence. I presumed they were taking a nap.

I considered the notion of crawling out from under the building and making my silent way back to the cover of the trees and boulders while the occupants of the house were slumbering. After a moment or two of pondering this idea, I discarded it. One or both of the men could just as likely be looking out the window as taking a nap, and I would have no way of knowing. I had little choice but to wait for a better opportunity, and it was looking like it would have to wait until dark. I had another problem: after six hours of lying underneath the building, I needed to urinate. It would have been a simple matter to relieve my bladder, but I feared the smell of urine would carry through the cracks between the floorboards and into the house. I would have to wait.

As I waited, I glanced around. I felt it was important to inventory the rattlesnakes that were taking shade under the building and to know where they were at all times. Earlier I had counted seven. With the killing of one, there should have been a half-dozen unless others had decided to take up residence. I counted and came up with only five. I felt like I needed to know where the sixth one was. Keeping as silent as possible, I squirmed my body around such that over the next few seconds I examined the entire area underneath the structure. I located the sixth rattlesnake, and it was slithering toward me.

The rattler wasn't a particularly large one—about four-and-a-half feet long. It was moving slowly, its muscular body slithering forward in a characteristic S-shape movement, its forked tongue darting in and out. The heat receptors in the tongue had located me, and the snake was coming over to investigate. I looked around for a stick or something to use to keep the reptile at bay. Nothing. In spite of the threat of the snake, I kept thinking I had to pee really bad.

The rattlesnake came to within eighteen inches of my face and stopped. It is unusual for a rattler to strike from any position other than a coil. This one wasn't coiled—yet. The tongue kept probing the air. I could swear I heard my heart hammering in my chest. For a full five minutes, the snake and I faced each other with nothing happening save for my breathing and the flicking of the reptile's tongue. I considered snapping my hand out and grabbing the serpent behind the head and killing it, but the angle was wrong. As I was trying to decide on an alternative, the snake, apparently perceiving that I was no threat, turned and slithered away to another location near one edge of the building.

Judging from the light, I guessed it was about two hours before sundown. I decided to Zen myself into a state of meditation and remove all thoughts of my having to urinate. After fifteen minutes of intense concentration, I was getting close to relaxing when I heard the unmistakable sound of a helicopter. At the same time, the men inside the building came out the front door and stood watching the approach of the craft. A few moments later, it landed on the pad and the two men walked over to it.

When the engine was shut off and the blades stopped spinning, I could barely make out conversation between the building's occupants and two new arrivals, but I was too far away to understand any of it. Following five minutes of exchange, items were off-loaded from the copter and carried into the building. Following this, packages I assumed were cocaine were carried from the building and loaded into the helicopter. Several trips were made back and forth and the exchanges took an hour. When completed, the two newcomers climbed back into the helicopter, started the engine, and lifted off. As I listened to the diminishing sound of the copter in the distance, I heard the remaining two men reenter the building. Now all I had to do was wait until nightfall to make my escape.

Relief from my predicament began to unfold a half-hour later. The building's temporary occupants packed up and loaded their belongings into the Jeep, locked the doors, and drove away. Only when I could no longer hear the sound of the vehicle's engine did I crawl out from under the building. The first thing I did was pee.

Assuming there was no lingering threat of danger, I made my away across the open canyon floor, crossed the little stream, and headed toward the camp. Waiting for me just inside the tree line were Stanley, Slade, and Poet. They looked as relaxed as if they had just completed a round of golf. They told me they had observed the day's events from hiding from the moment they first heard the arrival of the Jeep. I asked them if they had formulated a plan to rescue me from the potential danger I was exposed to, but they said no, that it was more amusing to try to guess what I would do.

I told them about sharing my space under the house with the rattlesnakes, and they said they were glad, that otherwise I would have had an easy time there with nothing to do. We discussed burning the structure down along with everything inside, but in the end opted to just leave the canyon and think about returning some other time.

We lost no time in breaking camp and packing our gear. Under a waxing moon and a bright starlit sky, we hoisted our packs and made our way out of the canyon. Though the lure of a large cache of silver ingots remained, we decided there were other challenges to select from, none of which, we were convinced, involved encounters with gunmen or rattlesnakes. As it turned out, we were wrong about both.

16

THE FINAL EXPEDITION

Luck is the residue of design.

—Robert B. Parker

The last expedition undertaken by Poet, Slade, Stanley, and me as a team started out like many of the earlier ones during the previous twenty years: Stanley would bring a translation of some document relating to a pack train transporting bullion to Mexico City, an attack by Indians or bandits or some other disaster, and the subsequent hurried caching of the gold or silver in some remote location. He had found one such promising document in 1974 and studied it off and on for twelve years before we ever mounted an expedition to go in search of it. The project involved a cache of silver bars in a remote canyon in the Sierra Madres somewhere along the Chihuahua-Sonora border, and Stanley was hell-bent for us to search for it.

"I can't explain it," he said. "It's calling to me. I dream about it every night."

Had we any inkling of the dangers we would subsequently encounter during our search for and recovery of the treasure, we would never have undertaken the quest. As it turned out, it nearly got us all killed.

During his research activities in Mexico for more than thirty years, Dr. Trenton Stanley learned that for more than a two-century period ending around 1850, hundreds of pack trains, loaded with Spanish or Mexican gold or silver from some mining location or another in what is now the United States, departed for church and/or governmental headquarters in Mexico City. According to existing documents, most of these pack trains made it to their destination, but many of them did not. A few were diverted by greedy Catholic monks, soldiers, or miners, the treasure being used to support lavish lifestyles or open business enterprises in one or more of the new settlements springing up in the American West. A number of treasure-laden pack trains were attacked by bandits and the contents spirited away, sometimes extravagantly spent, sometimes hidden or buried where many of them remain today.

More common were attacks by Indians as the burros or mules transporting the bullion were led across and through homelands of the Apaches, Yaquis, and other tribes. The leaders of the military escorts that often accompanied such pack trains assumed the Indians coveted the treasure and did their level best to keep them from it. The truth was, the Indians cared little to nothing about what the Spaniards or Mexicans transported. Instead, they resented the intrusion and trespass by the foreigners into and through their homelands. According to their cultural dictates, they attacked in the hope of driving them away or killing them. In addition, they often prized the horses and mules used by the Spaniards.

During their flight, the military escorts in charge often ordered the treasure hidden from the attacking Indians in the most convenient location, and then fled with plans to return with a larger force of soldiers to recover the riches. Because of dramatic shortages of manpower and the growing threat of Indians in the north, return expeditions to recover cached treasure were rarely undertaken. As a result, numerous caves throughout Mexico's Sierra Madres contain untold fortunes in gold and silver ingots.

Following months of research and translation relative to a document he found among some uncataloged museum items encoun-

tered in the Mexican state of Guanajuato, Stanley stumbled upon
the description of a cache of silver ingots hidden in 1726 in a remote canyon of the Sierra Madres along the Chihuahuan-Sonoran
border. The cache consisted of close to one thousand eighteen-
inch long ingots, a fortune estimated to be worth over two million
dollars. According to the document, the silver bars were hidden in
a cave in an unnamed canyon in the extensive range.

Stanley was passionately attached to this tale, to undertaking
an expedition to the area, and to locating the cache. The rest of us
were infused with his zeal, and since we had already experienced
several unforgettable adventures in the Sierra Madres, we agreed
to go.

During the late 1980s, decent topographic and geologic maps
of the Sierra Madres were difficult to obtain. When maps were
found, they were more often than not deficient in detail. On our
first expedition into the area, we operated on hunches. We drove
miles of unmaintained dirt roads into the foothills of the Sierras in
an attempt to get as close to a designated search area as possible.
From that point, we backpacked for three weeks through some of
the most rugged country we had ever been exposed to, searching
for the landmarks indicated on Stanley's document. By the time
we narrowed the search to the general area of the Indian attack,
we were weary and out of food, and Stanley was suffering from
pain in his left calf, the result of the rattlesnake bite a few years
earlier about fifty miles north of where we currently explored.
Our search area was thick with rattlers, and we could tell Stanley
remained in a nervous state.

Days later as we drove Stanley's Chevrolet Suburban out of
the foothills, we stopped at a ranch and made arrangements with
the owner to lease horses and mules for our next trip. We planned
to ride in, load the mules with a portion of the treasure we hoped
to find, and return.

Months later when we arrived at the ranch, however, we
found it abandoned. No rancher, no horses, no mules. Later, we

learned that the man Stanley had negotiated with was in prison in Ciudad Chihuahua. He was apparently in league with drug runners who used his ranch to store some of their goods. Area law enforcement officials caught wind of the arrangement, demanded a *mordida*—a bribe—for looking the other way, and didn't get one. As a result, the rancher was incarcerated until such time as he agreed to cooperate.

Once again, we entered the range on foot. As was our practice, we each packed a handgun. In addition, Slade brought a Winchester Model 94 .30-.30, and we took turns carrying the weapon. It was worth it, for he kept us in venison, a pleasant change from the trail food we normally carried. We dined on broiled rattlesnake from time to time to vary the menu, but Stanley eschewed this fare. On this trip, we narrowed down our search area to three canyons, each within a day's hike from one another. Because of some convoluted logistics, we were forced to return to Texas before having the opportunity to explore any of the canyons.

It wasn't until the third expedition into the range that we experienced some success. We were still unable to obtain riding and packing stock, so once again we backpacked in. Other than dodging rattlesnakes, the trip into the range was uneventful, and we set up camp at the mouth of one of the canyons we identified. In Stanley's opinion, it was the canyon that offered the greatest possibility of being the one through which the pack train of 1726 was led when it was attacked. It was here we hoped to find the cave that contained the one thousand silver ingots.

First signs were good. The canyon cut through eons-old limestone, the soluble sedimentary rock most likely to contain caves. On our first pass through the canyon, however, we found none. Ubiquitous were the narrow slit caves at the point of contact between different layers of the sedimentary rock, but no caves in the normal sense. It took a full day to hike from one end of the canyon to the other.

Though we found nothing, each of us voiced the suspicion that we were in the right place.

"There's something here," said Poet, as he scanned the steep walls. "I can feel it."

"I feel it, too," said Stanley. "We have missed something, something out of the ordinary. We owe this canyon one more look."

The next day, we made another pass through the canyon. Nothing. As we trekked through it on the way back to camp, Slade pointed to a spot at the base of the north wall that was shaded by a few poor oaks and suggested we stop for a late lunch. We climbed the low talus slope to the base of the cliff and dined on some venison Slade had jerked two days earlier.

After lunch we rested, jaws tired from masticating the dry, chewy meat, and sipped water. Stanley, with a full belly and delighted to be out of the warm sun, lay back and fell asleep. I decided to do the same. Poet said he had to go pee and crunched along the top of the loose talus until he was out of sight, some twenty yards away and around a slight curve in the cliff face.

Poet had been gone for perhaps two minutes when we heard him scream. Stanley bolted awake and yelled, "Snakes!"

Slade, his nine millimeter in hand, was already racing toward the sound. I grabbed my snake stick and fell in step behind him. When we arrived, we saw Poet on his knees under a scraggly oak tree and facing the canyon wall. He was pointing to something at the base of the wall. Slade and I skidded to a stop next to him and, still standing, looked in the direction of his point. It was a slit cave with an opening of no more than two-and-a-half feet high. A four-foot-long diamondback rattlesnake was slithering into the space.

Stanley arrived in time to hear Slade address Poet. "Jesus. When did you get so goosey about snakes? We've already seen forty or fifty on this trip."

Poet didn't respond. He kept pointing into the opening of the slit cave. Then he said, "Holy Mary, Mother of God, there must be hundreds of them."

Slade, Stanley, and I dropped to our knees and peered into the cave. In seconds, our eyes adjusted to the darkness, and what we saw caused our flesh to crawl and bumps to rise on our skin. In spite of the mid-afternoon desert heat, I felt a chill from the base of my skull down to my tailbone.

The slit cave extended into the cliff ten to twelve feet and about thirty-five feet along the base. On the blow-sand-covered floor, a carpet of hundreds of rattlesnakes writhed and twisted and twined. At our presence, a low buzzing sound started, and then grew in decibels as uncountable rattles whirred. The characteristic scent of a great cluster of snakes emanated from the dark space. Sounds and smells from Hades.

"Holy shit!" said Slade.

"God help me," said Stanley. "I'm going to be sick." With that, he stood and staggered back to where we had eaten lunch.

"This reminds me of all those snakes we found in that damn mine shaft north of here where Stanley got bit a couple years ago," said Poet, still pointing, "but this is incredible."

I was unable to take my eyes off the mat of coiling and twining snakes. Goose bumps formed on my arms, and the hair at the back of my neck stood out. As I watched, a ball composed of half a dozen rattlers broke several inches from the main body of snakes and thrashed around in the blow sand, their whipping tails stirring the dust and slicing through the fine sand less than four feet from the entrance. Then Poet and I saw it at the same time.

The constantly moving tails brushed at the loose sand and uncovered an object that seemed out of place in the cave. It was narrow and rectangular, and in an instant I knew what it was.

"There they are!" yelled Poet. "The silver ingots are right there!"

Slade stared into the opening, mesmerized.

"A fortune," said Poet. "Five feet away and covered with a zillion rattlesnakes."

As we stared into the cave, we saw more of the ingots exposed, uncovered momentarily by the stirring of the rattlesnakes.

"I don't like this at all," said Stanley, who had returned and stood behind us, bent over, hands on knees.

I moved toward the entrance of the slit cave. Two feet inside was a single three-foot-long rattler. Taking my snake stick, I flipped it onto the writhing mass toward the rear. Crawling farther, I used the stick to attack the ball of snakes twisting around over the ingot. After pushing them aside, I employed the hooked tip of the stick to pull the ingot toward me. I reached in, grabbed it, and hastened back out.

"You're an idiot," said Stanley.

I passed the bar around. It was eighteen inches long, two inches wide, and an inch-and-a-half thick. I estimated it weighed around fifteen pounds. The bar had clearly been molded in a length of split river cane, the joint being evident on the underside.

"A common procedure," said Stanley, "when they didn't have standard molds."

Slade took his pocketknife and cut into it. "Silver, all right," he said, "but not pure. Probably a lot of lead and zinc in it."

"It appears," said Stanley, speaking loud enough to be heard above the noise of the rattlesnakes, "that the Spaniards, while fleeing from their attackers, tossed their load of bullion into this slit cave and, now unburdened, continued fleeing toward the south."

Taking my snake stick, I crawled back into the slit to try to retrieve more of the ingots. Stanley continued, "The silver has remained in this cave for 264 years, untouched, until now."

I withdrew from the cave again with another ingot.

"Retrieving this silver could wind up being a lot of work," I offered.

"Not to mention dangerous," said Stanley.

Slade walked to the spot where we had taken a break, retrieved his snake stick, and crawled into the cave, returning in a minute with a third ingot.

"Let's head back to camp and figure out what we need to do about this," said Stanley, always the logical one.

"You guys go ahead," said Poet. "I'll be with you in a minute. I never did get to pee."

That night, around the campfire, we made plans. Stanley suggested we redouble our efforts to obtain horses and pack animals, return to the cave, and carry out as many of the silver ingots as we could manage to retrieve from under the snakes. After discussing our individual obligations and schedules, we made plans to return in six months, providing we could make arrangements for horses. The next morning, we returned to the slit cave, retrieved one more ingot, a total of one for each of us, and, after packing up, headed for home.

Through his numerous contacts, Stanley managed to acquire horses and mules for our next expedition to the slit cave. The ranch where we were to pick up the animals was seventeen miles from our previous starting point into the canyon, so it meant extra travel time.

Back home in Texas, Stanley had his ingot assayed. It was found to be only about 60 percent silver, the rest lead and zinc, which were worthless in such small quantities. We converted the four ingots into a little over one thousand dollars in cash, hardly enough to pay for our investment in time, energy, and money. Still, we were encouraged and optimistic: as far as we knew, we were the only people on earth who knew where the ingots were located and we now had pack animals to carry some of them out. Given that each ingot weighed fifteen pounds, we intended to return with at least eighty on this trip, an amount large enough to make us some comfortable money but small enough to be transported in Stanley's pickup truck and smuggled back across the border. Then we would return for more.

For the time being, our only concern was dealing with the rattlesnakes. Had we any inkling of what additional trials we were to face, we would have canceled the trip on the spot.

Things did not go as planned. In the months we were away from the area, a civil war broke out between the resident Indian populations in that part of the Sierra Madres and the American-owned timber companies that were encroaching into centuries-old native homelands to clear-cut pine trees. The Indians retaliated, launching guerrilla raids on the outlying camps of the timber cutters, killing several. The companies responded by hiring mercenaries armed with automatic weapons to exterminate the Indians. In turn, the indigenes sought help from the drug runners who frequented the region because of the remote routes they employed for their own smuggling operations. The *narcotraficantes* supplied the Indians with automatic weapons and grenade launchers and even lent them helicopter pilots once in a while. Things turned bloody, dozens on both sides were killed, and we arrived in the middle of the fray. Not only were members of the different factions killing one another, lone travelers found on the long and remote roads through the Sierra Madres were often slaughtered.

We decided to travel to the location during the winter when the threat of rattlesnakes was minimal to nonexistent. When we arrived in the area, it was clear the local Indians were convinced we worked for the timber companies, and the timber cutters thought we were helping the Indians. The drug runners, we learned later, thought we were government agents sent to spy on their activities. With a total of four handguns and two rifles, our arsenal was scant compared to everyone else's. Foolishly, we decided to buck the odds, continue into the mountains, and enter the canyon to retrieve some silver.

Because we felt that speed might be important when we were ready to leave the canyon, we only collected sixty ingots so as not to overload the pack animals. We debated whether to travel at night or during the day. We picked daytime because it would be easier to follow our escape route.

It started out well. After stuffing the sixty ingots into the packs, we left the canyon at dawn, and around mid-afternoon we were riding across the top of a treeless ridge, a spur that extended from a low mountain we had to cross on our return. The sides of the spur angled downward at forty-five degrees and merged with thick pine forest fifty yards below. Because we would be exposed on the bare ridge for about three hundred yards until we reached the forested mountain beyond, I was uncomfortable, but we had no other options.

About halfway across the ridge, rifle shots rang out from somewhere down the slope in the trees to our right. Slade, who was in the lead, spurred his mount and yelled, "Head for the timber!"

I was the last in line and hadn't covered fifty feet when I heard a bullet strike the horse I was riding, a sickening, thudding sound. The horse stumbled, the front legs buckled, and it went down. I went over the neck and head but tried to keep the horse between the shooters and myself. As a result, I rolled off the left side of the narrow ridge and down the slope, sliding for thirty feet before coming to a stop. I landed on top of a rattlesnake. After kicking the reptile away, I scrambled back to the top of the ridge with the idea of retrieving my rifle.

No luck. The dead horse was lying on its side, its back facing the attackers. My rifle was in the scabbard under hundreds of pounds of horse. I looked down the trail and saw my three partners, still mounted and pulling their pack animals along behind them, leaving the ridge and disappearing into the forest beyond. I was alone, unarmed except for a .44-caliber revolver. There was no sign of the ingot-laden packhorse I had been leading, and I presumed it had turned and fled back in the direction from which we had come, carrying its load of ingots.

I thought about trying to retrieve my personal saddlebags that contained two of the ingots but decided against it. I probably couldn't have pulled it free of the dead horse, and since I was now on foot, it would slow my escape. I had no choice. I had to make a run for it.

Sliding back down the slope and out of sight of the shooters, I began making my way toward the far end of the ridge along the incline. It was difficult. Here and there I could leap from one rock to another, but most of the time I was forced to run along a steep slope composed of loose rock. I fell numerous times, and by the time I completed the one hundred and fifty yards to the end of the crest, I was exhausted and breathless.

I poked my head up above the ridge and peered back to where my dead horse lay on the trail. There was no sign or sound of men. Keeping under cover, I made my way into the forest along the trail where I last saw Poet, Slade, and Stanley riding away. Carrying my revolver, I followed their tracks, constantly scanning the woods around me for any sign of an enemy. I spotted Poet and Slade walking down the trail toward me, on foot. They had tied off the horses up ahead and were making their way back to try to rescue me if I wasn't already dead. They informed me that Stanley had taken a bullet in his right calf.

I rode one of the packhorses and, after four days of avoiding settlements and timber camps, we finally made it back to the ranch where we had obtained the stock and parked the truck.

From the moment we rode off the mountain and headed toward the ranch, I had a feeling this would be our last expedition as a team. Stanley, whose calf was wrapped with bandages fashioned from two T-shirts and throbbing with pain, stated several times he had had enough, that he was "getting too old for this nonsense." Slade, who remained surly more often than not under the best of circumstances, was heard to say he'd had about all of Mexico he wanted and that if we returned we would do it without him. Poet and I exchanged glances and shrugged. Though unspoken, our thoughts ran to the notion that with the passage of some time, both men would change their minds and we would soon be embarking on another adventure. It was not to be.

We managed to return to Texas with only forty-three ingots. By the time we converted them into cash, paid the transaction fee, paid for the dead horse and the lost mule, and divided the money, we each pocketed just under $3,000. Not a lot of money for all that work and hazard.

At this writing, as far as I know, the rest of the treasure remains in the narrow niche in the remote canyon in the Sierra Madres. Unfortunately, the confrontations between the timber company, the Indians, and the drug runners wage on, thus making a journey into the region a perilous one. Still, the cache continues to call out to me.

SOME PARTING WORDS

You do what many dream of, all their lives.

—Robert Browning

Author Geoff Powter wrote a book titled *Strange and Dangerous Dreams* in which he examines the psychological motivations of men who seek, even crave, adventure, exploration, discovery. Powter refers to such individuals as being "off the map," and suggests there is a fine line between adventure and madness and that "there are dark motivations behind risk-taking." He refers to people like me as pathological adventurers and divides us into three categories: the burdened, the bent, and the lost.

The burdened, claims Powter, are weighed down with social pressures, such as a desire for fame. These pressures, he insists, cause them to make questionable decisions. Powter's burdened ones, I suspect, possess more ego than experience. The bent, he tells us, suffer from mild internal pathologies, which I think is psycho-speak for being almost crazy. The lost, according to Powter, suffer from exaggerated versions of the same pathologies, and some of these people can probably be labeled insane. He suggests that many so-called adventurers pursue danger because of an "indirect suicidal intent."

As I reread the selected treasure-hunting vignettes included in this book, it occurred to me that my partners and I spent an

249

inordinate amount of time crawling around in dangerous abandoned mines and remote caverns. It also struck me that nearly
every time we undertook an expedition, we had close encounters
with rattlesnakes and other poisonous vipers and arachnids. People
who know us have suggested that it required a certain level of
insanity to continue to expose ourselves to those kinds of circumstances time and again.

Not true. As it happens, old mines and caverns are the places
where the treasure can be found. If you want to locate caches,
then oftentimes that is where you have to go. It just works out
that way. In what may be an apocryphal story, Jesse James was
once asked by an interviewer why he robbed banks. "Because,"
responded Jesse, "that's where the money is." It's the same with
us, just substitute caves and old mines for banks. Case closed.

The location of rattlesnakes and other poisonous vipers is a
direct function of geography. Most of our expeditions took place
in the deserts of the southwestern United States and northern
Mexico, and that's where they live. The truth is, we were guests
in their neighborhood.

Were we insane to continue to explore dark, closed-in spaces
and rub shoulders with rattlesnakes? Perhaps, in the mind of some,
though we doubt it. Because of where we traveled, we expected
snakes, we understood them, and we treated them with respect.
Many of our expeditions were likely more fulfilling because of
them. It is a truth that people fear what they don't understand,
and most people don't understand snakes.

It is easy for me to disagree with Powter, a man who writes
about people taking risks but provides no indication that he has
taken any himself. I do, however, agree with Powter on a number
of other observations he makes in his book. He makes the distinc-
tion between selfish and self-full risk-takers. A selfish risk-taker is
one who is absorbed with himself and who is quite disengaged
from what is going on outside of himself, whether it is people or
place. The self-full risker regards such experiences and adventures

as enlightening and comes away from them a more fulfilled, more experienced, more rounded person.

Powter says adventurers are motivated by the same things: the desire to pit oneself against nature, to test one's limits, and a desire for acclaim. These are the responses, of course, of adventurers Powter knows personally or historical figures such as Robert Scott who he has studied. Powter also maintains that this has a lot to do with achieving what he calls a "remarkable sense of mastery in a harsh environment." I would take issue with Powter here. I never had any desire to master any environment we were in; I only wanted to get along with it and be part of it, to function effectively and efficiently within its realm. This is a significant difference.

Powter states, "There is no greater feeling than getting yourself in a treacherous spot and coming out the other side." This is likely true the first one or two times it happens, but after a dozen or more it becomes commonplace. For a professional treasure hunter, there is no greater feeling, after weeks or months of research and preparation, than that of coming upon a cache of gold or silver ingots worth millions of dollars. The feeling of surviving life-threatening episodes involving flash floods, rattlesnakes, ambushers, and cave-ins often pales in comparison. But then, professional treasure hunters were not among those studied by Powter.

Powter and I do agree on this: one is seldom aware of what a privilege it is just being alive, and the only time that is fully understood is when one has faced death and survived.

During the pursuit of a quest, adventure is a by-product, not an objective, of that endeavor, and it is far more complex than authors like Powter are aware. I claim that before society became anesthetized by television, video games, and related mind-numbing products, adventures, even life-threatening ones, were common, even ordinary, and entirely normal people experienced them on a regular basis.

I feel sorry for those who have never undertaken a quest, and whose only exposure to adventure is movies. Today, far too many live their lives vicariously through actors and via television "reality" shows, which have nothing to do with reality at all. This, to my way of thinking, is abnormal. This is not sane, but, importantly to people who undertake such things, it is safe and simple. And that's the way they like to live their lives: no risk.

Not so with a quest. It, along with the accompanying experiences, can be quite complex, physically and intellectually. It can also be remarkably healthy and deeply human.

I had the good fortune to have been involved in a number of unforgettable adventures. I have taken risks I doubt I would consider today. I have faced death on several occasions and always came away intact. During a recent talk, a member of the audience asked me if I was ever afraid of dying. I thought about it for a moment and came to realize I never experienced fear in those days. It occurred to me that one becomes afraid when one has time to think about it. I was never provided the time.

I was also asked once if I regretted not being able to return home with some of the treasures we found. I regret nothing. In many cases we were extremely fortunate to be able to recover and return with those we did. The ones we had to leave behind for logistical, legal, and other reasons are, as far as I know, still there.

Some who have claimed to know Poet, Slade, Stanley, and me have stated that we were fortune-hunting mercenaries after riches, and that obtaining wealth was our primary goal to the exclusion of all else. That has never been the case.

Wealth in the form of gold and silver ingots, coins, and precious artifacts was merely the catalyst for the quest. To varying degrees, neither Poet, Slade, Stanley, nor I ever planned on getting rich. We always remained hopeful we would find the stated object of any search, but we always knew the odds were against us. The treasure we sought, whether documented or legendary, seemed like a cloud, a will-o-the-wisp that more often than not eluded our grasp.

It is true that we found lost gold and silver, that we recovered some hidden treasure, and that for short periods of time we possessed a lot of money. There was some satisfaction and excitement associated with having a small fortune, but it was generally short-lived. Being practical men, we used whatever money we realized from a successful expedition to pay off bills and expenses, fund educational opportunities for our children, and invest toward other quests. Frankly, being wealthy never brought us the kind of satisfaction we thought it would. It was only money, and if the truth were known, none of us spent much time thinking about it.

Some have claimed we were in pursuit of adventure, that we were adrenaline junkies. Anyone who has ever been on a quest will tell you that adventure happens when plans go awry. The great explorer Roald Amundson once said, "An adventure is merely an interruption of an explorer's serious work and indicates bad planning." Our plans often turned out badly, which may give you some idea of our collective ability to arrange and organize a perfect expedition, to prepare for any and all contingencies.

I've discussed this notion of pursuing adventure with my partners many times, as well as with other professional treasure hunters and questers. In the end, when boiled down to its basic essence, we were all involved in the pursuit of life.

One doesn't experience life sitting in a recliner in front of the television, in the daily nine-to-five experience of a job, in going to the occasional baseball or football game, in hanging out with buddies and drinking beer and throwing darts at the local tavern. That kind of living is for amateurs, the perpetually frightened, for those who feel a need to be safe and secure. Those types of people confuse living with existing, and merely existing can be a slow death. If one is fulfilled by such ordinary things, it is because one's notion of a quality life is undeveloped and one's standard of living is low.

Life—in its purest and truest sense, from the standpoint of the explorer, the venturer, the bold and daring, the person who wants a bit more out of living, who wants to experience the taste, feel, and smell of the world—has to be chased down, captured, embraced, fondled, made love to, and then turned loose for another time.

Life. That was our ultimate goal. That is what we pursued. And, by God, we found it many times over. Life, a high quality of life, a life filled with delicious and rewarding adventure and experiences.

In many ways I envied and admired the successes of the late Mel Fisher. Mel was the treasure hunter who found the *Atocha*, the treasure-filled Spanish vessel that sank off the coast of Florida during a violent storm during the early 1700s. From the wreckage of this ship that lay partially covered amid the sands of the continental shelf, Fisher and his team brought up millions of dollars worth of gold and silver coins and ingots and artifacts. His family corporation continues the recovery enterprise.

During our forty or so years as professional treasure hunters, we never achieved the success of Mel Fisher. Finding lost caches and mines was seldom a problem. There are plenty of them out there, and we located more than our fair share. The principal difficulties we encountered were related to recovery. Many of our finds were in remote regions of Mexico or the United States. Since we never publicized our discoveries and refused to report them to state and federal agencies, we were forced to remain clandestine, operating under the radar. As a result, we could not afford to undertake recovery operations that would attract notice.

We learned this from observing Mel Fisher and other treasure hunters. Mel's recovery operations attracted attention, which were followed by articles in major newspapers and magazines. When Florida politicians realized Fisher was harvesting millions from the sea floor, they decided they needed to cut themselves in on it. As a result, the Fisher family was forced to pay millions of dollars in taxes to the state and the federal government. They were also required to pay for salvage licenses that did not even exist when they started.

Dozens of major treasure discoveries across the United States and along the Atlantic coast have been seized by local and federal governments or placed in legal limbo as a result of the intrusion of insurance companies and descendants of individuals originally involved with the treasure. Treasure hunters and salvage corporations have invested upwards of millions of dollars in research, exploration, and recovery only to have their find taken away from them with little or no recompense whatsoever.

We chose not to be involved with any of that. The politicians, the governments, the insurance companies, and the relatives of men who were responsible for losing or caching a treasure have never financed or contributed in any way to our research, to our preparation, or to our expeditions. They have never assisted us with any of the recoveries. Therefore, we were not about to share any of what we found with them.

Furthermore, recovery of gold, silver, and artifacts in Mexico is fraught with numerous hazards, not the least of which are associated with smuggling the goods back across the border. Sometimes it worked; other times it proved to be impossible.

While we recovered treasure, and while we made money from time to time, we never became wealthy, not in the monetary sense anyway. We did grow wealthy, however, from the experiences we gained along the way. Neither Poet, Slade, Stanley, nor I watch television or go to movies. We made our own entertainment, and it far surpassed anything we'd seen that ever came out of Hollywood.

Our final expedition represented a turning point in our partnership. Together, we had been on a couple of hundred expeditions and somehow managed to return home each time, despite dazzling arrays of hazards. Over mescals one evening, we decided the statistics related to surviving an expedition were no longer in our favor, that each time we went out we were closer to a disaster. We decided not to buck the odds.

At this writing, Stanley has been gone for several years. Between stiffness from a rattlesnake bite in one leg, a bullet wound in the other, and severe arthritis, Stanley's mobility was limited and his days of extensive hiking and backpacking were over. Worse than the injuries and arthritis, he said, were the dreams. He confided that he had dreams every night about the four of us leaving for an expedition somewhere in Mexico, but only three of us returning. In the dreams, he was the one who didn't make it. He said he jerked awake each time he had one of these nightmares, sweating, heart pounding. He told me once that the dreams were so real they frightened him. He said that the next time we went out together, he knew we would come back without him. He chose not to go, said his days of hunting for lost treasure were over. He has since passed away.

Slade and his wife are raising a granddaughter. The little girl has changed him. She has somehow managed to unwrap his warrior skin and underneath found a tender, sensitive, devoted, loving grandfather, one loath to leave the little girl. One afternoon while visiting him at his home, I watched as he held his granddaughter in his arms and told me he was staying home from now on, and she was the reason why. He said he would never return to Mexico.

Poet, a British citizen, located a long-lost and little-known shipwreck a short distance off the coast of a Caribbean island, one that went down while carrying a fortune in stolen gold during the days of pirate activity in the area. He was in the process of recovering the treasure from that wreck while trying to keep his activities from being detected. The last time I heard from him was during the summer of 1995. What became of him is not known. He simply disappeared.

Me? There are a lot of treasures we found but were unable to retrieve. I think about going back after them, but not alone. In the meantime, I content myself with writing books. Sometimes, late at night when I'm in bed, I think about the quest, the challenge, the joy of being on the trail, the hunt, and I think it may be just a matter of time before I head out again. Perhaps I may be able to mount yet another expedition and go back for them. Perhaps someone else will. It matters little who finds them and retrieves them. What matters is that they represent a reason for going on, for a quest.

May you find the treasure you seek.

ACKNOWLEDGMENTS

For years, poet, novelist, and memoirist Laurie Wagner Buyer encouraged me to write down accounts of a number of my treasure-hunting adventures and to consider putting them together as a book. I resisted for several reasons, most of them explained in the text. When I finally acquiesced, she edited the first, as well as two subsequent, drafts. Every writer should have an editor like Buyer.

Muchas gracias to Sandra Bond, my intrepid agent, who somehow always manages to find the right home for my manuscripts, who makes me work harder than I want to, and who is fun to hang out with.

I feel a boxcar load of gratitude to Rick Rinehart and the talented, efficient, and congenial cadre of professionals at Taylor Trade Publishing in Boulder, Colorado. All of my books are better for having received their attention.

Thanks to the efforts of publicist Stephanie Barko, the first edition of *Treasure Hunter* was introduced to the reading public, garnered some fine reviews, and won an Indie Reader Book of the Year Award.